Klaus Toft has been a documentary producer for
the Australian Broadcasting Corporation for
ten years. His work has won over forty awards.
This is his first book.

[THE NAVIGATORS]

Flinders vs Baudin

THE RACE BETWEEN MATTHEW FLINDERS
AND NICOLAS BAUDIN TO DISCOVER THE
FABLED PASSAGE THROUGH THE MIDDLE
OF AUSTRALIA.

Klaus Toft

DUFFY & SNELLGROVE
SYDNEY

Published by Duffy & Snellgrove in 2002
PO Box 177 Potts Point NSW 1335 Australia
info@duffyandsnellgrove.com.au

Reprinted 2002 (twice)

Distributed by Pan Macmillan

Cover design by Alex Snellgrove
Image of Baudin courtesy of Allport Library and Museum
of Fine Arts, State Library of Tasmania
Miniature portrait of Matthew Flinders, c.1805,
watercolour on ivory. (ML Ref: Z MIN 52)
Mitchell Library, State Library of New South Wales

Internal map by Alex Snellgrove
Typeset by Cooper Graphics
Printed by Griffin Press

ISBN 1 876631 60 0

visit our website: www.duffyandsnellgrove.com.au

[CONTENTS]

To Lee, Madeleine and Natalie

[AUTHOR'S PREFACE]

What an amazing piece of history this is. And how remarkable that it is not more widely known. Until I began preparing the television documentary *The Navigators* for the Australian Broadcasting Corporation, I was ignorant of this aspect of Australia's past. I was aware of the name Matthew Flinders. I had never heard of Nicolas Baudin.

My original brief was to produce a documentary about Matthew Flinders, to coincide with the bicentennial of his voyage being celebrated all around the country. As I began to research, however, it soon became apparent that to tell Flinders' story without reference to Baudin, might be like trying to tell the story of Napoléon Bonaparte without reference to Joséphine.

Fascinating research began to mount up and I soon found myself in the invidious position of trying to condense this epic tale into the time constraints of two hours of television. There was still so much to be told about these two incredible men and their race to explore Australia which simply could not be squeezed into the documentary. Thus was born the idea of this book.

Many other books have been written about Flinders and a few about Baudin, and I am grateful to the authors of those that I have relied on as sources. What makes *The Navigators* different is its focus squarely on 'the race' between Baudin and Flinders, one of the greatest ocean races the world has ever seen.

I have tried to tell much of the story from Flinders' and Baudin's own points-of-view. Fortunately, both men recorded a great deal about their voyages in their own words.

Klaus Toft, Melbourne
September 2002

Timor

Bonaparte
Archipelago

N O U V

H O L L

Shark's Bay

Cape Adieu

Geographe Bay

Recherche Archipelago

Cape Leeuwin

King George Sound

Gfe de. Carpentarie

Great Barrier Reef

ELLE

ANDE

Wreck Reef

Port Jackson

Encounter Bay

Port Phillip Bay

Tre de Diemen

D'Entrecasteaux Channel

[PROLOGUE]

'Baudin did well to die; on his return I would
have had him hanged.' So said Napoléon
Bonaparte when the official account of
Captain Nicolas-Tomas Baudin's voyage into the
unknown was finally delivered to the French Emperor.
So the story goes.

In 1800, Baudin had embarked on one of the
greatest ocean races the world has ever seen, a race to
explore the distant, mysterious world of Terres Australes. His British rival was Matthew Flinders. In
recounting what occurred on Baudin's ships, early
writers painted a most unflattering picture of the
French Captain. Depending on whom you read, he
was either cruel, ignorant, dishonest, or cowardly, or a
combination of all these. Some held Baudin responsible for France's failure in the colonisation of the
Pacific. Hubert de Castella suggested that 'if Australia

did not become French it was because Baudin withdrew in the face of the terrible croaking of the
Australian frogs'. In 1879 in his *Histoires des Grands Voyages et Grands Voyagers*, Jules Verne wrote with respect to
Baudin's expedition, that 'it is as though ... all the
biographical dictionaries and narratives of voyages had
agreed to say as little as possible about it'.

Slowly some came to question the 'official
account' of Baudin's voyage. As early as 1828, another
French explorer, Dumont d'Urville, had stopped at the
island of Mauritius, where Baudin had died. One
evening d'Urville found himself talking to an old sailor
who had sailed on Baudin's voyage. Listening to the
old man speak of his adventures, a very different picture of Baudin began to emerge. If the old man was to
be believed, d'Urville could see that a great injustice
had been done to Baudin's memory, leading d'Urville
to write that 'if he had lived things might have turned
out differently; on his return Baudin might have got
the advancement and credit due to him, and those who
had made such a clamour against him would have been
silenced'.

But back in France, d'Urville's story fell on deaf
ears. Someone had to be held responsible for France's
failure in the colonisation of Australia, and an enormous historical injustice was done to Baudin's
memory.

Chapter 1

[THE MISSION]

O n a crisp October morning in 1800, in the northern port of Le Havre, Captain Baudin stood on the deck of his corvette, *Le Géographe*, watching some late provisions being loaded. Further down the dock he could see his other ship, *Le Naturaliste*, all ready to depart. One of the greatest French scientific expeditions ever assembled was about to embark, with 46-year-old Baudin in command.

An extravagant banquet had been held in his honour back in Paris. The esteemed explorer, Comte de Bougainville, had raised his glass in the first toast: 'To the return of Captain Baudin and of the observers taking part in the expedition.' Other toasts followed. One of the members of the *Society for the Observation of Man* charged his glass fervently, 'To the amelioration of the lot of the savages.' Finally, Baudin himself stood up to express the wish, 'That I may once more, returning from my expedition, be in the same room with the same persons.'

When Napoléon had returned from his campaign in Italy and paraded his spoils of war along the Champs de Mars, some unusual trophies had appeared at the head of the procession. In front of the lions, bears, camels and works of art by Raphael, Titian and Veronese – in front of all these – were a coconut palm, a banana tree and some paw-paw plants. The cheering spectators soon learned that the plants had come not from Italy, but from the far-off world of the West Indies, brought back by the intrepid explorer, Nicolas Baudin. Accomplished in the face of cyclones, shipwreck and war, Baudin's Caribbean expedition had been a huge success. He had been lauded in the popular press as 'the greatest navigator and naturalist of all time', responsible for delivering 'the richest and most beautiful collection of living plants ever brought to Europe'.

That success had brought Baudin to the latest voyage, to explore and chart that mysterious world known variously as Nouvelle Hollande or Terres Australes. It was intended to bring glory to Revolutionary France. Napoléon's government was so confident of success that a medal had already been struck to commemorate the grand venture. Baudin, however, was all too aware that success was far from assured. Four other French captains had already visited Terres Australes. Not one had made it back alive. In 1772 Louis-François de St Allouarn had landed on the west coast of Terres Australes and claimed it for the French. Six months later, without seeing France again, he was dead. At the same time that St Allouarn landed on the west coast, Marion Dufresne landed on the east coast, in Terre de van Diemen. In a novel move Dufresne ordered his men to strip naked before going ashore bearing gifts to establish friendly relations with the local inhabitants. The naked Frenchmen were the first Europeans ever to meet the island's inhabitants and soon had fast-flying spears and stones hurled at them. Dufresne continued on to New Zealand where he was killed and eaten by Maoris. On January 26, 1788 La Pérouse landed at Botany Bay, the exact same day that the British First Fleet held an official ceremony founding the British colony at Port Jackson. La Pérouse would have been able to provide the French with information on just how precarious and fragile was the state of this British penal settlement except that he sailed out into the vastness of the Pacific and was never seen again. In 1791, Admiral Bruny d'Entrecasteaux was sent to search for him. A few months after the storming of the Bastille, an amazing 600,000 *livres* was allocated to sponsor the search. On January 21, 1793, the very same day that Louis XVI lost his head, d'Entrecasteaux reached Recherche Bay in Van Diemen's Land, having completed a full circle around Terres Australes. He did not find La Pérouse, and died on the way back. A curse seemed to befall French explorers who ventured there. Missions that required men to sail into the unknown were risky by nature. Nature. Baudin knew better than anyone that as well as great wonders, Nature had in store great terrors, great horrors.

And speaking of Nature, the emperor's wife, Joséphine, had added to his sailing orders, asking that he bring back live creatures from Terres Australes for her private collection. Baudin added the request to his already long list from the government and the scientific community.

Long lists seemed to be the order of the day. Baudin had asked for only eight scientists. Instead, he had been given twenty-two. And one of them was late in arriving. Eventually, the junior scientist, 26-year-old François-Auguste Péron, a late inclusion to the team, ventured up the gangplank. Finally, the wind blew onshore. At 9.00 am, on October 19, 1800, Baudin ordered that the sails be unfurled and the lines cast off. Péron later described the scene: 'A band of music played on the summit, and cheered our departure; an immense crowd from all parts covered the shore ... all seemed to express: "Ah, may you, more fortunate than Dufresne ... St Allouarn, La Pérouse and d'Entre-casteaux, return once more to your country, and the gratitude of your fellow citizens!"'

Two hundred and fifty-seven Frenchmen waved a final farewell to the thousands of well-wishers, and the grand departure buoyed Baudin's spirits. However, no sooner had he emerged from the port of Le Havre than he was reminded of an impediment that could thwart the success of his undertaking – on the horizon, a British frigate.

France and Britain had been at war for eight years. The English had watched with fear and dread events across the Channel since 1789, when the French masses began their revolutions. They had seen a monarchy deposed, a king beheaded. Fearing that the phenomenon might spread to their own shores, Britain and her allies were quick to declare war on the infant French Republic. Soon the war engulfed half the known world. Battle raged on land and sea. And in order for Baudin's ships to have any chance of safely navigating oceans gripped by war, the French had applied to their British enemies for a passport of safe passage.

Baudin needed this important document only five hours after leaving Le Havre. The frigate, the *Proselyte*, one of the British ships blockading the northern French ports, began to shadow *Le Géographe* and *Le Naturaliste*. Baudin sailed straight towards the enemy vessel. He hoisted a flag of truce, lowered a dinghy and grabbed his passport. On board the *Proselyte*: 'The captain received me politely and after he had read the passport from the English Admiralty, we were friends.' The two captains shared a drink, and Baudin presented his foe with one of the commemorative medals struck to celebrate his mission.

Later, the captain of the *Proselyte* reported the episode back to the Admiralty who thus received confirmation that Baudin's expedition had left France.

They had been alerted to the plans for the expedition after they received the application for the passport in June. And while the application had stressed the purely scientific nature of the expedition, the British had immediately been suspicious. Of course they had a penal colony at Port Jackson on the east coast of New Holland, or New South Wales, as they preferred to call it. The idea of founding such a colony, based on convict labour, may well have been borrowed from the French. In 1756, the respected French advocate Charles de Brosses had urged France to form a settlement, perhaps 'some part of Australasia' recommending that 'a certain number of convicts, male and female, should be sent to it every year to supply the necessary labour, and to be in time transformed from a danger and burden to the State into industrious and useful citizens'. Brosses then went on to warn his countrymen 'against the danger of waiting until some other nation had proved the practicability of a colony by trying the experiment'.

But wait the French did, and by 1800 the British penal colony at Port Jackson was twelve years old. The audacious social experiment was now in full swing, a strange Kafkaesque world, run by the notorious and corrupt Rum Corps, employing convict labour to create roads, buildings and pastures on the edge of the unknown. The colonists did not know how far the land extended to the west.

The experiment had been put into effect only eighteen years after Captain James Cook had first sighted this coast and claimed it in the name of Britain, but he had been fortunate. Two years earlier, in

1768, the French explorer Louis-Antoine, Comte de Bougainville, had been sailing west, half-way through his circumnavigation of the world, heading straight towards a more northern part of the same coast. He would have beaten Cook, had he not encountered a vast reef blocking his progress westwards. Having crossed the desolate vastness of the Pacific, with his supplies running low, Bougainville decided to search for a way through the reef by heading north rather than south. The decision cost the French the discovery of eastern Nouvelle Hollande. The reef stretched on interminably and Bougainville's course eventually took him north of Nouvelle Guinea from where he was forced to make a dash for France.

While Cook was lucky, a little bit of common-sense did not go astray either. The year after he landed on the east coast, another French explorer, Yves de Ker-guelen de Trémarec, mistakenly believed he had landed on the west. He returned in 1773 with 700 other Frenchmen to form an outpost on what they thought was a part of 'the southern continent'. Kerguelen de Trémarec had been St Allouarn's commander, before their ships became separated. While St Allouarn had continued his mission after the separation and did indeed land on the west coast of Terres Australes, Ker-guelen found another coast he claimed to be part of the South Land. Claiming the land as 'Austral France' he returned with his 700 colonists only to discover that 'Austral France' was no more than a group of frozen, desolate islands in the subantarctic. Kerguelen was forced to return to France where he was promptly court-martialled and sentenced to twenty years gaol.

By 1800, the British were jealous and protective of their enterprise in New South Wales. The Admiralty were sceptical regarding the French claim that Baudin's expedition had merely scientific objectives. And their suspicions were not ill-founded.

Napoléon was well aware that the colony at Port Jackson might ultimately give his British enemies a strategic advantage in controlling sea traffic in the Pacific, as well as providing a point from which the British could mount an assault on French allies in the Spanish American colonies. He realised that France might well require a presence to counter the British. At the very least, he needed better and more detailed reconnaissance of Terres Australes than had been provided by the four previous French missions.

Furthermore, like many Europeans, Napoléon harboured a great curiosity to know more about the unique world of Terres Australes. It seems that at the age of fifteen, Napoléon himself had applied for a position on the ill-fated La Pérouse expedition. His application was rejected so he instead forged a career in politics, war and world domination. Throughout his life, however, Napoléon's fascination with Terres Australes remained. Napoléon read Captain Cook's journals and was amazed at the first descriptions and sketches of strange creatures brought back from this unknown land, such as the furred animal with webbed feet and a duck's bill. For Napoléon, as with so many others, Terres Australes represented that part of the world where the lines of charts disappeared into imagination, into the Unknown.*

The British Admiralty may have been ignorant of Napoléon's personal interest in Terres Australes, but his strategic concerns would have been obvious enough to concern them. Particularly given one final, vital detail.

In 1800, it was rumoured that a vast strait separated the east part of Australia from the west, running north-south. Indeed by 1798, an American, Captain Williamson, had claimed to have sailed through the strait, from the south coast to the Gulf of Carpentaria. The existence of 'Williamson's Strait' could only simplify Napoléon's claim to the western part of Terres Australes where it was feared the French would soon 'hoist the standard of Bonaparte at some convenient point of the coast and establish a French colony'. Britain had to date only claimed the land of New South Wales as far west as longitude 135°. In the words of author John Dunmore; 'The natural inference was that the French hoped to found a settlement on the western island and even expel the British who had settled at Port Jackson.' Baudin himself had stressed, in his proposal to launch the French mission, that he would

---

* Napoleon was a great believer in the importance of Science and Discovery. When invading Egypt, Napoléon had taken with his military force more than 150 scientists. Returning from Egypt, Napoléon himself had delivered the very first scientific report on the Rosetta Stone. Welcomed as a member of the pre-eminent French scientific body *l'Institut National de France,* Napoléon later remarked that it was the only ovation 'that really touched me'. (Schom, p. 70). Napoleon wanted France to be at the forefront of scientific breakthroughs, as he declared: 'The true power of the French Republic must henceforth consist in not allowing there to be ideas which do not belong to it' (Hunt *et al*, pp. 24–25).

explore the lands of Terres Australes in order to clarify this point: '[I will] discover in a clear and precise manner whether or not … these form part of a single island.'

So it was hardly surprising that the application for a passport for Baudin's expedition had caused some consternation in London. However, the French had been rather canny in the way in which they had applied for British cooperation for their 'scientific mission'. The first French overtures seeking British support for a passport had been made not to the Admiralty, but to a prominent British scientist. Initially, the President of *l'Institut National de France*, Antoine-Laurent de Jussieu, had written to his British counterpart, the President of the Royal Society, Sir Joseph Banks. Banks was not only President of the Royal Society, he was also a corresponding member of the *Institut*. He was also a great friend and confidant of Earl Spencer, the First Lord of the Admiralty. The letter from Jussieu, urging him to support France's application for a passport, immediately placed Joseph Banks in a quandary. He had not only been present when Cook had claimed the east coast of Terres Australes for Britain in 1770, he had bankrolled some of the expedition from his own funds. Banks was utterly fascinated by Terres Australes. It had been his enthusiasm for the uniqueness of this new world that led to the naming of 'Botany Bay'. Banks felt as territorial regarding New South Wales, indeed all of New Holland, as the Admiralty.

At the same time, Banks genuinely wanted to

assist his fellow *Institut* members across the Channel to discover more about the unique nature of this distant land. The Brotherhood of Science demanded his support, as Jussieu had eloquently reminded him in his letter: 'The *Institut National* considers that it is precisely at the moment when war still burdens the world that the friends of humanity should work for it, by advancing the limits of Science …'

Sir Joseph eventually recommended to his friend Earl Spencer, First Lord of the Admiralty, that the French be granted a passport for Baudin's mission. The passport had been issued on June 25, 1800. Banks wrote back to inform Jussieu that the decision had been made 'without a moment's hesitation'.

Banks himself had been busy trying to organise a British exploratory mission to New Holland, to be led by the famous African explorer, Mungo Park. Alas, the plan had fallen through when Park had returned to Britain and fallen in love with a woman in Scotland. Then, in September, 1800, Banks received another letter:

> To the Right Honourable Sir Joseph Banks …
> Having returned from a station on the east coast
> of New South Wales … I presume to address
> Sir Joseph upon the subject … Probably it will
> be found, that an extensive strait separates New
> South Wales from New Holland by the way of
> the Gulph of Carpentaria … It cannot be
> doubted, but that a very great part of that still
> extensive country remains either totally

unknown, or has been partially examined at a time when navigation was much less advanced than at present. The interests of geography and natural history in general, and the British nation in particular, seem to require, that this only remaining considerable part of the globe should be thoroughly explored ... I should enter upon it with that zeal, which I hope, has hitherto characterised my services ...

The timing was remarkable. The letter came from an ambitious young naval lieutenant and aspiring explorer who had himself just returned from several years in Port Jackson. Joseph Banks sent a letter back to the 26-year-old Lieutenant, Matthew Flinders:

Joseph Banks presents his compliments to Mr Flinders he is ... happy to see him in Soho Square at any time he will be so good as to Call upon him.

Matthew Flinders was there the next day. As he stood on the doorstep of the Soho Square mansion, Flinders was nervous, excited and a little bit cocky. He knew that Sir Joseph could be the influential and powerful patron he required to propel him on the path to fame and glory, a path Flinders craved.

The door opened and Flinders was ushered in. No details of this meeting have survived, but presumably Flinders performed impressively, finding a suitable balance between his confidence in his own abilities and at least some degree of humility. When he was informed that a French mission led by Captain Baudin had already embarked, he knew that this could be his opportunity of a lifetime, as he wrote with confidence: 'It might appear, that the presence of the French upon these coasts would be much against me; but I consider the circumstance as favourable, inasmuch as the attention of the world will be more strongly attracted towards New Holland, and some comparisons will no doubt be formed between our respective labours.' After the meeting, Joseph Banks again contacted his friend Earl Spencer at the Admiralty. He urged that the Admiralty mount a British mission to rival Baudin's. He added that he thought the job of commanding it should be given to Lieutenant Matthew Flinders.

But Flinders, like Mungo Park, was in love. On September 25, 1800, he wrote a letter, this time to someone he had not seen since he was a teenager:

My dear friend …
My imagination has flown after you often and many a time, but the Lords of the Admiralty still keep me in confinement at the Nore. You must know, and your tender feelings have often anticipated for me, the rapturous pleasure I promised myself on returning from this Antipodean voyage … As you are one of those friends whom I consider it indispensable and necessary to see, I should be glad to have some little account of your movements, where you reside and with whom; that my motions may be

regulated accordingly … Indeed my dearest
friend, this time seems to be a very critical
period in my life … I have more and greater
friends than before, and this seems to be the
moment that their exertions may be the most
serviceable to me. I may now perhaps make a
bold dash forward, or remain a poor lieutenant
all my life.

But, like his previous three letters to Ann Chappelle, it seemed at first that this one too would go
unanswered.

Chapter 2

[LOVE AND OTHER
CATASTROPHES]

Ann Chappelle had good reason for not wanting
to fall in love with a mariner. Her father, John
Chappelle, had been a sea captain and had died
at sea. Even before his death, Ann had seen at first hand
the pain her father's long absences caused her mother.
So she had vowed never to marry a sailor.

Flinders, however, was nothing if not relentless.
Ann politely responded to this letter, so Flinders sent
another:

My dear friend …
I will begin by informing thee that a ship is
fitting out for me to go to New South Wales …
Everything seems to bespeak the utmost haste,
but my appointment is not yet given out … Let
us then, my dear Annette, return to the 'sweet,
calm delights of friendship' … Thou wilt write
me once more so as to arrive before the 26th –
of thy departure for Partney. By personal
conferences we may be able to come to a better
and more final understanding than by letter. Let
us meet as lovers …

Flinders pursued Ann Chappelle to Lincolnshire,
where they finally came face to face at Christmas,
1800. The romance gained momentum, but he still
struggled to overcome Ann's reluctance to marry a
sailor. Flinders suffered greatly, as he revealed in an ago-
nised letter sent two weeks later:

Excuse everything here, my dear dear friend –
tears are in my eyes – I am torn to pieces …
May thou meet with one whose mind and heart
is worthy of thy love and whose circumstances
unlike mine, can afford thee the enjoyment of
life. Adieu, perhaps the last time. This excess
of misery is too great to be often recalled. It is
seldom that I have written a letter in tears.

Flinders tried to forget Ann and focused on his
voyage. He had returned to Sheerness to oversee the

fitting out of his ship, an old collier named *Xenophon*, to be renamed the *Investigator*. By now Earl Spencer and the other Lords of the Admiralty had accepted Banks' advice and had officially appointed the young lieutenant to lead a voyage of discovery to New Holland.

Ann and Flinders had agreed that it would be best to let their relationship cool. Now he was not only a mariner, but the commander of a voyage estimated to last at least three years. He wrote again:

> Thou, my dearest friend, hast not perhaps occupations that claim the whole of thy attention; fortunate indeed it is for me that I have; otherwise I had become the demonisation of fool, madman or villain 'ere this. Forget me Annette … However dear to me thy thoughts are, still is thy happiness dearer … Banish every thing else from thee. On love I <u>must</u> not think; it has constituted the greatest happiness and the greatest misery of my life; but I will now <u>endeavour</u> to try what life is without it.

Though he said he would understand if she found someone else, the thought that this 'witty, generous, raven-haired beauty with the rich red-brown eyes' could fall in love and marry another man in his absence tore at his heart. Flinders was used to getting his own way. He had spent his life thus far doing more or less as he pleased, overcoming obstacles that stood in his way. After all, that is what explorers did.

One day, Ann received an extraordinary proposal from her young lieutenant:

My dearest friend,
Thou hast asked me if there is a possibility of our living together. I think I see a probability of living with a moderate share of comfort. Till now I was not certain of being able to fit myself out clear of the world. I have now done it; and have accommodation on board the INVESTI-GATOR, in which as my wife, a woman may, with love to assist her, make herself happy …
I will write further tomorrow; but shall most anxiously expect thy answer at 86 Fleet St London on my arrival on Friday; and I trust thy presence immediately afterwards … It will be much better to keep this matter entirely secret. There are many reasons for it yet, and I have also a powerful one. I do not exactly know how my great friends might like it …

The idea was as inviting as it was incredible. Flinders proposed to overcome Ann's misgivings of marrying a sailor, by inviting her to sail by his side. Ann would herself sail beyond the horizon and see with her own eyes the Unknown. Finally, Ann surrendered and gave her heart willingly, eagerly to the dashing young adventurer, as she gushed to a friend: 'I trust I shall be pardoned when I say, that in comparison with him, the whole human race appears to my no doubt partial imagination, as drawn with inferior colours …'

The two lovers began plotting. Flinders' father had expected a visit from his son at Christmas, but was disappointed. He had not seen him since his return from Port Jackson. Flinders finally showed up and surprised his father by asking for a loan of £200. He did not tell his father what the loan was for. Flinders' father was unimpressed, writing in his diary that 'coming upon me in the midst of the dearest winter ever known in living memory – with my strength, health and spirits very much impaired … I have put off Matthew's demand for another year – he asked for £200 – but I have promised but one …'

One hundred pounds was not enough. Flinders felt he needed £200 in order to be able to afford to marry and support Ann. He was hurt by his father's reaction and instead agreed to borrow the £200 from Ann's stepfather, the Reverend Tyler. Soon after, Flinders asked for and received a week's extension of leave. He did not tell Joseph Banks why he was travelling to Lincolnshire, but his diary records his mission: 'I set off on Wednesday evening from town, arrived next evening at Silsby, was married next morning, which was Friday.' Isabella Tyler, Ann's half-sister, described the wedding somewhat more effusively: 'Never a man more happy than poor Flinders & he determined to be so, in spite of the Lords of the Admiralty and Sir Joseph Banks. Yes, of all the merry group none more merry than he.'

Flinders' father-in-law to be, Reverend Tyler, performed the service and slipped Flinders the £200, which the groom rolled and stuffed in his boot.

The following day, the newlyweds surprised Flinders' father, who wrote: 'With concern I note that my son Matthew came upon us suddenly and unexpectedly with a wife on Sat. April 18 & left us next day – it is a Miss Chappelle of Partney. We had known of the acquaintance but had no idea of marriage taking place until the completion of his ensuing Voyage. I wish he may not repent his hasty step.' The older and more careful Flinders was concerned that by marrying Ann in secret, his son had jeopardised his voyage. Hurt and angered by his father's reception, Flinders told his father from now on to consider himself as having one less son.

Flinders was as confident as ever: 'Next morning I presented myself before Sir Joseph Banks with a grave face as if nothing had happened, and then went on with my business as usual. We stayed in town till the following Sunday, and came on board the INVESTI-GATOR next day ...'

In secret, at least from the Admiralty and Joseph Banks, since the fact could hardly be hidden from his crew, Ann moved on board the *Investigator*. Soon after, Ann's sister Isabella, who was herself, it seems, a little in love with her sister's husband, visited the happy lovers: 'I saw dear Flinders ... in his handsome uniform, his cocked hat put slightly over one eye – his sword by his side – did he not look handsome?'

Ann was more excited than anyone, though she was also daunted by the prospect of having to sail away from the people she loved, as she confided to a friend, 'I am scarce able to coin one sentence or to write intelligibly. It pains me to agony when I indulge the thought for a moment that I must leave all I value on earth, save one, alas, perhaps forever. Ah … but I dare not, must not, think. Therefore, farewell, farewell …'

It all seemed to be falling into place for Flinders, including his finances. Very conscious of the fact that he owed his father-in-law £200, at least Flinders was now receiving the salary of commander, 'A moderate computation made £300 or £400 a year on which a wife could be kept genteelly.' The British East India Company had also advanced the considerable sum of £600 to be shared between Flinders, his officers and the scientists. The *batta* was a down payment for a stake in the *Investigator's* discoveries. Of particular interest to the East India Co. was for Flinders to discover and chart 'Williamson's Strait'. As the Company pointed out, 'Any Discovery of a Passage into the Eastern Seas (which it is apprehended does exist) may be of great advantage to the Company's Ships …' Flinders was of course in total agreement: 'Should such a strait exist, the advantages that would result from it … by the very expeditious communication with India, seem almost incalculable.'

Then, all of a sudden, his great plans began to unravel.

One morning, the new First Lord of the Admiralty, Earl Saint Vincent, arrived on the *Investigator*, unannounced. He found Flinders in his cabin, 'with his wife upon his knee!' and worse, 'without her bonnet'. The sight shocked his Lordship. Joseph Banks learned that his protégé was living with his new wife on board the *Investigator* and, worse, that he planned to take her on the voyage with him. He wrote immediately to Flinders:

> The Lords of the Admiralty have heard that Mrs Flinders is on board the INVESTIGATOR, and that you have some thought of Carrying her to sea with you. This I am very sorry to hear, and if that is the Case I beg to give you my advice by no means to adventure to measures so contrary to the regulations and the discipline of the Navy; for I am convinced by language I have heard, that their Lordships will, if they hear of her being in New South Wales, immediately order you to be superseded …

Flinders found himself in uncharted waters before he had even left port. He tried to argue his case, suggesting that there had been precedents for wives accompanying their husbands on long voyages. He also pointed out that he only planned to take Ann to the colony:

> It is true that I had the intention of taking Mrs Flinders to Port Jackson, to remain there until I should have completed the purpose of the voyage … and I trust that the service would not have suffered in the least by such a step. The Admiralty have most probably conceived that I intended to keep her on board during the voyage, but this was far from my intention.

Then his efforts to placate Banks and the Admiralty suffered a further blow. He had been ordered to sail the *Investigator* from the Nore to Spithead. On May 28, 1801, while the newlyweds were below deck, the ship slammed into a sandbar known as the Roar. Flinders claimed that the watchman, rather than himself, was to blame: 'The leadsman ... at ten minutes before six, had very culpably quitted the chains when his watch was out.' Perhaps Flinders had also been distracted.

Luckily the weather was calm with a rising tide and within a short time the ship came off. Had the accident occurred on an ebbing tide, the ship would most likely have been lost. Flinders had no way of knowing it, but Baudin had experienced exactly the same embarrassment on leaving Le Havre. The incident was nevertheless a disaster. Joseph Banks was incredulous. He wrote again to Flinders:

> I yesterday went to the Admiralty to enquire
> about the INVESTIGATOR, & was indeed
> much mortified to learn there that you had been
> on shore in Hythe Bay ... in defence I could
> only say that as Capt. Flinders is a sensible man
> & a good seaman, such matters could only be
> attributed to the laxity of discipline which
> always takes place when a Captain's wife is on
> board ...

For Flinders, appointed to chart thousands of miles of unknown coastline, this was hardly an auspicious beginning. An inquiry was held. Flinders was acquitted of wrongdoing, but the English expedition lost further ground to Baudin while the *Investigator* was dry-docked to check the keel for damage.

Flinders was less concerned about the damage to his ship than to his reputation. He worried that an already angry Admiralty might be losing patience and confidence in his ability to lead this voyage. He knew that, having supported him, Banks had staked a good part of his own reputation on Flinders' success. His patron had already reminded him of as much in a letter, counselling his protégé of his 'firm belief that you will, in your future conduct, do credit to yourself as an able investigator, and to me as having recommended you'.

Flinders had to choose between Ann and the voyage. Eventually, he made his decision, writing to Sir Joseph that:

> … whatever may be my disappointment, I shall give up the wife for the voyage of discovery; and I would beg of you, Sir Joseph, to be assured, that even this circumstance will not damp the ardor I feel to accomplish the important purpose of the present voyage; and in a way that I shall preclude the necessity of anyone following after me to explore.

Ann was devastated. Her worst fears were realised. She would soon watch her new husband sail away for at least three years. With what must have been considerable bitterness, she later observed that 'no difficulty could stop his career, no danger dismay him: hunger, thirst, labour, rest, sickness ... Death itself were equally to him matters of indifference if they interfered with his darling Discovery ...'

Flinders achieved at least one objective – denying the woman he loved the opportunity of meeting and marrying someone else while he was away. All Ann had to look forward to for the next three years was village gossip, a meagre £40 per year allotment and a severely restricted social life as a married woman on her own.

Staring at the pain in her eyes, for Flinders departure could not come soon enough. He argued that he was committed, that their financial security, their future happiness, depended upon him fulfilling his mission. Whether Ann was convinced is debatable. Many years later she reminded her husband in a letter that 'Thou mayst gain reputation, fame, fortune, honour in this life, but Oh sweetheart these fading vanities have no tendency to qualify the soul for the kingdom of God ...'

Chapter 3

[THE DOLDRUMS]

On November 1, 1800, just after midday, the two French ships approached the Canary Islands. Baudin described the scene: 'The moment we sighted land, all the scientists and even most of the officers were so overjoyed that they behaved like madmen … pandemonium reigned on board. If a stranger had witnessed what went on and had not known when we had left Europe, it would have been impossible for him not to think that we had just completed a voyage lasting at least six months.'

They had been at sea for just twelve days. The

scientists implored Baudin to let them leave the ship immediately: 'More anxious than the rest, they had pestered me from the moment we dropped anchor to allow them to go ashore and I had been obliged to give my permission in order to be rid of them.'

Baudin hoisted out the dinghies, which soon raced towards the main port of Tenerife full of boisterous scientists and officers. In a parting gesture, Baudin warned the men to be wary of fraternising with the local women. He later suspected, rightly, that his warnings had been in vain: 'I have every reason to believe that the majority of the crew will be very sick as a result of their conduct with the native women, most of whom were infected with scabies, and other diseases even more disagreeable ... they came and went as freely as one does at a fair.'

Baudin was forced to reprimand Lieutenant Henri Freycinet, first for bringing a person of 'ill-repute' to dine at his table, and later for threatening to kick the chief steward in the stomach. Baudin was unimpressed: 'I sent for Mr. Freycinet ... I am very much afraid that this officer, whom I had fairly accurately judged at Le Havre, will eventually oblige me to deal severely with him in a way that will be disagreeable to us both.' Baudin was then informed of another incident between the surgeon and one of the painters: 'The second more disagreeable scene was a dispute which had arisen between Citizen Lebrun, an artist, and the ships doctor, Lharidon. Not content with abusing each other in a most ungentlemanly manner, they had seized each other by the collar, and if some men from the ship had not come along then, a fist fight would have developed in the middle of the pier.' Baudin ordered that Lebrun be confined to his quarters until they sailed from Tenerife.

Baudin again lamented the excessive number of artists and scientists he had been landed with: 'If attention had been paid to the observation that I made on the uselessness of embarking so many scientists for a voyage upon which half the present number would still be too many, then, perhaps, the personalities might have been better suited and I should have had fewer worries.'

Tenerife presented many frustrations. Baudin found it virtually impossible to secure adequate supplies. He had been quoted 70,000 francs for the 100 casks of wine he needed for the next leg of his voyage, almost three times what his budget allowed. When the fresh meat, fruit and vegetables finally arrived, many days late, only half of his order had been provided. After wasting, as he saw it, eleven days in Tenerife, Baudin decided to cut his losses and forged on. News of the lack of adequate food and wine rations did little to ease the frictions on board, Baudin observing that: 'The officers, like the scientists, found the fare unacceptable and were demanding more particular treatment, wanting all the food to come from on-shore and to consist only of fish, game, vegetables, fruit, etc., etc. And they wanted me to pay all these extra expenses.' Baudin struggled to maintain his sense of humour: 'I must say here, in passing, that those captains who have scientists … must, upon departure, take a good supply of patience. I admit that although I have no lack of it, the scientists have frequently driven me to the end of my tether and forced me to retire testily to my room.'

The men of *Le Géographe* and *Le Naturaliste* watched the Canary Islands disappear into the distance. Less than two weeks later, Baudin really found himself in the doldrums, 'Another day lost, for we were becalmed. The men began to be sick of this weather, and although I did not show it, I was certainly more vexed by it than anyone, but one must be patient in adversity.'

Baudin hoisted every last square-inch of sail to catch the faintest breeze. The ships remained listless. The ocean was like glass. There was little to do, but dangle lines over the side. Even this, as Baudin described, ended in tears: 'At about eleven o'clock we caught a fairly large shark and it was a great distraction, particularly for the scientists ... I was far from foreseeing that this poor creature would become the cause of a very serious dispute ... I saw Citizen Péron coming to me, dripping all over with blood, to complain that Mr Lharidon had snatched the shark's heart from him ... I did my best not to laugh at the complaint, which Doctor Péron considered very grave. But to console him, I promised him that the next one we caught should be his alone ...'

At first Péron bemused Baudin. The junior scientist, who had arrived late in Le Havre, made his first appearance in Baudin's journal creating some welcome light relief: 'Disagreeable as it was for citizen Péron, it nevertheless did not fail to delight all his scientific friends and most of the officers who witnessed it. Towards midday he was in the port head taking readings on a thermometer. A wave washed right over him and carried away his observation book as well as his thermometer. This accident ... did him no apparent harm, but he thought he was drowned beyond hope ... he was quite amazed not only to find himself alive, but still in the same place, for he had thought himself washed right out to sea.'

Péron was not amused. Indeed, he held Baudin responsible for their current predicament in the doldrums, which was interesting, for he was not himself a sailor. Péron, 26 years old, had been studying medicine in Paris when he heard of the mission. He quickly wrote an article titled 'Observations on anthropology, or the natural history of man ...', which he submitted to the *Muséum national d'Historie naturelle*. In the article he had argued that there should be additions to Baudin's expedition, 'young medical students, especially commissioned under the title anthropologists ...' Péron had of course recommended himself for the position, declaring enthusiastically to Jussieu, Director of the *Muséum*: 'Just let me be taken aboard, and you'll see what I can do.'

By that stage all the scientists had already been chosen, but a place was found for Péron – though he was commissioned as an assistant zoologist rather than what he really wanted to be, an 'Observer of Man'. Péron had been happy simply to get a berth. He was, by his own admission: 'Irresponsible, scatter-brained, argumentative, indiscreet, too absorbed in my own opinions, incapable of ever giving way for any reason of expediency, I can make enemies and alienate my best friends ... These failings are made up for by my good qualities. Virtuous, sensitive, generous, I have never knowingly hurt anyone ...'

The doldrums, however, did not seem to bring out Péron's good qualities. Péron accused Baudin of having taken the wrong course to round the Cape of Good Hope: 'The obstinacy of our commander in ranging the coast of Africa, was the chief cause of this delay ... We shall soon find, that from this preposterous obstinacy ... consequences at once grievous and irreparable!' In accusing Baudin of sailing the wrong course, Péron was in fact mistaken. Baudin was following the standard route used by nearly every mariner who travelled south from Europe towards the Cape. Captain Cook had followed the same course. Baudin had made this trip from Europe to Île-de-France, their next port of call, several times before. Péron was typical of many of the non-sailors on board; bored, irritable and not shy of showing it.

Baudin watched his ships drift, at the mercy of the currents: 'We were becalmed once more and the ship did not move until just after midday. We were already beginning to smell a bad odour on board.' The ships edged closer towards the Equator. 'A messenger came to announce that we were close to crossing the line and to ask permission to hold the traditional ceremony. I gave my consent willingly ...'

On Christmas Eve, 1800, Lebrun started a fight by

throwing a glass of water in the face of another artist, Milbert. Baudin had a chat with Lebrun: 'I summoned him to my room. As it was not the first complaint about him, I told him very seriously that if he continued to behave badly, I would put him under arrest in the artillery room and that he would only come out to disembark at Île-de-France.' A few days later, Baudin had to have a chat with Milbert: 'Citizen Milbert had spent such a restless night ... caused by his grief at being separated from his wife and children ... Someone, who no doubt held his behaviour against him, had given him the idea that I had written unflatteringly of him to the Minister of Marine at the time of our departure from Tenerife. I was astonished he could have believed this ... I thought the fairest thing to do was let him know what was in the letter, so I read it aloud to him. I wish that this act of condescension on my part may restore his spirits ...'

Baudin's expedition might have been the best equipped ever to sail out of France, but it was certainly not the most harmonious. Time and time again, Baudin found himself called upon to settle what he saw as terribly petty grievances. Baudin began to worry about the suitability of his young team for the task before them – a voyage into uncharted waters, the perils hidden and even unknown. He decided it was time to have a chat with the whole team: 'I assembled all the officers and scientists in the council room and informed them of the government's intentions concerning the conduct they were to uphold on board ... I took the opportunity of telling them all that I was disappointed to see that they were not getting on well together and that the reason for this lay in the ill naturedness of certain persons. I added that I had authority to get rid of them at the next port if they did not mend their ways.'

Baudin's good friend, Anselm Riedlé the gardener, saw the meeting as timely: 'The commandant observed to us that only good order and understanding would enable the voyage to succeed, that all Europe had its eyes on us, and if the voyage failed it would be due only to the bad understanding and the discord that were arising between officers and naturalists, and on our return to France we would be blamed by the whole nation …'

The meeting, however, did little to alter the behaviour of the malcontents. Indeed, it may even have spurred some on. There was another issue simmering away on board, perhaps the most contentious of all. Many of the young men simply found it impossible to respect their captain's authority. The more Baudin tried to enforce it, the more they resisted.

The young scientists, and even the officers, were 'children of the revolution', young men in their early twenties keen to make their mark and prove their worth. Baudin's 'team' had been selected, not by himself, but by the *Institut* and they did make up one of the largest and most impressive scientific teams ever assembled to prosecute a voyage of exploration – astronomers, geographers, botanists, zoologists, mineralogists, artists and gardeners. With the exception of three who had sailed with Baudin on a previous expe-

dition, they had been chosen for their academic quali-
fications and enthusiasm for the voyage. As Péron
gushed: 'Never was a display so considerable given to
this department of a voyage of discovery; never were
means so amply prepared for ensuring success.'

As Baudin had by now observed, however, most
of them had never before experienced life at sea. They
really had no idea of what was in store. With their
heads full of the notions of *Liberté*, *Egalité* and *Frater-
nité*, they had seen themselves heading off for the
adventure of a lifetime, and instead found themselves
wallowing in the Atlantic Ocean on reduced rations,
having to submit to the authority of their much older
commander. To the young Revolutionaries, Baudin
soon began to look more and more like a symbol of
the despised *Ancien Régime*. This was ironic, as many
of the young scientists and officers were in fact themselves descendants of the aristocracy. By 1800, the
guillotine had grown rusty and the aristocratic families
that had survived the purges were again rising to
prominence and filling the ranks of the intelligentsia.
Aristocratic lineage was ceasing to be a career impediment and notions of ascendancy were, with the
aristocrats at least, back in vogue.

Many of Baudin's team were proud sons of aristocrats and resented being ordered about by a man
who came from the lower classes. Péron was himself a
product of the middle-class, but he eagerly 'sided with
the younger officers, who, as openly as they dared,
called their captain a miser, no naval man, merely an
old merchant skipper with his head turned, unfit to

command real fighting officers'.

The irony would not have been lost on Baudin, who was far more a Revolutionary than his young officers and scientists. Indeed, if the Old Order had not been toppled, a man of his origins would never have received command of this expedition.

Baudin was born in 1754 a commoner, the son of a humble merchant, one of thirteen children. He realised at an early age that he should expect little in the way of financial support from his parents, and as a teenager determined to take his chances as a cabin boy on vessels plying the French coast. Baudin served a tough apprenticeship, beaten and abused until he grew big enough to defend himself. In his early twenties, he joined the Royal French Navy and served on the *Minerve* battling the British in the American War of Independence. He conducted himself so impressively that he was eventually given command of the frigate *Apollon*.

This all occurred before the Revolution, and Baudin was just settling in to his new command when he was suddenly relieved of it, for no other reason than to make way for an *officier rouge* – an officer of noble birth. When offered a choice between giving command to an *officier bleu*, as Baudin was – or giving it to an aristocratic *officier rouge* – for the French Royal Navy, there was no contest. The commanding officer in the port of Brest, the Comte d'Hector, as Baudin bitterly described 'used the pretext of service requirements, too common at that time, to deprive me of the command and give it to one of his protégés'. Baudin quit the French Royal Navy in disgust.

However, it was this decision that had really set him on his course in life. He returned to the merchant marine and began to broaden his horizons, travelling to the Caribbean, Santo Domingo and down the dark coast of Africa. One day he met a gardener, in fact Franz Boos, the Royal Gardener to the Emperor of Austria. Although Baudin was, at the time, trying to negotiate a slave-contract, he agreed to take Boos and his assistant to Île-de-France instead. During the voyage, watching the Austrians in action, began Baudin's fascination with the challenges of keeping natural history specimens alive on board a windswept, tossing ship. So successful was the trip that Baudin was then contracted to take all the specimens of the Austrian expedition back to the Austrian Emperor, Joseph II, brother of Marie Antoinette. The specimens arrived safely and Baudin soon found himself in great demand. He discovered that he enjoyed the work of botanical voyager immensely and, in stark contrast to his experience in the Royal French Navy, the Austrian Navy promoted him and he reached the rank of Naval Captain in 1792 – an honour normally reserved only for Austrian subjects. If not for the Revolution, Baudin might never have returned to France.

Now in late 1800, off the African coast, drifting in and out of the doldrums, he had need of every last one of his managerial skills as he strove to hold his fractious company together. He did not find it easy to warm to his young charges, instinctively offended by the pompous antics of the uppity young naturalists and his so-called *officiers rouge* – carrying on as if privilege was their right.

Finally, in early February, 1801, *Le Géographe* and *Le Naturaliste* rounded the Cape of Good Hope. The wind began to blow more constantly, if often from the wrong direction. Baudin kept a record of it all. 'The ship strained somewhat and shook violently.'

Chapter 4

[CRIME AND PUNISHMENT]

S till in England, Flinders was experiencing his own problems just getting out of port. The French were partly to blame. As a frustrated Flinders explained, 'Various circumstances retarded our departure, and amongst others, a passport from the French government, to prevent molestation to the voyage, had not arrived.' Since the English had already issued one for Baudin's ships, Flinders could not foresee there being any difficulty in the courtesy being reciprocated. Unless of course the French deliberately wanted to delay the departure of his mission.

At least, by now, Flinders had his own scientific team assembled. Compared with the French team of twenty-two, the British group was small, consisting of only six men: Robert Brown, twenty-seven, naturalist; Ferdinand Lukas Bauer, forty, botanical artist; William Westall, nineteen, landscape artist; John Crosley, astronomer; John Allen, miner. Peter Good was chosen as gardener to keep the plants alive at sea. Unlike Baudin's scientists, Flinders' team had been briefed as to what the British Navy expected of them in terms of discipline and the duty owed to their commander. Indeed, Sir Joseph ensured that each had signed instructions to that effect – stating that they would comply with 'voluntary obedience to the commander of the ship, and on all occasions conduct themselves peacefully, quietly and civily'.

Flinders had managed to secure his own brother, Samuel, a position on the voyage as a second lieutenant. Filling most of the vacancies on board had been a breeze. When Flinders was seeking seamen, he asked for volunteers. By chance, the men who came to stand before him were men from his last ship, the *Reliance*. Flinders was gratified by the response. 'Where eleven volunteers were to be received … about three hundred disposable men were called up, and placed on one side of the deck; and after the nature of the voyage … had been explained to them, those who volunteered were desired to go over to the opposite side. The candidates were not less than two hundred and fifty …' The last position Flinders filled was that of his second-in-command, or Master. He eventually offered the job to another man who had also sailed with him on the *Reliance*, the straightforward and dependable John Thistle, a 28-year-old sailor who had risen through the ranks.

Unfortunately Flinders' efforts to smuggle his wife along on the voyage had not been appreciated by the superstitious sailors. Everyone knew that to bring a woman on an ocean voyage only invited disaster. John Thistle visited a gipsy who delivered a most gloomy prophecy of the voyage ahead. The gipsy forecast that Thistle and several other men would be lost in a small boat, followed later by total shipwreck, not of the *Investigator*, but another ship. Thistle had tried to joke about the prophecy, but the story only heightened the sailors' unease. Mind you, superstition did not prevent the sailors bringing prostitutes on board while in dock. With departure imminent, the crew were paid two months salary in advance. No longer permitted on shore, in the evening the officers turned a blind eye as the Gunroom and Seamen's Mess became scenes of debauchery.

Daylight brought the sailors back to earth. One morning the Royal Navy paraded a salient reminder of the strict discipline expected of its crews. On Bastille Day, 1801, Flinders and his crew were treated to the spectacle of four deserters being rowed in a small boat from one ship to the next to ensure that every crewman in the harbour witnessed their flogging. The punishment was repeated in front of every ship. The harbour was full of ships and each man received in excess of a thousand lashes.

Flinders had lost a few deserters of his own and was impatient to get under way. The longer he delayed, the greater the possibility that the Admiralty might lose faith in his ability to lead this mission. Flinders himself remained cocksure of his talents; he was used to sailing his own path. He had been doing it since he was a child, since he had read *Robinson Crusoe* – that book with those intriguing opening words that both attracted and disturbed him:

> My father, who was very ancient, had given me
> a competent share of learning and had designed
> for me the Law ... but I would be satisfied with
> nothing but going to sea, and my inclination to
> this led me so strongly against the will, nay the
> commands of my father, and against all the
> entreaties and persuasions of my mother and
> other friends, that there seem'd to be something
> fatal in that propension of nature, tending
> directly to the life of misery which was to
> befall me.

Flinders' father had intended a career in medicine for his son. Matthew Flinders Snr was a surgeon, as had been his father before him. But young Flinders began to dream of new horizons and far-away shores. He later confessed that he was 'induced to go to sea against the wishes of friends from reading *Robinson Crusoe*'.

Flinders seems always to have been confident that he was best qualified to chart his own path in life. As he grew older, he realised that a career in the Royal Navy would not only broaden his horizons, but also offer a much better opportunity for social and financial advancement, compared to the limited prospects of a country doctor. England had again declared war on France, a situation that promised even greater opportunities, since bounties would be paid on the capture of enemy ships.

His father had grave misgivings in supporting his son in such a foolhardy endeavour. Donington, where Flinders grew up, was twenty miles from the sea. It did not produce sailors, but men of the land. But as Flinders pointed out, Cousin John had done it, and so could he. The point did not entirely convince his father. Cousin John had spent a lifetime in the service and only reached the rank of Lieutenant. Cousin John helped Flinders, though, suggesting that the aspiring mariner read other books besides *Robinson Crusoe* – such as Robertson's *Elements of Navigation* and Moore's *New Practical Navigator*. Flinders read his books well, so well that his father could not fail but be impressed, and slowly he began to support his son, delivering young Matthew in person to his first commission on the *Scipio* in 1790. Flinders' father confided his lingering doubts to his journal: 'It has long been his choice, not mine … I shall heavily miss him.'

Only a year later, when Flinders secured a berth sailing with Captain Bligh, his father struggled to conceal his pride: 'My son Matthew … is going with the famous Captain William Bligh in the *Providence* … to circumnavigate the Globe. They expect to sail about

1st June and will be near 3 years performing this great undertaking.' At seventeen, Flinders set off on the ultimate boy's adventure. Bligh was attempting his second trip to transport breadfruit from Tahiti to the West Indies. The trip allowed Flinders ten weeks with the Tahitians. Like most of his companions, Flinders could not resist beautiful women who traded their favours for European goods, Flinders noting that 'The ladies are fond of Shirts or Sheets. Ironwork they will take but do not care much for.' There was also another price. Amongst the surgeon's list of men who afterwards sought medical treatment for venereal disease was the name 'Matthew Flinders'. As the ship's surgeon noted, 'We chased the girls only to find the girls were not chaste.'

The other low point of the voyage, as far as Flinders was concerned, was the fact that he had to surrender his log to Captain Bligh. As his father had urged him, young Flinders had kept a detailed journal describing his adventures. Along with the diaries kept by all the men on board his ship, Bligh confiscated Flinders' diary at the end of the voyage. This was the standard practice of captains at the time. Flinders, however, was angry and decided that he could not continue to serve with Bligh, 'Since the credit, if any be due to my labours, would be in danger of being monopolised.'

Flinders had transferred to the *Bellerophon* and soon found himself in the heat of battle. On June 1, 1794, nineteen-year-old Flinders stared at the approaching enemy vessels of the French Revolutionary Navy. As the opposing fleets manoeuvred to try to annihilate one another, sensing that an opportunity might be missed, Flinders tried to sink a French ship single-handedly, as described later by his wife: 'Mr Flinders … seized the lighted match, and at the instant his ship was passing under the stern of a large French three-decker, fired off in succession as many of the deserted guns as would bear, right into her: Commodore Pasley having observed his actions, shook the young hero violently by the collar & sternly said "How dare you do this, youngster without my orders." ' Fortunately, Flinders' commander did not pursue his insubordination, perhaps because his initiative, at least according to Ann, helped secure British victory in the battle subsequently dubbed the 'Glorious First of June'.

Flinders, though, saw little that was glorious: 'About 5, we had taken possession of seven sail of the line … the last of which sunk very soon after, about 200 of the men were picked up by different boats. The rest, about 600, were lost … How an idea of liberty, and more so, that of fighting for it should enter their heads I know not …' Flinders had not joined the Navy for this, as he later wrote: 'My employments and inclinations lead to the extension of happiness and of science, and not to the destruction of mankind …'

So now in July, 1801, Flinders stood entrusted with the lives of 80 other human beings for the next three years, in what could only be described as a risky undertaking. He wrote optimistically to Ann: 'I trust that a very short period indeed will now see me absent from England and each wasting day will then bring nearer the period of my return … I go, beloved, to gather riches and laurels with which to adorn thee; rejoice at the opportunity which fortune and circumstances give me to do it.'

Finally, the passport from the French arrived. On July 19, 1801, Flinders left England. Ahead lay an unexplored world, pristine and vast. And a Frenchman.

Chapter 5

[ISLAND OF FRANCE]

With a head-start of nine months, Baudin approached the lonely outpost of the French Republic, Île-de-France (today known as Mauritius). The initial reception was hardly encouraging: 'The lookout men had reported us as enemy vessels … all the troops and national guards had been ordered to their respective posts … I could not help laughing at the fright caused by such peaceable ships as ours.'

Even on learning that the ships were not British but French, the islanders remained suspicious. A pilot boarded *Le Géographe* and the impression Baudin received was one of general paranoia: 'They asked if there were any secret agent on board entrusted with putting into execution the decree concerning the liberty of the natives.'

Baudin had to reassure the island authorities that he was not there to enforce the 1794 decree guaranteeing the emancipation of all French slaves. The local administrators and land-holders were not yet ready to follow the lead of the Revolutionary Government in Paris and undermine their own economy. On learning that Baudin was just passing through, and on an entirely different mission, he was eventually greeted warmly by the Governor, General Magallon. He was then led to meet Chauvalon, the administrator or 'Intendant'. Baudin found this man far less forthcoming: 'I did not find at all in the administrator … the polite and gracious welcome that I had met with everywhere else.' He was now desperate for fresh supplies. But when Baudin requested that the Intendant provide his mission with fresh food, he was refused. Baudin was stunned: 'His reply was that we could eat what we liked, but he would replace nothing for us.'

With the British blockade of Le Havre and most French ports, supplies in France had been at a premium. Baudin had been guaranteed that government stores would replenish his ship at Île-de-France. The supplies at the Canary Islands had proved inadequate and the expedition's two-month delay due to the doldrums meant that Baudin's predicament was now acute. Baudin found Intendant Chauvalon unmoved:

'In the morning the crew complained to me about the way they were being fed while in port. I took their representations to the Intendant … It was in vain that I told him that such an unfair measure could not fail to serve as a pretext for desertion.'

In fact, desertion was exactly what the Intendant desired. For the islanders, two hundred more fighting men, and two fine ships, were a tantalising prospect. Baudin eventually recognised the ploy for what it was: 'I really began to see that an effort was being made to force my crew to give up the rest of the expedition … a constant fear of attack by the English made it desirable that I should remain longer so that my men could be conscripted if they did appear.' Many of Baudin's men needed little convincing to desert. The miserable rationing of the last few weeks had persuaded many of the adventure-seeking scientists, and even some of the young officers, that this was not a trip for them.

On his way back to the dock, Baudin was greeted by an unusual sight: 'In the evening as I returned aboard, I noticed a placard which had been put up at the corner of some streets and upon which was written in large letters: The Expedition that Failed …' Baudin suspected that the placard was the work of Intendant Chauvalon. He confronted him: 'I asked him if he had been the one who had posted up "the Expedition that Failed" and if he really thought he should succeed in it … as the conversation was growing too heated, I left …'

He soon found himself fighting battles on several fronts: 'As a result of the Intendant's behaviour toward the crews several men convinced that I would not be able to leave, began to grow unruly and even impertinent. A few were put in irons on the ship to serve as an example, but they made light of the punishment.'

As the islanders had hoped, the expedition began to unravel. Several of the officers and scientists claimed to be too ill to continue on the voyage and booked themselves into the Port Louis hospital. Baudin visited the men: 'I went ashore and visited the hospital to see the officers and naturalists who, according to the certificates given me were to be found there. The trip was quite useless for I found nobody. The Sisters of Charity who run the hospital assured me that these gentlemen sometimes returned in the evening and even rather late.'

In an attempt to win Chauvalon over, Baudin wrote a letter to the Intendant, inferring that his mission had a secret political agenda with orders directly from Napoléon:

> The mission the Government has charged me
> with … includes some political aspects … I
> know that Administrators as enlightened as
> you will easily conceive that the Government
> has not undertaken in today's circumstances
> an expedition like mine without having an
> objective of a utility more solid and useful than
> the simple collection of objects of curiosity …

This is one of the very few times that mention of Baudin's 'secret instructions' was actually recorded.

Interestingly, while several authors have noted the references to such 'secret instructions', many dismiss the claims, pointing to a lack of evidence. This interpretation seems somewhat illogical, since 'secret instructions' by definition do not necessarily leave evidence of their existence. Even a superficial understanding of Napoléon's character and motivation would suggest that he did little without a strategic interest. Jean-Paul Faivre wrote: 'In spite of the almost total absence of documents I still persist in believing in the political character of the Baudin expedition.' 'Secret instructions' were not unusual in voyages of exploration. Captain Cook had his secret orders as did La Pérouse. The latter landed at Botany Bay to 'explore the coasts of New Holland, doubtless with some more or less definite designs of settlement'. There was a very good reason for secrecy. If the British found evidence of any political or strategic instructions, then a passport issued in the spirit of scientific investigation would have been rendered void. In terms of what such instructions may have stated, an educated guess may suggest that Baudin was ordered to scout for suitable sites for settlement, but also to gather the intelligence La Pérouse failed to bring back – that is, spying on the settlement at Port Jackson; determining the size of the garrison there and charting approaches for a possible invasion. Since La Pérouse's disappearance after his visit in 1788, no other Frenchman had seen the British colony and Napoléon may have been very curious as to the nature of it.

The letter had little effect on the Intendant's

attitude and Baudin determined upon a different course of action. He estimated that he needed to find 10,000 *piastres* in order to purchase the minimum amount of supplies he required for the next leg of the voyage from private merchants. He enlisted the help of an old friend to loan the funds. 'The Danish consul Pelgrom … invited to dinner the following day all the Danish captains who were in the colony … he proposed to several captains, who had remittances to send to Europe, that they give me the sum of ten thousand piastres … The Danish captains found this sum so reasonable that they all wanted to make it up in equal portions.'

Baudin then turned his attention to the trickier problem: the deserters. While in port, thirty slaves had been employed in repairing Baudin's ships. The islanders suddenly became very worried when Baudin refused to send the slaves back on shore: 'As a result of these fears, the Intendant sent a port official to me to ask for them, but I refused to hand them back … I did not hide from them the fact that it depended upon them alone to have my missing men returned to me.'

The threat eventually had the desired effect. With the administrator's assistance, some of Baudin's deserters were returned. Baudin was satisfied: 'On the *Géographe*, leaving the scientists aside, I was 15 men short of the number I had had on arrival … I had 100 men all told and the *Naturaliste* 85. We were thus in a position to put to sea without worry.'

The next morning Baudin hoisted his sails as soon as possible: 'At seven o'clock we felt a breeze and although it was weak, weighed anchor immediately to my great satisfaction …'

Anselm Riedlé, Baudin's best friend the gardener, felt that Baudin had shown his mettle in preventing them becoming 'The Mission that Failed'. Riedlé was convinced that, 'Without the actions of the commandant, the ships would have remained in the port of Île-de-France.'

Chapter 6

[A L L   A T   S E A]

The *Investigator* pounded its way through the
waves, the sound reverberating through the hull.
Another update on the situation below was
delivered to Flinders. The news was more of the same,
more water: 'We had the mortification to find the ship
beginning to leak so soon as the channel was cleared,
and in the three last days she had admitted three inches
of water per hour.' Flinders knew that the ageing
Xenophon, though grandly renamed the *Investigator*, was
already well past its prime. Perhaps Ann's presence
had distracted him from keeping a closer eye on the

quality of the workmanship while the ship was being refitted.

Flinders cursed himself for not having examined the ship more carefully, though he also realised he had had no other options: 'Should it be asked, why representations were not made, and a stronger vessel procured? I answer, that the exigencies of the navy were such at that time, that I was given to understand no better ship could be spared from service; and my anxiety to complete the investigation of the coasts of Terra Australis did not admit of refusing the one offered.'

Flinders' initial impression of his ship had been quite favourable, not least because it was a flat-bottomed collier, the exact same kind of vessel employed by another navigator charting his way to fame and glory: 'The *Investigator* ... nearly resembled the description of vessel recommended by captain Cook as best calculated for voyages of discovery.' At any rate, it was too late for regrets. There was nothing to do but sail on.

On the first leg of the voyage two ships fired on the *Investigator*. Flinders ordered the hoisting of the ensign and prepared for action. Though he possessed the passport, he knew that he might get a cannonball through his cabin before anyone had a chance to read it. The smaller ships hesitated and eventually retreated.

On reaching his first port of call, Madeira, Flinders organised for the *Investigator*'s entire hull to be recaulked. Unlike Baudin's problems on Île-de-France, Flinders had no difficulty securing further provisions: 'Water, wine, and fresh beef, were the supplies procured at Madeira. Wine for the ship's company was charged at the enormous price of 5s. 8d. per gallon ... I therefore took only small quantities ...' Flinders knew that he had to be careful not to skimp too much with the men's grog. The standard daily ration for a British seaman was a quarter of a pint of rum (spirits) per day, anything less might lead to mutiny.

The *Investigator* and her crew sloshed their way onwards, towards the Equator. As the British expedition crossed the line, the rum ration received a further boost: 'I permitted the ceremony of shaving and ducking as usual in crossing the equator to be performed in full latitude. At the conclusion they had as much grog given to them as they could drink, the ship having been put under snug sail.'

Continuing down the coast of Africa, they avoided the doldrums that had delayed Baudin and began to gain on their French rivals. Flinders reached the Cape of Good Hope only ninety days after leaving England.

Again Flinders had no trouble taking further good provisions on board, stocking up on ample fresh meat. However he had one loss at this early stage. At the Cape, Flinders had one 'deserter', the astronomer. John Crosley had spent most of the trip thus far clinging to the *Investigator*'s gunnels, retching. This was a serious blow to Flinders. A mission heading into uncharted waters, intending to chart those waters, had serious need of an astronomer. Flinders found it impossible to find anyone to take Crosley's place in Cape Town. So he persuaded Crosley to leave the Board of Longitude instruments on the *Investigator*. Flinders would take on the duty himself, in conjunction with his brother Samuel: 'The loss of the astronomer was severely felt by me … but through an increase in effort, and with the assistance of my officers, I hoped to carry on the surveys and fulfil the most essential parts of the instructions from the Board of Longitude.'

In addition to the extra workload, Flinders of course also expected to take on part of the astronomer's salary, money he felt that he and his wife could well use. Flinders kept Ann informed of his progress, posting three letters to her from Cape Town. Even after leaving that port, with no prospect of reaching another for many long months, he continued to write to her:

> Write to me constantly; write me pages and
> volumes. Tell me the dress thou wearest, tell me
> thy dreams, anything … think of me, my love,
> and write me the uppermost of thy thoughts.
> Fill me half a dozen sheets, and send them when
> thou canst … Think only, my dearest girl upon
> the gratification which the perusal and reperusal
> fifty times repeated will afford me … Adieu, my
> dearest, best love.

While in Cape Town, Flinders had had the *Investigator* caulked again, this time insisting that not only the sides but every part of the deck be done. Continuing on, heading deeper into the Indian Ocean, all the efforts seemed to have been in vain: 'The leakiness of the ship increased with the continuance of the southwest winds; and at the end of a week, amounted to five inches of water an hour ... [this] could not be contemplated without uneasiness ...'

Flinders decided that it was too risky to descend to the Roaring Forties. Here he was, representing the world's greatest naval power, embarking on a three-year voyage, sailing in an impossibly leaky tub. Unbeknown to Flinders and his carpenters, the main support timbers behind the planks of the hull had begun rotting almost immediately on leaving England.

Nicknamed 'Indefatigable' by his friends, for Flinders there was only one option. To press on.

Chapter 7

[THE FAR HORIZON]

On the far side of the Indian Ocean, in the face of endless complaints, Baudin too pressed on. Meal rations were the main issue: 'I arranged things so that every day I invited two people to dinner, an officer and a naturalist … I always had four at my table, and at my expense. I had correctly foreseen, upon leaving France, that there would be malcontents and that no matter how good the meals were, there would always be someone who was dissatisfied with them. Still, I must admit that the scientists never complained.'

Not to his face that is. Baudin was not privy to the scientists' journals, in particular the journal of Péron who wrote: 'We were informed by our commander, that ... we should have but half a pound of new bread once in ten days; that instead of the allowance of wine, we should have three sixteenths of a bottle of bad rum ... a sad prelude, and chief cause of all the miseries we in the end experienced.'

Many of the deserters on Île-de-France had been surprised that Péron had not deserted with them. Of course, Péron had seen that in the mayhem of desertions, with the number of scientists dwindling, there was a great opportunity for a junior scientist to be promoted. And he was right. After leaving Île-de-France Baudin appointed the young assistant zoologist to the position Péron had originally lobbied and applied for, the important duty of official 'Observer of Man'.

Baudin was not entirely displeased with some of the changes that had been forced upon him at Île-de-France: 'I was not very sorry about the officers and scientists who had abandoned the expedition.' In particular, Baudin had been happy to see the backs of the two painters: 'I filled the positions uselessly occupied by M. Milbert and Garnier with Citizens Petit and Lesueur.'

This appointment was a bold move. Baudin promoted two young gunners, whom he himself had employed to make sketches in his private journal, to be the new official artists of the expedition. This was not a decision to be taken lightly. Baudin understood his responsibilities to the *Institut National* and, indeed, to

Napoléon himself, to provide images of what he and his crew would find in the unknown. Paintings and sketches were the only way for the benefactors of the expedition to experience vicariously the spectacle of new sights.

Entrusted with painting landscapes, Baudin appointed 23-year-old Charles-Alexandre Lesueur. Portraits would be executed by Nicolas-Martin Petit, also twenty-three. As Baudin said: 'We shall see from the work of these two young men whether my choice of them was good or bad.' He need not have worried. Baudin's choice of painters was a masterstroke.

While Lesueur and Petit practised their craft, sketching their shipmates and the different hues of the endless horizon surrounding them, *Le Géographe* and *Le Naturaliste* crept eastwards across the Indian Ocean. One afternoon, even Baudin was surprised by the height of the watery hills towering over them: 'The sea was so big that the two ships, although only half a canon-shot apart, were hidden from each other when the waves rose between them. And although a fresh breeze was still blowing, our sails hung windless in the troughs of the waves.'

The tossing of the ship did nothing to allay the grumbling of the malcontents. Below deck, in the nooks and crannies of *Le Géographe*, Baudin's detractors continued to conspire, to whisper, to build grudges. Some even began to spy on their commander's log-book and official correspondence. Baudin ignored them as best he could. He knew that the uninspiring rations and still overcrowded conditions could not fail to breed dissatisfaction.

Baudin steeled himself with patience and toler-
ance. And when he needed companionship and a
laugh, Baudin always had his two good friends to rely
on. Anselm Riedlé, the gardener – tireless, full of life
and vigour, a man who shared Baudin's passion for all
things botanical. René Maugé, the zoologist, Baudin's
own age, wise and fair, and an expert on the *Muséum*'s
collection, even if he could not read or write. Both
men had sailed with Baudin before. They had volunteered for this trip only because Baudin was in charge.
They knew that they had entrusted their lives to a tal-
ented, fearless man. They had seen Baudin in action.
Riedlé and Maugé had been there, one dreadful night
in 1797 on an earlier expedition, Baudin standing
calmly on a disintegrating deck, yelling orders into the
teeth of the howling hurricane. Another scientist had
recorded the scene: 'Amidst the greatest dangers his
example inspired the company, his coolness spread
confidence … Although badly wounded in the head,
although deprived of food and sleep he was heedless of
his own needs, and concerned himself only with our
own. His experience and his skill rescued us from the
horrors of shipwreck.'

Baudin had a running feud with hurricanes. In
previous encounters, eight years earlier, they had
gotten the better of him, as he wrote begrudgingly: 'I
was off the coast of New Holland when two consecu-
tive forced me to turn back.'

Not this time. On an autumn morning in 1801,
Baudin knew he was near, 'at half past seven the

topmen unfurling them told us of land lying East by North East … It was about half past ten before we began to distinguish it from on deck …'

At last Baudin saw it shimmering there on the horizon, beckoning. The lands of Terres Australes. The land of Nouvelle Hollande. Seven months after leaving France, the Frenchmen had arrived at the true beginning of their adventure. As Baudin had predicted, all the officers and scientists immediately forgot their grievances. The excitement was palpable.

Baudin had in his possession a thirty-year-old chart of Cap Leeuwin, the south-western tip of Nouvelle Hollande. The chart had been drawn by St Allouarn, one of the French explorers who had previously stepped onto the soil of this unknown land. One of the four who had never returned. Baudin knew he had to be wary in these waters, and spent most of the day creeping slowly towards the dark outline on the horizon. By dusk, the coast was still several miles off and Baudin decided it would be safer for the two ships to spend the night tacking, in order to maintain position until the following morning. To maintain the sense of excitement on board, Baudin suggested that they all spend the evening fishing. 'To make the night seem shorter … I decided to put down one of our dredges. I was convinced that despite the great depth of the water, I would find some beautiful shells or other curious objects … it was pulled up and to our great satisfaction, we found it full of different objects which we were most impatient to look at.' At last, Baudin and the scientists and even the officers seemed to share a common purpose. Together Baudin and Péron pored over the marine samples brought up to slither across the deck.

The next morning, with the return of light, the expedition crept closer to the coast and began heading north. Soon after, Baudin discovered a great bay not marked on his old charts. Baudin named the feature in honour of the ship that had brought him to this point, Géographe Bay. The great moment then arrived: 'At 9 o'clock we left to go ashore. All the scientists as may easily be imagined wanted to be of the party … I had as travelling companions Citizens Maugé, Riedlé and Depuche.' Approaching the shore, Baudin's party spotted a man: 'Until then, we had not seen a single one of the natives of the country, but as we landed, we saw one … At first he appeared to pay little attention to us and concerned himself solely with his fishing. But when we landed at about the distance of gunshot from him, he left the water … the native began to shout violently, signalling us to go back. As his signs were in the direction of the ships, we were in no doubt as to what he was saying to us.' Baudin ignored the signal. The Frenchmen pursued the *Wardandi* man. He disappeared. Baudin continued inland, conscious of Napoléon's instructions: 'It was the wish of the 1st Consul, that as Deputies of Europe, we should conciliate these uninformed people, and appear among them as friends and benefactors.'

As they travelled, Baudin noticed that the soil, although sandy, offered some scope for cultivation. Unable to locate any more of the local inhabitants,

Baudin instead left a gift from Europe: 'On the short tour inland, I had maize, apple and pear seeds … and various other types of vegetable planted on the plain that we crossed … If all these things flourish, it will mean additional sustenance for the individuals in this part of New Holland.'

Péron too failed to find the *Wardandi*. The newly promoted official 'Observer of Man' had approached the shore in another boat: 'As soon as we landed on the beach I ran towards the interior in search of the natives, with whom I had a strong desire to be acquainted. In vain I explored the forests, following the prints of their footsteps.' In his enthusiasm to test his anthropological skills, Péron lost his way: 'After a three hours fatiguing walk to no purpose, I returned towards the sea shore, where I found my companions waiting for me and rather alarmed at my absence.'

This was the first of many times on the voyage that Péron was to get himself lost. It happened again the following day, when Baudin sent a boat to investigate what appeared to be a possible source of desperately needed fresh water. The longboat was launched before dawn along with two smaller boats. Included in the party of twenty-five was Péron. Baudin stayed on board *Le Géographe*.

Scraping bottom on a sandbar near the beach, the landing party waded to shore, then scattered. Scientists and officers raced in every direction to explore. Only two young sailors remained on the sandbar with the longboat. The young men discovered a keg of brandy left in the boat. The find was too tempting and soon the keg was empty. With waves building on the incoming tide, the two lads eventually lost control of the longboat, which was suddenly swamped and sank.

Péron had ventured off on his own and late in the afternoon found himself on the banks of a lagoon. He stared in wonder at the semi-circle of glowing white melaleuca trees, stripped of bark, surrounding another semi-circle of coloured sand. Péron gushed: 'This charming place … is probably dedicated to some public or private mystery. The worship of gods may be the particular object … A new race of Egyptians, who probably like the ancient inhabitants of the Nile, have consecrated by their gratitude the stream which supplies their wants.'

Heading back towards their landing place, Péron struggled to locate his companions. He eventually stumbled across the painter Lesueur walking with Lieutenant François Ronsard, the chief engineer. Péron listened enviously to the two men's account of their encounter with a *Wardandi* woman on the beach: 'Lesueur and Ronsard had just had a somewhat extraordinary interview with a female savage … who was very far advanced in a state of pregnancy … Despairing of her situation of being able to escape from strangers … she stopped from the first moment, and sitting down on her heels and hiding her face with her hands, she remained as one stupefied and overcome with fear and astonishment.' Lesueur explained that the woman was so alarmed at the appearance of the strangers that she prostrated herself. Ronsard had placed gifts beside her to try to reassure her, but one of the other men had put his finger inside her mouth, ostensibly to check whether she had her two front teeth. The woman had then begun to cry.

Péron insisted that Lesueur show him where the meeting had taken place. Lesueur thought it unlikely that the woman would still be there, but obliged. The woman was gone, but Péron and Lesueur found evidence of her presence, and her terror, 'the woman had disappeared, leaving behind her the most unequivocal proofs of her great trepidation … spontaneous evacuations.'

Lesueur then helped Péron find his way back to their landing spot. Péron was surprised to see no sign of the longboat: 'This alarmed me as it was now five o'clock, while the weather … had changed.'

Back on board *Le Géographe*, Baudin too was concerned. The other two dinghies eventually returned but there was no sign of the longboat. He suspected that the scientists might have had a hand in the delay: 'The only likely explanation was that M. Le Bas de Ste Croix, to whom I had given command of the longboat, had allowed himself to be swayed by the fine talk of the naturalists.'

The wind continued to strengthen and the hours dragged by. Baudin became increasingly agitated: 'After sunset, seeing no sign on the horizon of their return, I gave orders for the lights to be put on the masts and for the cannon to be fired every two hours.' Still there was no response from the shore.

With the return of the morning light, increasingly worried for the welfare of twenty-five of his men, with the storm continuing to build, Baudin adopted a risky manoeuvre: 'I filled my topsails only and, having paid off on the port tack, came parallel to the shore … and sailed along it, watching very carefully.' Baudin sailed perilously close to the shore, hoping to spot the missing men: 'At half past eleven several very thick columns of smoke rose from behind the dunes. They seemed to indicate that someone was there.'

Into the treacherous, pitching waves Baudin launched one of the dinghies and watched it struggle towards shore: 'I scanned the coast incessantly to see if I could spot someone … seeing the boat drop its grapnel without anyone's coming in sight … I could not hold back my tears and withdrew to my cabin to ponder the next steps I should have to take.'

At 3.00 pm, some good news. Finally a signal had been fired, indicating to Baudin's great relief that the missing men had been found: 'This calmed my anxiety and freed me from the painful existence I had led … At nine o'clock my boat returned, bringing only Citizen Péron who was more dead than alive. He had been forced to swim to the boat, which had not been able to reach the shore.'

Péron informed Baudin of the longboat disaster. He described how, after some more searching, Lesueur and he had eventually found the others and the stranded craft. As the storm had built around them the twenty-five Frenchmen had spent their first terrifying night on the shore of this unknown land, huddled together without food or shelter, surrounded by the strange nocturnal noises of Nouvelle Hollande.

Baudin sent another crew, together with the carpenters, to attempt to refloat the precious longboat. With the wind and swell increasing by the minute, the men were forced to abandon the effort, and their tools. They struggled just to reach the dinghy, having to swim back out to the waiting boat. Worse followed. Just before dusk, in the dying light and driving rain, Pierre Milius, the second-in-command on the *Naturaliste*, on his own initiative, approached the beach in a dinghy. Milius determined that he would try to retrieve some of the lost equipment. Trying to land, Milius' boat was then swamped. Half-drowned, a new bunch of castaways struggled onto the beach.

Milius' absence was soon noticed and Baudin sent yet another boat. Perhaps embarrassed by the new dilemma he had created, Milius was instrumental in helping to rescue his men who had to be dragged by rope through the now massive surf to the waiting dinghy. Suddenly a nineteen-year-old sailor, Timothée Vasse, lost his grip. The large swell and ferocious undertow tore the man away. Milius lunged to grasp Vasse, but the ocean was too strong. In the roaring surf and gathering darkness, though he was known to be a good swimmer, Vasse could be neither seen nor heard. Fearing for the lives of the other men, Milius ordered that they make for the *Le Géographe*. Struggling on board, Baudin interrogated Milius about the latest disaster, Baudin recording that: 'Mr Milius, who was in the small boat, told me that having gone to the place where the long boat was … this attempt had cost the life of one of his boatmen. He was carried away by a wave – and drowned.'

Baudin was dismayed. He had no time to ponder it, however. The *Naturaliste* and the *Géographe* were soon themselves in danger of being washed ashore by the raging storm. Baudin ordered both ships to depart immediately for the relative safety of the open ocean. *Le Naturaliste* was forced to cut its lines and abandon her anchor. The ships barely cleared the bay, both tacking constantly, always a dangerous proposition in confined waters. In the darkness it was even more terrifying. Milius described the angst of all on board: 'One can readily judge the sort of night we spent, having to tack every two hours and the wind still aft. Although I had come on board with a very high fever, I remained constantly on the bridge and directed all the manoeuvres until the evening of the next day, by which time I could no longer speak or stand upright. The fever, anxiety and pain exhausted me and I fell into an alarming state of depression.'

Baudin took stock of the losses – the precious longboat, so necessary for inshore charting; the unique, irreplaceable scientific equipment; specimens; a good deal of the carpenter's tools and one nineteen-year-old seaman's life. Of course the life of Timothée Vasse was the greatest cost. Baudin named the spot Ance des Maladroits, Bay of the Clumsy.

The storm raged for a further two days. The *Naturaliste* disappeared. Baudin watched most of the cattle die. He listened to a sanitised account of the meeting on shore with the pregnant woman: 'According to the report it seems that our people did not frighten her in the least and she waited most patiently for them at the place where she had stopped ... They gave this woman various presents which she appeared to like very much.'

After several days of waiting and searching, there was still no sign of *Le Naturaliste*. Baudin began to head north: 'I no longer have any hope of finding the *Naturaliste* until reaching the Swan River which I had given her as the first meeting place in case of separation.'

Baudin's sailing orders were explicit:

> The aim of the Government ... has been to
> have examined in detail the southwest, west,
> northwest and north coasts of New Holland,
> some of which are still entirely unknown ...
> By combining the work ... with that of the
> English navigators on the east coast and of
> D'Entrecasteaux ... we shall know the entire
> coastline of this great south land.

Baudin was to pay particular attention to the truly unknown coastline of the south-east, where 'Williamson's Strait' was rumoured to have its southern opening. The orders stressed that: 'This section of the coast has not yet been discovered; no navigator has seen it, and Citizen Baudin must apply himself to ... drawing up an accurate chart of the whole ...'

In terms of his itinerary, Baudin was specifically instructed to head first to Terre de van Diemen (Tasmania) to reconnoitre the D'Entrecasteaux Channel: 'He will sail the full length of this channel in order to ascertain whether or not the English have established a settlement there …'

From the geopolitical viewpoint, the D'Entre-casteaux Channel was very strategically positioned as one of the best points from which to command sea-traffic into the Pacific. It was also a part of Terres Australes that the French could lay legitimate claim to, following Dufresne's early landing, which had in turn been followed by d'Entrecasteaux's detailed charting. Terre de van Diemen was the first priority in Baudin's instructions; his orders could not have been clearer:

> Upon leaving Île-de-France, he will proceed directly to D'Entrecasteaux Channel … He will be able to reach it about 10 Germinal (late March), at which time autumn in the southern hemisphere begins.

But it was now June, not March. Baudin was running three months late thanks to his delays and problems suffered off the coast of Africa and at Île-de-France. If he headed south now, it would be the icy depths of winter by the time he reached Terre de van Diemen. Baudin was gravely concerned by the poor seamanship of many on board. He was not keen to expose his inexperienced officers and scientists to the winter gales of the Southern Ocean. He had read enough to know that this region produced the most tempestuous seas in the world, especially in winter. Baudin did not plan to disappear without a trace, like La Pérouse had done.

So he had determined to change his itinerary: 'I decided to head Northeast by North to reach a more suitable latitude for navigation work.' They would spend the winter charting the west and north-west coasts and then head for Terre de van Diemen in spring.

The decision was sound. Péron, however, was critical: 'This important determination gave us much concern, because it was not absolutely necessary from our actual situation … it appeared to us to be more prudent to pay respect to the instructions we had received from the government … We shall see in the end the consequences produced by this first deviation from our orders.' In light of the debacle in the Bay of the Clumsy, if anything, Péron's comments demonstrated Baudin's commonsense in not wanting to expose his inexperienced team to dangers they did not know how to handle, or it seemed, even understand. But the ocean demanded respect. To Baudin, it was obvious that many of the young men on board still had to learn to appreciate the true fury of which it was capable.

Péron, like many of the young team on board, was impatient to make the great discovery – to pursue one particular aspect of their sailing orders, that is 'to visit the part of the continent … where it was supposed that a Strait existed communicating from this point with the bottom of the Gulf of Carpentaria, which would have cut New Holland into two great islands of practically equal size'. All in good time, as far as

Baudin was concerned. Had he known that an English expedition was pursuing him, his decision might have been very different.

Chapter 8

[THE WILD WEST]

Baudin had already informed the captain of *Le Naturaliste*, Emmanuel Hamelin, of his plans to head north. Together, they had arranged a number of rendezvous points in case of separation. There was no sign of *Le Naturaliste* at the first two meeting places, so Baudin pressed on for the next, Shark Bay.

While waiting, hoping that *Le Naturaliste* would arrive soon, Baudin allowed the scientists further excursions on shore. For the second time, to his annoyance, one of the scientists got himself lost and delayed the landing party's return: 'By five o'clock everyone was back except Citizen Péron. Carried away, no doubt, by his enthusiasm … I shall refrain here from saying what I could say. However, I firmly promised him that when he went ashore again, I would send someone with him who would keep him constantly in sight …'

The conduct of some of the officers also continued to worry Baudin: 'Mr Freycinet … arrived in the large boat to receive my orders and carry out the task I had told him of the preceding day, before coming ashore. But as he had brought only two days' provisions, when he needed four to do the work well, I put his departure off until the following day, but not without vexation at his lack of foresight.' Baudin noticed that Freycinet did not seem in the least concerned by the delay: 'The pleasure seekers, and I have plenty of them, set off kangaroo hunting.'

At least Péron continued to provide light entertainment: 'Citizen Péron, whose extreme enthusiasm leads him to undertake everything without thought for the dangers to which he is exposing himself, went on a visit to the western part of the island and, as usual, went alone … At first he amused himself at the expense of the crabs … wanting to climb some rocks, where the sea appeared not to break too roughly, he was knocked head over heels by a wave … this decided him to return … for the second time he became completely lost. It was nine o'clock before he rejoined us … having had to abandon on the way his tin box, his shirt and his crabs.'

Departing Shark Bay in yet another storm, Baudin did not find the antics of his officers so amusing: 'I had been on deck for 26 hours without a break. I noticed again at that stage that not one of the officers appeared on deck, except for the person on duty, and that our frequent tacks did not prevent their sleeping more soundly than [if] we had been in the most comfortable position.'

They had waited three weeks at Shark Bay for *Le Naturaliste* to show up. Baudin had instructed Hamelin that they should wait for one another at each rendezvous point for only fifteen days. He was increasingly concerned, and continued his charting of the west coast alone.

The risk of shipwreck on this isolated, desolate coast was all too obvious. The further north they sailed, the greater the dangers. Having avoided the perils of winter in the south, the northern coasts presented their own terrors. Baudin soon found himself having to thread his way through a maze of islands: 'Generally speaking, they are fairly high and appear to be linked under water by shallows, over most of which a big sea rolls. This, no doubt, is caused by the violence of the currents … all the hazards that one finds more than a league out to sea from these shores … would terrify anyone caught here.'

Progress was slow. *Le Géographe* had a draught of sixteen feet. Some of the tides dropped by as much as thirty feet. Baudin was extremely wary of approaching too close to the coast and risked few excursions on shore. The landings that were made hardly revealed an inviting prospect for a French colony. 'A land with neither fresh water nor harbour for the safety of ships … it will not suit anyone to attempt a settlement on it − at least in this part.'

Baudin charted the Napoléon Archipelago. The expedition did not encounter any more of the local people, though Baudin was very aware of their presence: 'We saw four or five large clouds of smoke on various parts of the coast. There is no doubt, therefore, that this area is inhabited …'

Primarily, however, it was the inhabitants of his own ship that mostly occupied Baudin's thoughts: 'Citizen Picquet was on duty. He was occupied solely in tormenting the signal men because he found that the clock was not moving fast enough to suit his impatience.' Irritated by the voices yelling outside his window, Baudin yelled to the men above: 'Mr Picquet, you must pay attention to the lead and not the clock!' Baudin described Picquet's appearance at his door a few seconds later: 'He said in so many words, "Confound it sir! You're quite ridiculous to find anything wrong with my watching the clock!" … I relieved him of the command of a watch until I could get rid of him altogether.'

By August, 1801, the situation on board *Le Géographe* was acute. Ten of the crew were debilitated by scurvy. Baudin's failure to get adequate fresh supplies was catching up with him. It was now almost four months since they had departed Île-de-France with their modest rations. The desolate coasts they had been exploring had offered little in the way of fresh food.

The water casks were almost completely exhausted. Baudin was forced to make another important decision: 'I decided to head north to the anchorage that everyone hankered after with so great an impatience. This news had such an effect upon some of the sick on board that several of them found strength enough to come up on deck to make sure that it was really true.'

A few days later, the *Géographe* limped into the lonely Dutch outpost of Kupang, in west Timor. Baudin found the town in ruins. 'The English had captured the fortress last year, but had been obliged to evacuate it by night, having failed to conciliate the natives ... the town is mostly destroyed. What the sword could not reach fell victim to the flames.' A British man–of–war had tried to take the trading-post from the Dutch, but as Péron explained, had failed: 'Seventy or eighty Englishmen had been cut in pieces and eaten by the savage Malays ... from that moment the most implacable hatred had subsisted among the whole Malay nation towards the English.'

In contrast, the French were welcomed warmly, as described by Pierre Milius: 'The women are beautiful and walk with a voluptuous gait. Some go naked ... their appearance is quite seductive overall ... Although the men are generally very jealous of their wives, they are not above prostituting them to us ... Every night these wretched men come to trade with us for their wives' favours – as well as their daughters'. I do not need to make the observation that we complacently avail ourselves of this type of commerce.'

Fresh fruit and vegetables soon cured the scurvy,

but brought with it something far worse. One of the first to be affected was Baudin's best friend, Riedlé the gardener. Péron described the terrible symptoms: 'The unfortunate Riedlé was very ill … the inflammation had spread from the rectum to the rest of the intestines, and the pains he suffered were horrible …' He watched the dysentery attacking one man after the other. Soon 'eighteen men were confined to their beds, all severely and dangerously ill with a most cruel dysentery'. Baudin watched his dearest friend die after nine agonising days. Baudin was devastated: 'Nobody knows how much I love him how attached I am to him … No one onboard can even partly replace him.'

Baudin himself became seriously ill, stricken by a fever. He was so sick at one point that Péron thought the expedition might soon have a new leader: 'Our commander, who had been ill for some time with a dangerous ataxic fever, experienced successively three such violent attacks, that for some hours he was thought to be dead.'

Adding to Baudin's depression, by late September, the *Naturaliste* had still not arrived. Péron, like most of them, began to fear the worst. 'Our anxiety for the fate of the *Naturaliste* increased every day … This cruel uncertainty grieved us all; we began to lose all hope, and to despair of ever again seeing our friends …'

Then, one day, the ship appeared. 'On the 21st of September, in the morning, a signal was made that the *Naturaliste* was entering the bay. The joy was general and we were soon among our companions.' The captain of *Le Naturaliste* came to Baudin's bedside. Baudin ordered that Hamelin assume command of the mission upon his death. Baudin prepared to relay his 'secret instructions', as he explained to Hamelin: 'He would find in the place I designated a particular instruction to which he would have to conform strictly, or he would be personally responsible to the Government …'

But Baudin was not done yet. He slowly began to recover and immediately set to rid himself of his most insubordinate officer. He informed him by letter:

> To Citizen Picquet.
> I give you warning, Citizen, that you must, as quickly as possible, find a lodging on shore … you are no longer a member of my staff …

Baudin described the scene that followed: 'Mr Picquet arrived asking to speak to me in private. He was in uniform with his sword at his side … Mr Picquet came towards me and said: "… I trust that you would be so good as to explain your treatment of me. I have come ashore expressly for this."'

Baudin simply stared back at the arrogant young *officier rouge*: 'I gazed sternly at him for more than two minutes without saying a word … my silence which he took for a fresh insult, made him furious and he asked me why I did not reply, adding that it would be well worth my while to do so. I then told him as calmly as I could, that if I had not yet replied as I ought, it was from fear of having misunderstood him … I asked him to be kind enough to repeat himself.'

Picquet stared back at his commander, eyeballing

him. Picquet struggled to find words in his rage. He reached for the sword hanging by his side and 'he then answered: "*Foutre!* If you haven't understood, follow me." Then, grabbing his sword, he said, "If you dare come near me, you'll soon see what I use this for."'

Baudin went outside and ordered one of his men to fetch four fusiliers to take Picquet to prison: 'This order which no doubt he did not expect, made him tremble with rage, and for two or three minutes he stood cursing and swearing. Then he vanished in a flash.'

This was simply too much. Baudin summoned his second-in-command, Le Bas, to find and arrest Picquet. Baudin decided against ending Picquet's life: 'When the Government learns of this, it will no doubt blame me for not having had him shot then and there ... But I am determined to endure this reproach, not on his account ... but on his family's.'

As ordered, Le Bas arrested Picquet, who was interned in the local garrison. Secretly, however, several of the officers, Le Bas included, sympathised with Picquet, as did a few of the scientists. In the words of Péron: 'M. Picquet, one of our most deserving officers, was ... arrested by order of our commander, whom he had the misfortune to offend ... Every day one of our officers ... went to keep him company.'

As he convalesced, Baudin had no idea that some members of his senior staff began to whisper thoughts of mutiny. Le Bas led the charge, organising a meeting at which he discussed ways of assisting Picquet. He also accused Baudin of having embezzled some of the expedition's funds at Île-de-France. After the meeting,

Le Bas installed himself in the captain's cabin on board *Le Géographe*.

The chief engineer, François Ronsard, informed Baudin of what was happening. For his efforts, Le Bas challenged Ronsard to pick his second and meet for pistols at dawn. As Baudin was pleased to record, Le Bas came off second best, 'incapacitated by a well deserved shot wound in the left arm received while fighting a duel'. Baudin had been looking for an excuse to leave Le Bas behind in Kupang and he now needed to look no further. For his part in the illegal duel, Baudin ordered Ronsard be gaoled, but released him after two days.

Baudin watched his expedition once again sliding perilously close to the point of disintegration. As soon as enough men were well enough, he was keen to set sail: 'We prepared to weigh anchor. Although I had a fever on this day, I was too impatient to leave the country where disease had dealt us such a blow.'

The day after departure, Baudin watched another man's health deteriorate, the assistant gardener, Sautier: 'He was immediately given all the usual remedies for such a situation, but they were in vain, and towards midday he died.'

Baudin had lost twelve weeks in Timor. With the return of summer, he was determined to return to his main sailing orders – aiming straight for Terre de van Diemen – to discover whether the British had yet established a colony there.

The British threat, however, was not in Terre de van Diemen, but closing in from the west.

Chapter 9

[T H E   R A C E]

Entirely invisible to Baudin, who was unaware of the rival on his track, Flinders now approached the south-west coast of New Holland. In stark contrast to Baudin's men, Flinders' team were in fine health: 'At this time we had not a single person in the sick list, both officers and men being fully in as good health, as when we sailed from Spithead … I had the satisfaction to see my people orderly and full of zeal.'

Flinders had made great ground in the leaky *Investigator*. He was proud of their efforts so far: 'The average distance … was a hundred and forty miles per day; and the *Investigator* was not a frigate, but a collier-built ship, and deeply laden.'

Although Flinders had left Europe nine months after Baudin, he approached Cape Leeuwin just over six months after Baudin had landed there. On December 6, 1801, he showed the typical trepidation at approaching an unknown coast that gave no hint of its closeness: 'Notwithstanding the nearness of the land, there were no signs of such proximity: no discolouring in the water, no sea weed, no new birds.'

But Flinders knew he was near. He had in his possession copies of the charts of the d'Entrecasteaux expedition. He took advantage of the previous French reconnaissance to guide the *Investigator* carefully towards what was marked on the French chart as a small group of islands. 'According to their position by the French rear-admiral d'Entrecasteaux; a traced copy of whose general chart of this coast had been furnished to me … these isles are called Îles St. Alouarn.' Flinders then took pleasure in correcting what he saw as an error on the French chart. 'We saw hills extending from behind, and, to all appearance, joining it to the main land. This supposed isle is, therefore, what I denominate CAPE Leeuwin.'

Flinders hit the coast a mere ten nautical miles from where Baudin had first sighted New Holland. But unlike Baudin, Flinders did not head north, but immediately sailed east to explore the southern coasts, as stressed in his sailing orders:

> ... make the best of your way to the coast of
> New Holland, running down the said coast from
> 130 degrees of east longitude to Bass's Strait ...
> discover such harbors as may be in those parts;
> and in case you should discover any creek or
> opening likely to lead to *an inland sea or strait*,
> you are at liberty to examine it.

Except for Baudin's orders regarding Terre de van Diemen, Flinders' orders of priority were much the same. He was required first to chart the south-eastern coast from longitude 130° where 'Williamson's Strait' was believed to lie, and following that to chart the north-west coast, then the Gulf of Carpentaria, Torres Strait and finally, only if time permitted, parts of the east coast.

Before he could proceed, though, Flinders again had to make repairs to the *Investigator*. 'The first essential requisite was a place of secure shelter, where the masts could be stripped, the rigging and sails put in order.'

Flinders made landfall and set up camp in King George Sound on December 12, 1801. The local *Minang* people were no more welcoming than the *Wardandi* had been to the French in Géographe Bay. Flinders could hardly misunderstand the signals of the first *Minang* he encountered. 'These men did not seem to be desirous of communication with strangers; and they very early made signs to our gentlemen to return from whence they came.' Flinders found the Aboriginal men intriguing: 'They seem to have no idea of any superiority we possessed over them; on the contrary, they left us, after the first interview, with some appearance of contempt.'

Flinders stayed three weeks at King George Sound (near present Albany), where his scientists marvelled at the number of alien species they quickly discovered; in the words of the botanist, Robert Brown: 'In this Port ... our collections of plants made chiefly upon its shores and a few miles into the interior of the country, amount to nearly 500 species.' Flinders himself was intrigued by one of the new discoveries: 'Amongst the plants collected by Mr Brown and his associates, was a small one of a novel kind, which we commonly called the pitcher plant ... these were generally found to contain sweetish water, and also a number of dead ants ... a contrivance of nature to obtain the means necessary either to the nourishment or preservation of the plant.'

On Christmas Eve, 1801, Flinders and a small party climbed a peak overlooking the Sound. The summit afforded a stunning view in every direction. Flinders had no way of knowing, but as he looked west, over the horizon, his French rival was passing by about 150 miles away.

Chapter 10

[THE CRUEL SEA]

The situation on board the French ships was grim. Forty days after leaving Timor, on Christmas Eve, 1801, Baudin found himself back near the point where he had begun his survey of Nouvelle Hollande. This time, he was not stopping. The day before, *Le Naturaliste* had signalled to him that an eleventh man had died since leaving Kupang. This time, the news was particularly upsetting. The dead man was the young zoologist Stanislav Levillain. Levillain had, like Riedlé and Maugé, sailed with Baudin on his previous mission, and while his younger age perhaps prevented him from becoming as close a friend to Baudin as the other two, Baudin had still been very fond of the young zoologist. Baudin knew that Levillain had, like the other two, joined the mission out of respect and affection for him. He was again torn by guilt: 'It seems I am destined on this expedition to be parted from my best friends, and to have not only the pain of seeing them die, but also my own reproaches, since it is only through friendship for me, and in order to accompany me, that they have joined it.'

Baudin feared for the life of his last friend: 'Citizen Maugé, who likewise had dysentery, did not look well.' Sailing from Timor towards Terre de van Diemen, Baudin lost men at the rate of one every four days: 'The symptoms of this terrible illness are so frightening that the moment one is struck down by it one feels dead already.'

One of the gunners afflicted by the painful illness tried to commit suicide by jumping overboard, as Baudin described: 'He wanted to drown himself and would have done so had he not been promptly rescued. When he was lifted back on board he said to us with great calmness: "You have done me a great disservice, for I know well that I shan't recover. In this way you are only prolonging my sufferings for a few more days."' Sure enough, three days later the gunner's dead body was thrown overboard. Péron, like the rest of the men, wondered who would be next: 'This terrible disease … pursued us, as we shall soon see, to the extremity of the globe, and strewed the seas with our dead bodies.'

Baudin noticed that even the seemingly indomitable Péron was losing hope: 'While we were all talking on the quarter-deck, the conversation turned on the great humidity that there was at night. I then asked Citizen Péron, who was in charge of this part of our observations, if he were continuing to take them from his bed … it so happens that I was just teasing him. But to get out of the difficulty, he told me that as his mother was no longer producing children and he was the family's sole hope, he did not want to kill himself taking observations at night … For a scientist, his replies were disjointed and inappropriate, and I was astonished by them.'

The expedition could hardly afford further losses. The ships that had left France crowded with 257 men, now carried less than 170. Never before had Baudin experienced losses like these. Never before had his men experienced such hardship. Baudin had faced four hurricanes and numerous other perils, yet he had prevailed.

When he was thirty-six years old, he had sailed out of Genoa on a mission for the Austrian Crown to pick up a collection of botanical specimens at the Cape of Good Hope. The same day France had declared war on Austria. He had not learnt of the declaration until reaching his first port of call, Malaga. He had immediately approached the French Consul and tried to re-enlist in the French Navy. When his Austrian officers learnt of this, they reported him to the authorities, who imprisoned him. He was released with strict orders to continue and complete the voyage.

He had continued the voyage and after filling the hold with botanical specimens collected mainly on Africa's east coast, he sailed back to The Cape, where his ship *La Jardinière III* was wrecked. Only Baudin's impressive display of determination and courage managed to save the botanical collection, which he then, in an unusual move, transported across the Atlantic and deposited with a friend in Trinidad. He then made his way back to France via the new American Republic.

Baudin had returned to Paris, which was once again on the verge of anarchy. On October 5, 1795 the Revolution was under siege as 20,000 well-armed Royalists marched on the capital. Assigned with suppressing the insurrection was 26-year-old brigadier-general, Napoléon Bonaparte, whose swift and decisive actions saved the day, with the death of 1,400 Royalists. Back in Paris for the first time in ten years, Baudin had immediately contacted the *Muséum national d'Historie naturelle*, taking with him a few African seeds and plants from the collection he had left in Trinidad. Baudin described the other wonders contained in the collection stashed at Trinidad and offered to retrieve the collection for France, requesting in return simply a ship and crew.

By now Louis XVI and Marie Antoinette had ascended the steps to the guillotine. The night before losing his head, Louis reputedly asking his gaolers: 'Is there any news of La Pérouse?' Nothing, it seemed, including Revolution, war or death, diminished the insatiable French passion for Discovery. Baudin secured the backing for his proposal. The *Muséum* appointed the naturalists and Baudin met his future friends: Riedlé, Maugé and Levillain.

Baudin had set sail, finally, as the commander of a French vessel, the *Belle Angélique*. He soon found himself pitted against a hurricane. His courage and cool head saved the night, though he did clock up his fourth shipwreck. The collection, however, was saved again, this time deposited at Tenerife while Baudin continued collecting in a new ship. He ultimately delivered the entire collection back to France, some of which was paraded as part of Napoléon's spoils of war from Italy. The Director of the *Muséum*, Antoine Jussieu, proudly proclaimed that 'the experience of the past and the knowledge of his former achievements make us believe that he follows worthily in the steps of Bougainville, La Pérouse, and d'Entrecasteaux, and that he will be more fortunate than the last two'.

So what had gone wrong? What was different this time? Why was this mission so much harder than all the others?

Baudin pressed on. He intended to succeed. Again.

Chapter 11

[INDEFATIGABLE]

It took three weeks for Flinders' men to make the necessary repairs to the *Investigator*. They then left King George Sound, shortly after New Year's Eve, 1802 and headed east. However, contrary to his orders to proceed directly to 130° longitude and then begin charting, Flinders instead began charting the moment he left the Sound.

He argued that this would add little delay to his itinerary: '[It] was not prescribed in my instructions … but the difference of sailing along the coast at a distance, or in keeping near it and making a running survey, was likely to be so little, that I judged it advisable to do all that circumstances would allow whilst the opportunity offered.'

He was wrong. The extra effort delayed his progress by about five weeks and added extra pressure to an already extremely ambitious itinerary. But Flinders was determined to do things his way: 'My leading object had been, to make so accurate an investigation of the shores of Terra Australis that no future voyage to this country should be necessary.'

Soon after, his resolve was put to the test. On January 8, the *Investigator* reached the Archipel de la Recherche, as marked on his French chart. (This is located almost half-way along the southern coast of Western Australia.) The archipelago had been named by the French in honour of d'Entrecasteaux's ship and consisted of a maze of over 200 reefs, rocks and islands. Flinders found the maze inviting: 'The French admiral had mostly skirted round the archipelago, a sufficient reason for me to attempt passing through the middle …'

Flinders steered straight into the archipelago. He argued that it could only be useful to do so: 'A ship on discovery; whose business it is to encounter, and even to seek danger … may produce an important benefit to geography and navigation.'

By late afternoon, the *Investigator* found itself heading deeper and deeper into jeopardy. There were islands, rocks and breakers in every direction except from where they had come: 'The chart alone can give any adequate idea of this labyrinth of islands and rocks, or of our track amongst them …' Soon they were running out of light: 'I found myself under the necessity of adopting a hazardous measure; we steered directly before the wind for the main coast.' Basically, Flinders staked everything on finding a safe anchorage in the dying light, and sure enough: 'At seven in the evening we entered a small sandy bay … The critical circumstances under which this place was discovered, induced me to give it the name of LUCKY BAY.'

Flinders felt the ordeal had been worthwhile. 'From the French ships having sailed round the archipelago, and not through the middle of it as I did in the *Investigator* … my survey … will afford much new information; and useful also, since it has brought to light a well sheltered cove affording wood and water …'

With their nerves perhaps not quite of the same calibre as Flinders', some of his fellow thrill-seekers requested a breather: 'I had intended to pursue our route through the archipelago in the morning; but the scientific gentlemen … expressed a desire for the ship to remain two or three days.'

When the English expedition continued, the wind was now against them, as Flinders noted with annoyance: 'From D'Entrecasteaux's Archipelago westward … westerly winds seem to be much the most prevalent. These foul winds and our detention in England favoured Mons. Baudin.'

Chapter 12

[THE DIEMENESE]

Having dropped down into the gales of the Roaring Forties, Baudin had made good headway. The trip was nonetheless horrific. Men continued to die. On January 13, 1802, the Frenchmen's relief at their first sight of land since leaving Timor was described by Péron: 'Every eye was now fixed on the land: we admired those lofty mountains, which nature has placed like so many ramparts of granite to oppose the rage of the stormy sea ... a long rank of white muzzled dolphins, with several large whales, played around us; in a word, every thing seemed to unite in giving a sort of solemnity to our arrival off these shores, and all proclaimed that we touched the extreme boundaries of the southern world.'

Finally the Frenchmen had reached the first priority of their sailing orders, a full year behind schedule. The ships dropped anchor in Great Cove in the D'Entrecasteaux Channel. Baudin was pleased to discover no sign of a British settlement. He sent scouting parties further afield to make sure: 'Captain Hamelin came aboard … we agreed that the following day his longboat should head for Port Esperance and examine it to ascertain that the English had made no settlement there.' Baudin could see for himself what great potential D'Entrecasteaux Channel promised: 'It offers an infinite number of harbours and resources … The area known as Port Cygnet is, of all places along the channel, the one that seemed most suitable for the establishment of a European Colony.'

From the moment they had entered D'Entrecasteaux Channel, it was obvious to Baudin that the place was already densely inhabited: 'As we coasted D'Entrecasteaux Island, we saw a group of fifteen to twenty natives, who came to the water's edge to watch us go by. They stood close together for some time and appeared to be making signs to us, which we could not understand too clearly.' The following day a crowd of fifty local *Nuenonne* surrounded six Frenchmen fishing on the shore: 'The natives gathered in large numbers at the place that had been chosen for hauling the net ashore. Men, women, children and Europeans all mingled together without any distrust or fear of each other.'

The *Nuenonne* seemed to be as curious about the visitors as the French were about them. As Baudin described: 'If several of the men are to be believed, the women used various ways and means to draw some of them aside, and the signs that they made were too expressive for anyone to mistake their intentions. Some of the oarsmen from the *Naturaliste* even affirmed that upon their following them, the women had entirely voluntarily satisfied their curiosity, but not their desire.'

Midshipman Maurouard challenged one of the *Nuenonne* warriors to a wrestling match. The Frenchman defeated his opponent. The warrior seemed to take the defeat in good humour, but as the Frenchmen departed, the vanquished man suddenly threw a spear, hitting Maurouard in the neck. Luckily the wound was fairly superficial and the Frenchmen returned to *Le Géographe*. On learning of the incident, Baudin insisted that there be no retaliation. His men claimed that the spearing incident was unprovoked, but Baudin saw another explanation: 'It seems likely to me that the natives upon seeing their comrade defeated by strength, sought later to make it known that they were not the weaker in skill and cunning.'

In the mossy, ancient forests of Terre de van Diemen, Baudin resumed his passion for exploring, collecting, observing and trying to understand. After all their recent hardships, the thrill of discovery had returned. He was well aware of the violence and bloodshed that ensued when Dufresne had encountered the people of Terre de van Diemen thirty years earlier. Baudin outlined the policy he expected to be upheld in encounters with the local people in a letter to Lieutenant Freycinet: 'If you should meet any natives … you are absolutely forbidden to commit a single act of hostility towards them … According to what is known of their character, the people of this country do not appear to be savage, except when provoked.' Baudin was very conscious of his responsibilities in leading the very first scientific expedition with specific aims of studying – and 'observing without judgement' – the customs of indigenous people. He was himself, after all, a founding member of the *Société des Observateurs de l'Homme*. The *Société* had only recently been formed, in December, 1799, by members of the *Institut National*, to study 'the science of man, in his physical, moral and intellectual existence'. Joseph-Marie Degérando, the author of the *Société*'s manifesto, best described their aspirations: 'The philosophical traveller, sailing to the ends of the earth, is, in fact, travelling in time: he is exploring the past … Those unknown islands that he reaches are for him the cradle of human society.'

The *Société* was concerned with learning not only about the habits of Natural Man, but about all people, including themselves. In the long, now murky shadow of the Revolution, many still dreamt of a better, perhaps a simpler, world. The opening words to Rousseau's 'Social Contract' still resonated through the times: 'Man is born free; and everywhere he is in chains. One thinks himself the master of others, and still remains a greater slave than they.' It was Rousseau who had argued that the inequalities of society had resulted in part from people becoming alienated from the natural world; that man was good by nature, but had been corrupted by civilisation. Rousseau had reignited Europe's fascination with the ancient Greek notion of the 'noble savage'. Such ideas were still popular in Europe, though seasoned travellers such as Baudin recognised much in them that was overly romantic. Baudin, like the other members of the *Société*, wanted to remove himself from the romance, to truly study and learn about the cultures and habits of indigenous people. Above all, one had to 'observe without judgement'.

Baudin, however, was not the official 'Observer of Man'. He had bestowed that honour on Péron, who described his first encounter with 'the Diemenese', as he termed them: 'His physiognomy had nothing fierce or austere. His eyes were bright and spiritual ... we could readily perceive his artlessness and good nature.' While Péron had great enthusiasm for the job of 'Observer of Man', he had little experience other than his reading of Rousseau. He was not a member of the *Société des Observateurs de l'Homme*.

Péron experienced his next intimate encounter with 'the Diemenese' while on an excursion with Henri Freycinet. The Frenchmen met a small family and shared a meal of cooked shellfish. Soon a young girl, Ouré-Ouré, joined the group, as described by Péron: 'The young lass ... attracted our more particular attention by the softness of her manners, and by the affectionate and expressive regard with which she appeared to observe us. Ouré-Ouré, like her parents, was entirely naked, and did not seem at all to be aware that any person could imagine there was any indecency or immodesty in this absolute nudity.' Péron and Freycinet were inspired to sing a song: 'While our good Diemenese thus enjoyed their simple repast, the idea of treating them with a little music entered our heads ... We chose the hymn which was so unhappily prostituted during the revolution, but which is nevertheless so full of enthusiasm and spirit, and so likely on this occasion to produce effect.'

A rendition of 'La Marseillaise' drifted through the trees, while the *Nuenonne* children danced around the Frenchmen. Péron was convinced that he had indeed discovered the 'noble savage': 'Thus ended our first interview with the inhabitants of Van Diemen's Land ... The confidence which the inhabitants showed us, the affectionate testimonies of goodwill which we could not but understand, the sincerity of their demonstrations, the frankness of their manners, the affecting ingenuousness of their caresses, all seemed to unite in developing the kindest and most interesting affection and friendship ... I saw realised, with inexpressible pleasure, those charming descriptions of the happiness and simplicity of a state of nature, of which I had so often read, and enjoyed in idea.'

A few days later, however, another group of *Nuenonne* were less forthcoming, as Baudin noticed: 'I left to go to the place where our men had seen the natives the day before ... Seven natives ... appeared on the other side of the hill facing our landing-place ... we made friendly gestures to persuade them to wait, for they retreated as we approached.' Baudin took his time: 'We stood rather a long time inviting each other over, so seeing that they were not moving, I went across to them. They waited for me very quietly.' Baudin persuaded the men to walk with him, but as he presented them with some glass beads and other trinkets, 'they asked us to go back to our boat. Among the different words that they spoke, one, "Kaoué, Kaoué", kept recurring, and was even said in a tone of command. In the language of the negroes of Mozambique and the African coast, it means "Go away", but I cannot say if it has the same meaning with the natives of Van Diemen's Land.'

Baudin was familiar with some African customs. He had, after all, worked as a slave trader. He bid the men goodbye, but met them again later in the afternoon: 'Their "Kaoué" began again as we advanced and they still kept a fairly long way off.' Baudin ordered his men to sit down. Sitting on the sand with his boat just behind him, he invited the *Nuenonne* to join them. Eventually they did: 'They went and put their spears down behind some trees and came over to us … When we were all together again, they made signs for the sailor beside me to put down my gun, which he was carrying.' Sitting together, Baudin let the men go through his pockets: 'After this inspection, they turned to our clothes, and in order to humour them in everything, we showed them our chests, about which they seemed very curious. But only the doctor's gave rise to astonishment. Being hairless, it caused great exclamations and even greater shouts of laughter. After satisfying themselves in this region, they passed on to our legs … They would have very much liked to see something else, but we did not think it advisable to show them.'

Baudin was surprised at the men's language skill: 'We said various words for them, which they repeated very clearly, and I was amazed even, at the small amount of trouble they had.' With words and hand-signals, the Frenchmen and *Nuenonne* began to barter: 'Captain Hamelin wanted to exchange something for one of their spears … and it was agreed that they would hand over a spear in return for a uniform button.'

Soon after, the mood suddenly changed: 'Citizen Petit, who had done a drawing of one of them had the paper snatched away from him … he snatched it back again and we continued towards the shore. We had scarcely reached it when the three natives, with whom we had been on such friendly terms … began to pick up stones and throw them at us … I was not so lucky as the others as a fairly large stone hit me just as I was bending over to examine a shell and grazed my hip. I immediately aimed at the one who had thrown it … he put his head down and ran … this movement was sufficient to scatter them all, so I was not obliged to fire.'

Baudin was surprised at the sudden shift in tone of the encounter: 'On the way back we tried to work out the reason for their hostile behaviour at the moment of departure. The only explanation that we could find was regret at having exchanged their spears with us.' Péron had a different explanation and a change of heart, quoting Leschenault the botanist: 'These last hostilities were committed on the part of the natives, without our having given them the least provocation; on the contrary, we had loaded them with presents and civilities, and nothing in our conduct could have given them offence; and I am astonished, after so many examples of cruelty and treachery which are related in all voyages of discovery, to hear sensible people aver, that men in a state of nature are not wicked.'

Baudin was nevertheless determined to re-establish good relations with the *Nuenonne*: 'Despite what had happened to us, we went ashore the following day ... We were amazed to see the same men who had thrown stones at us the day before coming up to us without the slightest sign of distrust. That alone, proved to me that either they are not naturally wicked or they consider us incapable of doing them harm.'

The afternoon ended very pleasantly. 'In half an hour they were as familiar with us as if we had been old friends. As I wanted the portraits of the women and some of the children, I asked them to sit down, which they did very obligingly ... There were no bounds to the delight of the children and even the grown men when they saw the fish caught in the net ... We offered to share our catch with them, but they would accept nothing.' Baudin was pleased: 'When the net was pulled in, everyone went to watch as on the first occasion, in particular the children who hauled on the ropes with all their might, imitating our men and repeating very intelligibly everything they said. I was truly amazed that these children at first so timid, and fearful, should have become so friendly as they were in so short a time. When our men did not want to dance, play or run with them, they tormented them until they did what they wanted.'

Baudin then gave a new order: 'I decided not to give the men guns in future and to limit their means of self-defence to a sword.' Many of his officers were horrified. Péron simply ignored the order: 'A little boat … was at my command; it held only three men, and our only protection was a single musket, which M. Petit had secretly taken with him …'

In the space of a few short weeks, Péron's attitudes to the *Nuenonne* changed dramatically. The 'Observer of Man' became increasingly ambivalent regarding his 'subjects'. Landing on Bruny Island, Péron and his party encountered a group of twenty women who had been fishing. The younger girl caught Péron's eye: 'Fifteen or sixteen years of age … pleasant features, with a round well formed bosom, though the nipples were rather too large and long.' One of the women, Arra-Maida, invited Péron and the others to join them: 'Calling aloud to us *medi medi* (sit down sit down); she seemed also to desire us to lay down our arms, of which they seemed to be in some fear. These preliminaries being settled, the women squatted on their heels, and from that moment seemed to shew all the natural vivacity of their character without the least reserve, and speaking altogether, asked us a number of questions, seeming often to criticise our appearance, and laugh heartily at our expense.'

The kind of impression Péron had initially had of the young girl Ouré-Ouré when they had first arrived seemed now but a distant memory: 'Their black skin disgustingly greased with the fat of the sea-wolf, their short woolly hair, which was black and dirty, and which some of them had powdered with red ochre; their figure besmeared with the dust of charcoal; their shape generally lean and shrivelled; with their breasts, which were long, hanging down: in a word, all the particulars of their natural constitution were in the highest degree disgusting … . They were besides, almost all of them covered with sores, the sad consequences of the ill treatment they had received from their ferocious husbands: one only, among all her companions, had preserved any degree of confidence.'

Péron stared at this woman, Arra-Maida: 'After M. Bellefin had concluded his song, she began to mimic his action and the tone of his voice, in a very pleasant and truly original manner … she next began herself to sing, with such a rapidity of expression … so different from the general principles of any European music.'

When Arra-Maida had finished her song, she approached Péron with a piece of charcoal. 'She came close to me … and with an obliging air she began to apply it to my face … Thus it appears that the fairness of skin, of which Europeans are so vain, is an absolute defect, and a sort of deformity, which in these distant climates must yield the palm of beauty to the blackness of coal.'

On their return, Baudin hardly recognised Péron

with his face all blackened: 'When they came … we no longer recognised them except by their clothes.' The *Nuenonne* men sitting with Baudin, however, immediately recognised their wives and were not amused. For their part, on recognising their husbands, Péron noticed that his female companions became very nervous: 'At this unexpected rencontre … [they] seemed greatly terrified; and their savage husbands gave them such looks of rage and anger, as were not at all likely to reassure them.' Baudin ordered his men back to the ship.

That night, the Frenchmen found themselves surrounded by forest fires. Péron found the heat stifling: 'It was scarcely possible to breathe even in the open air: the wind seemed like the heat from a furnace, and immediately all the surface of the sea appeared to smoke … we were as if plunged in a bath of hot vapour.' Péron was convinced that some of the fires were directed at them: 'Wherever we turned our eyes, we beheld the forests on fire: the savage inhabitants of these regions appeared to wish, even at this price, to drive us from their shores.' In contrast, Baudin was more puzzled than alarmed by the fires, also speculating as to their possible cause: 'There is no doubt of its being the natives who are responsible for this great conflagration … It is possibly not just for the pleasure of destroying that they set fire to their forests in this way, and it is reasonable to suppose there is some useful purpose behind it … it may have been for hunting some quadrupeds sighted in the area.'

By the end of their stay in Terre de van Diemen,

however, the 'Observer of Man', Péron – had made up his mind about the *Nuenonne*. Péron was happy to share his views with anyone willing to listen: 'They were treacherous and insincere … fierce and ferocious in their menaces, they appear at once suspicious, restless and perfidious. In their joy, the figure displays a convulsion that has the appearance of madness …' Baudin was of a different opinion: 'Their glance is restless. This is perhaps the result of the distrust that men so different from themselves must have aroused in them.'

After almost five weeks in the D'Entrecasteaux Channel, Baudin was keen to move on. The fires continued to blaze all around and Maugé's cabin was like an oven. Baudin was worried. His last remaining friend had still not shaken the dysentery.

Baudin was now desperate to leave, but the wind would not allow it. Day after day, the ships sat motionless in the dead calm. When the wind finally returned, it blew from the wrong direction, fanning the fires.

Baudin watched the days come and go surrounded by a strange mistiness: 'The sky was so dark throughout the day and the atmosphere so obscured, that we could scarcely see the coast … this day too, was lost.' Every few hours Baudin visited Maugé, who 'spoke of nothing but his imminent death, and his regrets for the friends whose advice he had disregarded by undertaking the voyage … I was so upset by this new opinion that I had a very miserable day'.

The wind stayed away and Baudin began to have second thoughts on the suitability of the

D'Entrecasteaux Channel as a harbour for settlement. After more than twelve days, finally the wind swung to the south-east: Baudin wasted no time in getting under way.

Chapter 13

[THE BIGHT]

Flinders stared at the impenetrable wall that they had been sailing below for over two hundred miles. It seemed to extend forever. He had never seen cliffs like these before: 'Their elevation appeared to be from four to six hundred feet ... nearly destitute of vegetation, and almost as level as the horizon of the sea.' There was certainly no chance of landing. He noticed that the cliffs were made of a sedimentary deposit and began to speculate as to what lay behind them. 'Nothing of the interior could be seen above it ... The bank may even be a narrow barrier between an interior, and the exterior sea.'

Every day took Flinders closer to where 'Williamson's Strait' was suposed to exist. After nine days and 435 nautical miles, the cliffs finally came to an end. On his chart, Flinders wrote a new name, the Great Australian Bight.

Now Flinders approached the true unknown, passing the eastern limit of d'Entrecasteaux's discoveries on January 27, 1802. The following day he passed the limit of Dutch exploration at Cape Nuyts.

The heat was soon scorching, 'such as to make walking a great fatigue … The thermometer stood at 98° in the shade'. Flinders' excitement, however, could not be dampened. He knew that he could come across the mysterious strait any day now. Should he be the first to discover it, his status as a renowned explorer would be assured. Perhaps Baudin was already there, and had already beaten him. Perhaps he has not. Perhaps Baudin had been delayed, wrecked. Why lose confidence … 'Flinders the Indefatigable', wasn't that what his friends called him?

A few days later he had to contain himself. Flinders landed on a beach and struggled to the summit of St Peter Island to see how far the promising body of water stretched to the north: 'My strength was scarcely equal to reaching the highest hill near the middle of the island. I had no thermometer, but judged the temperature could scarcely be less than 120°.' The summit, however, offered a disappointing sight, not a strait, but a bay: 'The bay to the northward, between these islands and the main land, I named DENIAL

BAY ... as to the deceptive hope we had formed, of penetrating by it some distance into the interior country.'

Flinders took his frustrations out on the birdlife: 'At dusk a sufficient number of sooty petrels were taken from the burrows to give nine to every man; making, with those before caught, more than twelve hundred birds.' They forged on, and on February 20, 1802 the prospect of a great discovery loomed larger than ever. The coast disappeared to the north. A strong tide ran from the same direction. Flinders ordered his company to bring the *Investigator* to anchor in the lee of an island. He later described the animated discussions on board the ship that night: 'Deep inlets, inland seas, and passages into the Gulph of Carpentaria, were terms frequently used in our conversations of this evening, and the prospect of making an interesting discovery, seemed to have infused new life and vigour into every man in the ship.'

Chapter 14

[CATASTROPHES]

The same evening, over a thousand miles away, Baudin's mood was very different as he watched the last of his close friends die. Dysentery finally claimed René Maugé. Baudin was shattered: '[His] death and dying words filled me with sorrow. A few moments before the end, he said to me: "I am dying because I was too devoted to you and scorned my friends' advice. But at least remember me in return for the sacrifice that I have made for you."'

The French expedition had reached Oyster Bay on the east coast of Terre de van Diemen, at Maria

Island.* The next morning, while Baudin prepared to bury his friend, Péron went on shore to explore. By coincidence, he soon discovered a tomb: 'In the shade of some ancient Casuarinas stood a conical structure roughly made of pieces of bark ... I soon made up my mind to push ahead with an examination of it. Removing several large pieces of bark, I gained access within the roof ... Scarcely had I lofted off some upper layers of grass than I perceived a thick heap of white ashes which seemed to have been gathered together with care. I plunged my hand into the middle of these ashes and felt something which was solid. Drawing it out, I found it to be a human jawbone to which shreds of flesh still clung. A feeling of horror filled me.'

Péron reported his discovery to Baudin who then ordered that Maugé be buried between two ancient casuarinas, like the tomb Péron had described. Baudin watched the body of his friend leave the ship. 'All the guns fired a salute ... half-way to shore a second was fired and a third just as we landed.'

After the funeral, Péron continued his explorations and made contact with a group of Maria Islanders, the *Paredarerme*. Comparing genitalia with the *Paredarerme*, the 'Observer of Man' concluded that the Diemenese men were far less virile than Frenchmen: 'Several of them showed with a sort of scorn their soft and flaccid organs and shook them briskly with an expression of regret and desire which seemed to indicate they did not experience it as often as we did.'

---

* The island had been named after Abel Tasman's wife.

Péron then found himself in the company of some women and decided to investigate whether they kissed: 'In vain did I address a number of them one after the other to try and make them understand what I wanted to know. Their comprehension was at fault. When in order to leave no doubt of what I was asking, I approached my face close to theirs to kiss them, they had all that expression of surprise which a strange action evokes.' He speculated that perhaps the Diemenese of Maria Island had to come 'on heat': 'Like most animals, do they only experience the need for love at fixed and intermittent periods?'

Baudin began having serious concerns about the usefulness of the findings of his 'Observer of Man'. He found Péron's commentary on the diet of the Diemenese preposterous: 'One of our scientists claims that … they live on grass in times of scarcity. As he finds the evidence for his theory in some dried excrement, one can judge how far his hypotheses is well founded.' Baudin missed his friends more than ever: 'Citizen Maugé's death is an irreparable loss … alone, he did more than all the scientists put together.' Maugé's last words continued to haunt him, for they were true: 'I realise with pain that he and Riedlé, the only two genuine friends that I had on board, have fallen victim to their friendship for me.'

§ § §

The same day that Baudin buried Maugé, Flinders prepared to make his great discovery. On February 21,

1802 he rose early. In the dawn light he climbed down into the waiting boat. The cool of morning was a relief from the heat of the night before. Flinders nodded to the man travelling with him, his trusted Master, John Thistle. Together they covered the few hundred yards to shore in a few minutes. They stepped onto the island and began to ascend. Stomping their way through the scrub, they soon encountered a snake: 'In our way up the hills, to take a commanding station for the survey, a speckled, yellow snake lay asleep before us. By pressing the butt end of a musket upon his neck, I kept him down whilst Mr Thistle, with a sail needle and twine, sewed up his mouth … ' Soon after, the two men were attacked by birds: 'A white eagle, with fierce aspect and outspread wing, was seen bounding towards us … Another bird of the same kind discovered himself by making a motion to pounce down upon us as we passed underneath.'

The men continued on and reached the summit. Flinders' hopes soared even higher: 'From a clear spot upon the north-western head of the island, I traced the main coast to a cape bearing N.18 W., where it was lost … More to the right were three small islands … but no other land in a north-east, and none in an eastern direction …' Surely, this was 'Williamson's Strait'.

Flinders and Thistle returned to the ship. By now it was late afternoon. As so often happens, disaster began with a small detail: 'On comparing the longitude observed … with that resulting from my bearings, a difference was found which made it necessary to repeat the observation on shore; and as this would prolong the time too near dusk for moving the ship, Mr Thistle was sent over with a cutter to the main land, in search of an anchoring place where water might be procured.' Thistle, and the seven men who accompanied him, were never seen again.

The cutter was eventually recovered, 'stove in every part, having to all appearance been dashed against the rocks … nothing could be seen of our unfortunate shipmates'. Flinders had known Thistle for several years now. They had been in Port Jackson together: 'I had known him, and we had mostly served together, from the year 1794 … His loss was severely felt by me.' That evening, Flinders was informed for the first time of the gipsy's prophecy, which had foretold Thistle's drowning. The further prophecy of total shipwreck cast a gloom over the company. Flinders scoffed at the prophecy, but he was devastated: 'The recovery of their bodies was now the furthest to which our hopes extended; but the number of sharks seen in the cove and at the last anchorage, rendered even this prospect of melancholy satisfaction extremely doubtful.'

Flinders named the cape 'Catastrophe'. He named the island on which he had so recently scaled a hill with Thistle in honour of his friend. 'And further to commemorate our loss, I gave to each of the six islands nearest to Cape Catastrophe, the name of one of the seamen …'

Searching for the missing men to the north, Flinders discovered a huge port he named after his home province, Lincoln: 'Fresh water being at this time the most pressing of our wants … I caused a hole to be dug there … water drained in, which was perfectly sweet, though discoloured.' It took nine days to replenish all the water casks and the delay allowed further time to hunt for the missing men. While searching, Flinders briefly glimpsed the local *Pankarla* people, who withdrew on their approach. Flinders found a few trinkets belonging to his dead sailors, but never their bodies.

He finally decided to continue north, through what he hoped was the strait that would transport him all the way to the Gulf of Carpentaria. At first the signs looked promising, the shore continued running northwards and there was still no land visible to the east. Slowly however, Flinders began to lose faith. 'Although nothing had been seen to destroy the hopes formed from the tides and the direction of the coast near the cape, they were yet considerably damped by the want of boldness in the shores, and the shallowness of the water; neither of which seemed to belong to a channel capable of leading us into the Gulph of Carpentaria …'

The following day, a dark line appeared on the horizon to the east. Not a good sign. Over the coming days the line grew bolder and land began to close in from both sides. After sailing north for more than a week, with mountains looming ahead, Flinders' disappointment was confirmed: 'Our prospect of a channel or strait, cutting off some considerable portion of Terra Australis, was lost.'

Flinders was determined to at least chase the

water to its source: 'We still flattered ourselves with the prospect of a longer course, and that it would end in a fresh-water river.' Even this ambition proved frustrating. 'We continued the examination upwards, carrying 4, 3, and 2 fathoms in mid-channel; but at ten o'clock our oars touched the mud on each side, and it was not possible to proceed further.' There was no sign of fresh water: 'It seemed remarkable, and was very mortifying, to find the water at the head of the gulph as salt nearly as at the ship.'

A party landed to climb a nearby mountain. The view to the north revealed nothing but dry land: 'In almost every direction the eye traversed over uninterruptedly flat, woody country; the sole exceptions being the ridge of mountains extending north …'

Flinders named the gulf after the man who had officially sent him on this mission, the First Lord of the Admiralty, Spencer.

Chapter 15

[L O S T]

The gulf between Baudin and many of his men
continued to grow. He lost *Le Naturaliste* again.
He pressed on, kept charting. The man responsible for that charting, the hydrographer Charles
Boullanger, asked to sail closer to the coast. As Baudin
described: 'Citizen Boullanger, our geographer, is
unfortunately very short sighted and can only take
bearings and angles with his nose on the ground.'

Baudin agreed for Boullanger to embark in one of
the dinghies, and gave command of the dinghy to Maurouard, the wrestler: 'Before he left, I recommended

him most particularly to return before nightfall and not to go out of sight of us. All these cautions were in vain for at midday we could no longer see him.' By nightfall there was still no sight of the dinghy. Worse, a thick fog had rolled in, enveloping the ship as if in a dream. The slumber was broken by an almighty thud as *Le Naturaliste* suddenly reappeared from the mist. But not for long, as an exasperated Baudin explained: 'Because she was afraid of colliding with us a second time, she rapidly disappeared from sight heading in the opposite direction from us. I am not too sure how to interpret this manoeuvre.'

The next morning, the mist cleared, but there was still no sign of either the *Naturaliste* or the dinghy. Baudin was deeply troubled and his anxiety brought on a colic so severe he was soon confined to bed. *Le Géographe* searched for the missing men all day, and all of the following day, without success. From his bedside, Baudin tried to rally his fractious company, adopting an unorthodox approach: 'I sent the following command to Citizen Freycinet ... Citizen, tonight at eight o'clock, or earlier if possible, you are to assemble the staff and naturalists in the large cabin to discover, if in spite of all our unhappily fruitless searching over the past three days to find our dinghy ... there is anyone amongst them who still hopes that we might meet it by returning South. A report of the opinions and replies will be drawn up and signed by everyone.'

What an extraordinary suggestion! A vote. The officers were stunned at the Revolutionary idea. They nevertheless obliged and delivered the verdict to

Baudin. The majority suggested continuing the search south: 'I was of a completely contrary opinion, for I could not believe that the dinghy had gone South off Cape Pele, since it had express instructions to proceed North. However, I fell in with the wish that everybody expressed to turn South and manoeuvred all night accordingly.'

He asked Henri Freycinet to take over the task of charting. Freycinet refused. The task was beneath him. The arrogance, verging on insubordination, stunned Baudin. Too ill and miserable to pursue it, Baudin let the issue drop.

After two further days of fruitless searching, however, Baudin ordered another vote. This time the officers agreed that it would be better to turn north, notifying Baudin by letter:

> The staff and naturalists declare that it would be useless to go further South … it is a moral certainty that the dinghy could not have passed [here] and that it has only too unhappily been lost at sea.

Baudin turned for the north. He disagreed that the men had been lost: 'The more I thought about what had happened, the less I was able to convince myself that any unpleasant accident had befallen it if it had remained on the coast. I still hope to find it somewhere at the entrance to the strait. It is true that the men will have suffered greatly through lack of food and possibly water, but in short, if they have had courage, they will still be alive.'

Four days later, Baudin began to recover his health. 'I was able to leave my cabin, suffering much less than I had hitherto.' But he remained deeply concerned not only for the dinghy, but also the *Naturaliste*, which failed to arrive at the rendezvous point: 'The more I have pondered over the motives that could have decided Captain Hamelin to leave me on the East coast of Van Diemen's Land, the less I have been able to imagine the reasons for them.' All Baudin could hope was that the *Naturaliste* had located the missing men and sailed on to the next rendezvous point.

After two weeks of searching, he was finally forced to make an agonising decision. He presumed that *Le Naturaliste* had found Boullanger and the dinghy and headed for the next rendezvous point. The decision was partly forced upon him. On March 19 a storm was brewing. So *Le Géographe* left the jagged coast of Terre de van Diemen and ran for the safety of open water. To the north was a large strait, marked on an English chart in his possession as 'Bass's Strait'. Baudin watched the storm continue to build, and mountains of water began crashing over the deck. He studied the English chart carefully. It had been drawn by two young explorers: George Bass and Matthew Flinders. He hoped that the two Englishmen had done a good job and discovered most of the perils of Bass's Strait. Just by looking at the chart, however, Baudin could see that the work was incomplete. The fact was confirmed soon after. The chart marked the area they were sailing in as open water, but outside, in the raging tempest, in the darkness, the bottom of the ocean was climbing towards them: 'The depth decreased successively from 45 to 41 fathoms, and between midnight and one o'clock we went from 41 to 35 ... During the midnight to four o'clock watch I did not want any soundings to be taken for the sake of everyone's greater peace of mind. If the depth had been found to be still decreasing, most people might have thought themselves lost beyond all hope.'

On such a night, there was little a sailor could do but hope, as Pierre Milius noted: 'Most of them, therefore, go below to their hammocks, and wait patiently till the sea either becomes calm, or swallows them up.'

Chapter 16

[*TERRE NAPOLÉON*]

S ix hundred nautical miles to the west, Flinders
found himself sailing into the very same storm.
The gale was ferocious and 'blew the hardest that
we have yet experienced upon the coast of New Holland ...' He had just left Spencer's Gulf and continued
southwards to reach the sanctuary of the open sea.
Suddenly, the wind began to ease. Something had
changed. Flinders sensed that the storm had not finished raging: perhaps the *Investigator* had sailed into the
lee of an island to the south. Sure enough, an outline
began to appear and towards dusk, some of the young

officers reported having seen strange things on the ridges. 'Every glass in the ship was pointed there ... Several black lumps, like rocks, were pretended to have been seen in motion by some of the young gentlemen, which caused the force of their imaginations to be much admired.' Through the mist, some of Flinders' crew thought they could see elephants.

The next morning Flinders led a party ashore. The creatures they had seen were not elephants, but kangaroos. Massive numbers of kangaroos. They were also fearless: 'Never perhaps had the dominion possessed here by the kanguroo been invaded before this time.' Flinders led the invasion: 'I had with me a double-barrelled gun, fitted with bayonet, and the gentlemen my companions had muskets. It would be difficult to guess how many kangaroos were seen; but I killed ten, and the rest of the party made up the number to thirty-one ... they suffered themselves to be shot in the eyes with small shot, and in some cases to be knocked on the head with sticks.'

That night, the crew feasted: 'Half a hundred weight of heads, fore quarters, and tails were stewed down into soup for dinner ... and as much steaks given, moreover, to both officers and men, as they could consume by day and by night.' Flinders had no trouble in finding a name for the new coast soon marked on his chart: 'In gratitude for so seasonable a supply, I named this southern land KANGUROO ISLAND.'

§ § §

Baudin had also survived the gale, and on the morning of March 24, 1802 he admired a different but equally stunning view of nature's bounty: 'From sunrise until eight in the morning we were surrounded by an immense number of dolphins which came and played near us and entertained us with their leaping and antics.' He had still seen no sign of *Le Naturaliste* and was confronted by constant reminders of Maugé's absence: 'On this day we sold a portion of the belongings of Citizen Maugé ... These articles consisted of wine, arrack and gherkins.' Baudin knew he was near the mainland coast and approached slowly, warily: 'We were about 6 or 7 leagues from the coast of New Holland ... as indicated by the English chart that we are using.' When he could finally see the coast with his own eyes, his spirits began to lift. As he explored westward, the lines on his English chart disappeared into nothingness and he began heading into the true unknown, with the possibility of finding 'Williamson's Strait' at any moment. Though somewhat muted, the thrill returned. Others struggled to contain themselves, such as Péron: 'As the point in question was nothing less than to resolve by this exploration the problem of New Holland being a continent ... we every one felt an additional degree of zeal and courage.'

Baudin was pleased that Freycinet had changed his mind and agreed to take on the task of chart-making. Freycinet was assisted by Bernier the astronomer. In the evening, Baudin pitched in too, helping Bernier with the time-consuming nightly astral observations. They sailed west along the coast that would come to be known as Terre Napoléon. He charted a series of bays and capes along the eastern end of the South Australian coast, naming them in turn Rivoli Bay, Guichen Bay, Lacepede Bay, Capes Dombey and Jaffa. There was no sign of the strait, however, and in early April, almost ten miles from shore, he sailed within 300 yards of disaster: 'We were quite amazed to see a rock at water-level which we had not noticed until then and which even the look-out men had not sighted ... Future navigators would be wise to be on their guard against it on account of its distance from the mainland ...'

The following day, in what is today known as Encounter Bay, Baudin was greeted by a sight even more amazing: 'We sighted a ship ... we were far from thinking that there would be any other Europeans in this region ... this ship made a signal which we did not understand and so did not answer. She then ran up the English flag and shortened sail.'

Flinders too was shocked, and watchful: 'On approaching nearer ... we cleared for action, in case of being attacked ... The stranger was a heavy looking ship ... and our colours being hoisted, she showed a French ensign.'

Chapter 17

[THE ENCOUNTER]

Like fighters, the vessels drew ever closer. Flinders saw the French ship hoist a white flag: 'We veered round … so as to keep our broadside to her, lest the flag of truce should be a deception.' Approaching nearer still, Flinders could finally spy the ship's name: 'I learned, as the stranger passed to leeward with a free wind, that it was the French national ship *Le Géographe*, under the command of captain Nicolas Baudin!'

Baudin was astonished by the next manouevre: 'They asked what the ship was. I replied that she was

French. Then they asked if Captain Baudin was her commander. I was very surprised, not only at the question, but at hearing myself named as well. When I said yes, the English ship brought to.' Flinders removed his hat in salute and ordered his officers to do likewise. Baudin saw the gesture and he and his officers returned the courtesy. Baudin and Flinders laid eyes on one another, for the very first time, in the middle of the unknown.

Flinders was keen to meet his rival, so 'a boat was hoisted out, and I went on board the French ship ... As I did not understand French, Mr. Brown, the naturalist, went with me in the boat. We were received by an officer ... and by him were conducted into the cabin.'

There the two captains came face to face, two men representing two nations at war. Baudin greeted his visitor politely: 'As soon as I learnt his name, I paid him my compliments and told him of the pleasure that I had in making his acquaintance.' Flinders insisted first on formalities: 'I requested captain Baudin to show me his passport from the Admiralty; and when it was found and I had perused it, offered mine from the French marine minister, but he put it back without inspection.' Baudin may have sought to show that he did not feel that two ships needed passports to meet in peace, so far from the known world. Baudin was still ignorant of Flinders' mission. He did not know that he had a rival.

Flinders did. Baudin tried to circumvent their interpreter, Robert Brown, by speaking directly to Flinders in faltering English. Flinders was quiet. Baudin noted his English guest's coolness: 'The English captain, Mr. Flinders ... expressed great satisfaction at this agreeable meeting, but was extremely reserved.' Baudin was more forthcoming: 'I informed him of all that we had done up till then in the way of geographical work.' Flinders listened carefully: '[He] informed me that ... he had explored the south coast from Western Port to the place of our meeting.' What Flinders found more interesting was where Baudin had *not* been. Flinders began to realise that he had beaten his French rival in charting a huge part of the unknown southern coastline, even though his rival had had a nine-month head start. Baudin continued, telling Flinders about their long stay in Terre de van Diemen. Flinders was surprised that Baudin was so talkative. He thought that perhaps Baudin had not yet realised who he was: 'It somewhat surprised me, that Captain Baudin made no enquiries concerning my business upon this unknown coast, but as he seemed more desirous of communicating information, I was happy to receive it.'*

Possibly annoyed at Flinders' continuing reserve, Baudin informed his English visitor that he had used an English chart while navigating Bass's Strait, but that he had found the chart rather incomplete. Offended, Flinders set the Frenchman straight: 'Captain Baudin was communicative of his discoveries about Van Diemen's Land; as also of his criticisms upon an English

---

* Oddly, Flinders would later claim that Baudin had not immediately recognised him or deduced the reason for his mission. But, as author Frank Horner points out, 'Flinders' passport, even unread, would have suggested to Baudin a voyage of discovery' (Horner, p. 219).

chart of Bass's Strait, published in 1800. He found great fault with the north side of the strait … On my pointing out a note upon the chart, explaining that the north side of the strait was seen only in an open boat by Mr Bass, who had no good means of fixing either latitude or longitude, he appeared surprised, not having before paid attention to it.'

Flinders suggested that they compare charts over breakfast. Baudin agreed: 'As it was already late, Mr Flinders said that if I were willing to stand off and on till dawn, he would return the following day and give me various pieces of information concerning the coast that he had examined from Cape Leeuwin as far as here. I was very gratified by his proposal and we agreed to remain together during the night.'

That night, in sight of each other's cabins across the water, both men had a lot to think about. Baudin's mind was racing, the Englishman's parting words no doubt disturbed him, *he had examined from Cape Leeuwin as far as here*. Had the Englishman really beaten him in discovering all that lay to the west? Was Flinders really what he appeared to be – a rival mission? Baudin began to realise that this young Englishman, who had left Europe nine months after him, had just in the last few weeks, if he was to be believed, charted thousands of miles of coast to the west. Had he discovered 'Williamson's Strait' before him? Again, Baudin cursed his delays on the voyage out. That evening, the mood on *Le Géographe* was tense. As rumours regarding the purpose of the English mission began to circulate, many of Baudin's officers and scientists blamed their commander for the delays.

Flinders could sleep more easily. He could even feel smug at the memory of Baudin's reaction on meeting him: 'Finding that we had examined the south coast of New Holland thus far, I thought he appeared to be somewhat mortified ... I did not apprehend that my being here at this time, so far along the unknown part of the coast, gave him any great pleasure.'

Of course, Flinders had known all along that he was in a race. He had done very well. With his nine-month handicap, he had still managed to catch the French, and even beaten them in charting a great part of the south coast. Flinders had just one uncomfortable thought. Had he not delayed his progress by charting part of the coast not stipulated in his sailing orders, he would probably have beaten Baudin in charting all of it.

The next morning Flinders arrived back on board *Le Géographe* at 6.30, dressed immaculately. In the words of one of the midshipmen: 'Monsieur Baudin received him looking like a tramp.' Over breakfast, Baudin was determined to enjoy the company of his new guest, even if he was a rival. The young English commander was certainly far more civil than most of his own young officers and this morning seemed far less reserved than yesterday.

After breakfast, the two men compared their all-important charts. Flinders felt that only now did Baudin show any detailed interest in the purpose of Flinders' voyage: 'He had become inquisitive, some of his officers having learnt from my boat's crew that our object was also discovery. I then told him, generally, what our operations had been, particularly in the two gulphs ... explained the situation of Port Lincoln, where fresh water might be procured ... and as a proof of the refreshments to be obtained at the large island opposite to it, pointed out the kanguroo-skin caps worn by my boat's crew.'

Flinders realised that it would be to his own benefit to make Baudin totally aware of the extent of his discoveries. He did not intend to give the Frenchman any opportunity of sailing on to claim discoveries that he had already made. And as Baudin listened to Flinders and examined his charts, he realised that there was no 'Williamson's Strait'. They both did. Unless, of course, one of them had missed something.

In response to Flinders' proud display showing the extent of his discoveries on the south coast of the mainland, Baudin ordered an assistant to fetch some of the artists' sketches of the people of Terre de van Diemen. He spread the drawings on the table and as Flinders and the English naturalist looked at them, Baudin outlined with pride the general aims of the *Société des Observateurs de l'Homme*.

Robert Brown, in ignorance and presumably arrogance, dismissed the sketches: 'There were figures of their huts, of their tombs, & their canoes ... All the natives were painted with woolly hair & Captain Baudin on being questioned on this had assured us that it was really so. The hair of all the figures was an ochry red ... it seems at least extremely improbable that the natives of New Holland should have merely curld hair while their more southern neighbours in other respects exactly resembling them so as to leave little doubt of their being the same race should have the wool of the negroe.' Brown took it upon himself to question the accuracy of the sketches depicting the *Paredarerme* of Maria Island and the *Nuenonne* of the D'Entrecasteaux Channel, even though he had never been to Terre de van Diemen while the French had just spent two months there. It may be that Brown missed the subtext of Baudin showing the sketches of the Diemenese – that the French mission was, as stipulated in their passport, scientific.

The two expeditions did have some things in common. They realised that they had just endured the same dangers, as Flinders noted: 'In Bass' Strait Captain Baudin had encountered a heavy gale, the same we had experienced in a less degree on March 21, in the Investigator Strait.' The two men could also compare disasters. Baudin went first: 'I told him of the accident that had befallen my dinghy and asked him to give it all the help he could if he should chance to meet it, he told me of a similar misfortune that had happened to him, for he had lost eight men and a boat.'

As he had promised, Flinders then gave Baudin copies of several maps that he had in his collection, maps which Baudin did not have. Baudin mentioned that he had been separated from his consort ship and asked Flinders to pass on a message to Captain Hamelin, should he chance upon him: 'At parting, the captain requested me to take care of his boat and people, in case of meeting them; and to say to *Le*

Naturaliste, that he should go to Port Jackson so soon as the bad weather set in … On my asking the name of the captain of *Le Naturaliste*, he bethought to ask mine; and finding it to be the same as the author of the chart which he had been criticising, expressed not a little surprise.'

Flinders would seem to be stretching credibility to breaking point by claiming that Baudin had not yet realised who he was, and had not even asked his name until this exchange. More likely, Flinders either had misunderstood what Baudin was asking, or, writing later in his journal, was rewriting the facts to suit himself. Perhaps Flinders simply refused to believe that someone could criticise one of his charts, directly to his face, and then follow it up with a parting reminder.

Baudin shook Flinders' hand one final time and watched the Englishman climb down into his boat: 'We parted at eight o'clock, each wishing the other a safe voyage.' As he clambered down, Flinders noticed again the ravages of scurvy written in the faces of so many of the French sailors. As his own healthy seamen rowed him away, he stared back at the receding French ship, 'at half past eight in the morning … we then separated from *Le Géographe*; Captain Baudin's course being directed to the north-west, and ours to the southward … The head of this bay was probably seen by Captain Baudin in the afternoon; and in consequence of our meeting here, I distinguish it by the name of ENCOUNTER BAY.'

On the French chart, Baudin wrote the names Baie des Mornes and Cap de la Rencontre. Baudin then watched the English ship depart, the two missions again heading in opposite directions.

There was one final misunderstanding between the two men which was crucial and also pertained to Flinders' charting accuracy. Before parting, Baudin had been careful to show Flinders his own chart of Baie des Mornes and Baie des Guichen, warning the Englishman of the submerged rocks on which his own ship had almost come to grief only two days before. Flinders gratefully acknowledged the warning: 'He gave me … a memorandum on some rocks he had met with, lying two leagues from the shore, in latitude 37°1', and he spoke of them as being very dangerous.' Flinders had marked the hazard on his own chart as 'Baudin's Rocks.'* He had, however, drawn 'Baudin's Rocks' in the wrong place.

That night, in a rising squall, in the darkness, the *Investigator* sailed perilously close to the hidden reef. Although Flinders had no way of knowing it, he passed within only a few hundred yards of catastrophe. Ten miles off shore, had he hit, it would almost certainly have spelt the death of all on board. The entire expedition and its findings might have disappeared without a trace. It is uncertain why 'Baudin's Rocks' were marked incorrectly on Flinders' chart – whether the mistake lay with Flinders, Baudin, or a simple misunderstanding of language.

Baudin continued west, though he knew he

---

* Today this hazard is still known to the locals as 'Baudin Rocks', but on official charts the rocks are referred to as Godfrey Islands (Horner, p. 220).

would be charting features Flinders had already passed. At the same time, Baudin knew that Flinders might have missed some important details, perhaps even the entrance to 'Williamson's Strait'. At least he now realised that he was in a race. A race to explore and perhaps to conquer. Baudin also knew that the race was still far from over. Both expeditions were still far beyond the known world. This unknown world had already claimed the lives of La Pérouse and others. Perhaps one of the missions would not make it back to Europe. Perhaps neither would. Baudin read his sailing orders again: 'After making a rapid inspection of Bass's Strait, he will examine the southern part of New Holland from that strait to the point on the coast where d'Entrecasteaux's reconnaissance ends.' He determined to follow his orders and keep sailing west until he reached Cape Adieu, the eastern limit of d'Entrecasteaux's charting. Only then would he take up Flinders' invitation to winter in Port Jackson.

Chapter 18

[THE SHIPWRECK COAST]

Flinders sailed directly for Port Jackson, his supplies now running very low. He conducted only a rough running survey of the coast as he sailed, knowing that Baudin's mission would claim it as a French discovery. Flinders was also increasingly concerned that the leaky *Investigator* needed to reach Port Jackson before the winter gales became too fierce. Another storm arrived on April 20, just as Flinders entered 'Bass's Strait'. Rushing to reach Port Jackson, sailing by day and night, Flinders was taking a greater risk than he would have if he'd sailed more slowly. He sailed on, through the rising gale, into the pitch-blackness, towards a coast that would later be known as the 'Shipwreck Coast'. Flinders' confidence may have stemmed from a feeling he was near familiar territory. He was, after all, co-discoverer of 'Bass's Strait'. He had been here before.

That had been in November, 1798. Flinders was twenty-four and had just been promoted to lieutenant. Stationed in the wild, infant colony of Port Jackson, he was well aware of the rumour that had been circulating for a long while that Van Diemen's Land was not joined to the mainland at all, but was in fact an island, separated by a strait. Governor Hunter was also aware of the rumours. He had helped start them. When Hunter had first sailed out to the colony, passing up the east coast, the magnitude of the swell coming from the west near the Furneaux Islands had made him suspicious.*

After eight years in the colony, Hunter felt it was time to solve the puzzle. Someone had to confirm or deny the existence of the strait and who better than the two young adventurers who had already made such a name for themselves, on their own initiative, conducting exploratory missions north and south of Port Jackson in their tiny boat the *Tom Thumb*. Everyone in the colony had heard of the two young men – George Bass and Matthew Flinders. The odd couple; Bass a huge bear of a man, loud and gregarious;

---

* Interestingly, the French Admiral d'Entrecasteaux had had the same suspicion during his passage down the east coast in 1791 (Dunmore, 1965, v.1, pp. 308–9).

Flinders, short and reserved.

Flinders had met Bass on his voyage out to Port Jackson while serving as master's mate on the *Reliance*. The two had much in common; both were Lincolnshire lads, both were supposed to have followed careers as surgeons (and Bass had), both longed to be explorers. Flinders had taken the direct career path, via the Navy, whilst Bass's career had been more circuitous. Upon finishing his medical studies he was employed as the ship's surgeon on the *Reliance*.

Bass was two years older than Flinders, and as far as the younger man was concerned, exactly the type of fellow Flinders himself aspired to be – cultured, aristocratic and wealthy. Flinders soon became very fond of Bass. As he indicated in a letter to his friend: 'I was so completely wrapped up in you, that no conversation but yours could give me any degree of pleasure; your footsteps upon the quarterdeck over my head, took me from my book, and brought me upon the deck to walk with you.'

Their greatest shared passion was discovery and they had made a very good team. They convinced Governor Hunter that they should be the ones to search for the strait supposed to separate Van Diemen's Land from the mainland and departed in the *Norfolk*, with a crew of eight men, one of whom was John Thistle. It had been Flinders' first command and his first test as a leader of men. He conducted himself impressively. Seven weeks later, although Flinders had barely stepped ashore, he circumnavigated Van Diemen's Land and proved that it was indeed an island.

Flinders had been very pleased with himself. He had named some small islands in the strait the Chappelle Islands in honour of the young woman who was increasingly on his mind, and he recommended that the strait be named after his best friend.

Now here he was, two and a half years later, back in 'Bass's Strait', in a south-westerly gale, in the middle of the night, being pushed closer and closer to the mainland coast. Soon, Flinders did not feel quite so at home as he would have liked. 'The gale increasing … when the night came on, we were uncertain of the trending of the coast … by favour of moonlight and a short cessation of rain, land was perceived on the lee beam.' The sight was not encouraging – sheer cliffs and jagged outcrops. As the gale intensified, the *Investigator* was pushed ever nearer, the easterly coastline appearing to jut out to meet them.

It was a terrifying sight really, visible in the occasional flashes of lightning; the rocks today called the Twelve Apostles towered ominously. Then, miraculously, at 2.00 am the *Investigator* cleared Cape Otway. From here the coast veered suddenly away to the north-east. Flinders was more than a little relieved: 'Our anxiety was great until daylight, when it was dissipated by not finding any land near us.'

Soon after, Flinders came across a small opening. Creeping closer, Flinders' excitement grew. 'Advancing a little westward the opening assumed a more interesting aspect … A large extent of water presently became visible within side.' Although he had passed this way, Baudin had not mentioned seeing any gap. Indeed, it was so small that had Flinders been just a little further out to sea, he too would have missed it. He forgave Baudin: 'It surprised me not a little … from the narrowness of the entrance he must have missed this.'

It seemed inconceivable that such a small entrance could provide passage all the way to the Gulf of Carpentaria, but it was certainly worth investigating. The strong current passing through the opening seemed to indicate a truly massive body of water to the north. Pressed for time, Flinders again threw caution to the wind. 'Although the entrance seemed to be very narrow, and there were in it strong ripplings like breakers, I was induced to steer in at half past one … every man ready for tacking at a moment's warning.'

Flinders sailed the *Investigator* straight into the narrow gap today known as 'The Rip', one of the most dangerous shipping channels in the world. As his ship began to be tossed about by the incoming tide squeezing through the narrow channel, Flinders began to appreciate the danger to which he had exposed his ship. But he was now committed: 'The depth varies from 6 to 12 fathoms; and this irregularity causes the strong tides, especially when running against the wind, to make breakers, in which small vessels should be careful.'

Flinders safely navigated The Rip but then got stuck on a sandbar. Luckily the rising tide allowed the ship to draw free soon after. Flinders was through. He scanned the horizon to the north. No sign of land. The body of water stretched as far as the eye could see. Flinders landed on the eastern shore and scaled the nearest peak (today known as Arthur's Seat). The view from the summit continued to excite: 'Even at this elevation its boundary to the northward could not be distinguished … it was almost incredible, that such a vast piece of water should not have a larger outlet than that through which we had come.'

Charting north, Flinders was enchanted by his new discovery: 'Quantities of fine oysters were lying upon the beaches … and appeared to have been washed up by the surf; a circumstance which I do not recollect to have observed in any other part of this country.' Behind the beach were other delights: 'In the woods are the kangaroo, the emu or cassowary, paroquets, and a variety of small birds.' Even the people were friendly. Flinders met three *Wathaurong* men: 'They came to us without hesitation, received a shag and some trifling presents … They afterwards followed us along the shore; and when I shot another bird, which hovered over the boat, and held it up to them, they ran down to the water side and received it without expressing either surprise or distrust.' Flinders was puzzled that the *Wathaurong* men were not more surprised as to the nature and use of a firearm. It suggested they were familiar with Europeans. Later, he and his three *Wathaurong* companions shared a meal of roast duck.

The ship continued north. Again the land closed in from either side and Flinders realised he had discovered a vast bay. It was beautiful, with terrific potential: 'It is in great measure a grassy country, and capable of supporting much cattle, though better calculated for sheep ... the hills rose one over the other to a moderate elevation, but so gently, that a plough might every where be used ... Were a settlement to be made ... as doubtless there will be some time hereafter, the entrance could easily be defended; and it would not be difficult to establish a friendly intercourse with the natives, for they are acquainted with the effect of fire arms, and desirous of possessing many of our conveniences.'

Flinders was chuffed with his discovery of what would one day be known as Port Phillip: 'I congratulated myself on having made a new and useful discovery ...' The fact that his French rival had missed the discovery only heightened his pleasure. 'Captain Baudin who had coasted along from thence with *fine* weather ... had found no inlet of any kind.'

Chapter 19

[THE POINT OF ADIEU]

Baudin pressed on westwards, in the face of increasing hardship. He reached the gulf Flinders had named 'St Vincent's', and bestowed a name in honour of weariness: 'I gave this gulf the name of Golfe de la Mauvaise because of the fatigue that it caused the whole crew.' Later, he would change the name, giving the feature an even more telling appellation, Golfe de la Misanthropie.

His officers and scientists increasingly irritated Baudin. They argued every point: 'As we still had plenty of work to do on the coast of New Holland,

and had only enough water for another two months, I judged it right to begin cutting down … it produced malcontents – not amongst the sailors, but in another quarter.' By late April, 1802, almost half of the crew were incapable of performing their duties, struck by scurvy and malnourished. The ship's biscuits were so worm-ridden the men refused to eat them, throwing them overboard. Dysentery still lurked between decks and claimed another life. One afternoon, every helmsman was incapable of performing his function. Baudin requested that the midshipmen take over the task of manning the wheel, suggesting that each do one ninety-minute shift in the evening. To Baudin's amazement, all but one of the junior *officiers rouges* obeyed the order, 'for all these men regarded it as dishonouring and schemed to evade it'. Baudin reacted irritably and perhaps irrationally: 'They all expected that I would punish them in various ways, but were quite mistaken. I contented myself with prohibiting them from any kind of duty on board, saying that I would do without them for steering quite as easily as I had done for other things.'

Such action only increased the pressure on himself and his health suffered further. A week later, a sense of utter lethargy seemed to permeate the ship: 'We had no more wood and every day had to resort to various expedients to obtain some; and our water supply could not last long. Like everyone, I felt these privations, but the wish to carry out the Government's design made me better able to bear them than the others. Scurvy, which was beginning to get a hold on several members of the crew, was what worried me most.'

Two days later, at last, the eastern limit of d'Entrecasteux's discoveries loomed ahead. Baudin had reached Cape Adieu. He turned his ship around, not a moment too soon: 'The weakness of my crew, which now consisted of only thirty men for the handling of the ship … decided me to abandon the coast and to head for D'Entrecasteaux Channel, where the anchorage is good, and from there to proceed to Port Jackson.'

Via D'Entrecasteaux Channel! The officers and scientists were dumbfounded: Why not take the most direct route, the short cut through 'Bass's Strait'? Péron was vocal amongst the dissenters: 'Our commander, without any kind of apparent reason, gave orders to steer to the south extremity of Diemen's Land. So extraordinary a resolution, spread a general consternation among us.'

Baudin had his reasons. As well as the certainty of where they could replenish wood and water in the D'Entrecasteaux Channel (as opposed to the uncertainty in Bass's Strait), Baudin seems to have been determined to consolidate his charting of the east coast of Terre de van Diemen. Perhaps he even wanted to have a last search for his missing hydrographer, Boullanger, and his boat's crew, before winter set in. Since Henri Freycinet had refused to chart the east coast of Terre de van Diemen after the loss of Boullanger, Baudin did still not possess detailed maps of this coast. And since his meeting with Flinders and his own confirmation of the non-existence of 'Williamson's Strait',

Baudin must have been keener than ever to consolidate French explorations and any potential French claim to the one land mass definitely not joined to the mainland. From his explorations he now realised that the forests and fertile plains of Terre de van Diemen offered far better scope for a colony than many other places he had so far seen on the barren and dry coast of western Nouvelle Hollande.

But the approaching winter opposed his plan. Again *Le Géographe* was battered by ferocious storms: 'More than once we were in danger of being lost on the east coast of Van Diemen's Land ... A continual blow with rain, hail and thunder, and a sea threatened every moment to engulf us.'

The slow progress and mounting hardships encouraged both officers and scientists to question Baudin's judgement publicly: 'Everybody especially the scientists claimed to recognise the cape that I had named as Cape Pele and I was the only person not to recognise either the cape or the aspect of land to the North and South of it ... This mistake on my part pleased more than one person on board and did much to persuade each one that he was more fit to manage the ship than I was.'

Even some of the crew began to become insubordinate: 'During the morning one of the helmsmen ... kicked up a diabolical row ... Tired of all this din I gave the order for twelve strokes of the lash to be administered to him. This was about to be done when he jumped overboard to escape ... As he was not a good swimmer it was not hard to recapture him. I intended to have twenty strokes of the cat-o'-nine-tails given him when he returned, but the doctors found him not in a state to receive them, so the business was put off.'

Some of the dying men held Baudin alone responsible for their misery, and told him so. Memories of Maugé and Riedlé, and all the others, haunted the decks: 'Most of the sick men were complaining loudly that by not seeking rest in some place where they could find relief, I wanted to bring about their deaths at sea … they regarded me as the prime cause of their illnesses for having stayed too long at sea. The staff and scientists murmured likewise.'

Finally, simple logistics forced Baudin's hand. 'There were only four men able to remain on deck, including the officer of the watch. That decided me to sail off the wind and make for Port Jackson, for we were no longer in a condition to keep at sea.'

Four more Frenchmen died leaving Terre de van Diemen. Two others soon followed. Of the living, thirty-one appeared close to death. Baudin could hardly bear to look at them: 'Their faces were the worst: leaden complexions, gums so swollen as to protrude from their mouths, ulcerated or without feeling.'

Chapter 20

[PORT JACKSON]

At 4.00 pm, on May 8, 1802, the same day that Baudin reached Cape Adieu, Flinders approached the Heads of Port Jackson. In contrast to the miserable condition of the Frenchmen, the Englishmen were in great condition, as Flinders proudly pointed out: 'There was not a single individual on board who was not upon deck working the ship into harbour; and it may be averred, that the officers and crew were, generally speaking, in better health than the day we sailed from Spithead, and not in less good spirits.' It had been 295 days since they had left

England. Flinders left the ship with a skip in his step: 'So soon as the anchor was dropped, I went on shore to wait upon his Excellency Phillip Gidley King … governor of New South Wales … to whom I communicated a general account of our discoveries and examination upon the South Coast.'

Flinders immediately learned that the great bay that he thought he had discovered in the last thirteen days, had in fact been discovered by the commander of the brig *Lady Nelson*, and had been named Port Phillip Bay. Flinders' high spirits were dampened somewhat: 'I [had] congratulated myself on having made a new and useful discovery; but here again I was in error. This place, as I learned at Port Jackson, had been discovered ten weeks before by Lieutenant John Murray.'

His spirits received a further jolt when he discovered that there were no letters awaiting him from Ann. Flinders wrote to her immediately:

> A moment snatched from the confusion of performing half a dozen occupations … is a poor tribute to offer to a beloved friend like thee. That I am safe and well … is to tell thee something. How highly should I value such short information reciprocated from thee! But alas, my dearest love, I am all in the dark concerning thee, I know not what to fear.

The lack of a letter from his wife worried Flinders greatly. It was ten months since he had last heard from her. He had no way of knowing whether her feelings for him had changed, or worse, whether something had happened to her. Flinders knew that Ann's health had always been delicate. His only comfort was that there were no other letters from friends or family informing him of her death. A positive sign, surely.

Less positive was the news that France, Britain and the Allies appeared close to signing a treaty of peace: 'We have a flying report of a peace having taken place, which to naval officers is no very welcome intelligence ... I hope that the difficulty in obtaining promotion which usually follows a peace will not extend to the *Investigator*.'

Flinders found a French vessel anchored close to his own ship: '[I saw] the French national ship *Le Naturaliste*, commanded by captain Hamelin, to whom I communicated captain Baudin's intention of coming to Port Jackson so soon as the bad weather should set in.'

To Flinders' great surprise, Captain Hamelin ignored Baudin's message to wait for him and on May 17 sailed out of Port Jackson. Hamelin had informed his British hosts that he was sailing south to search for *Le Géographe*, but his own officers were in no doubt of his real intentions, as one noted, 'Captain Hamelin was looking only for separation ... [and did not wish] to have to consult anyone but himself.'

§ § §

On June 14, *Le Géographe* finally found itself off Port Jackson Heads. Contrary winds and currents, however, meant several days elapsed before a frustrated Baudin could navigate his way through the Heads: 'So many and such continual setbacks only increased the unhappiness that reigned on board. Unable to put up with it patiently, everyone imagined fresh troubles in their displeasure.'

Finally, Baudin entered Port Jackson, and Flinders himself was witness to the miserable condition of the Frenchmen: 'Captain Baudin arrived in *Le Géographe* on the 20th, and a boat was sent from the *Investigator* to assist in towing the ship up the cove. It was grievous to see the miserable condition, to which both officers and crew were reduced by scurvy; there being not more out of one hundred and seventy, according to the commander's account, than twelve men capable of doing their duty.' Péron, like most of the Frenchmen, was grateful at the reception: 'With what universal joy, then, on the 20th, we saw a large English longboat coming towards us! ... the Governor, having correctly judged by our manoeuvres that we had need of urgent assistance, had sent his longboat with a pilot and the men necessary to bring us in to port.'*

On landing in Sydney, Baudin received good

---

* The story of Baudin's arrival at Port Jackson has several versions. In Péron's account he failed to mention that it was a common occurrence for ships to be delayed several days waiting for favourable winds to navigate Port Jackson Heads. Nor did the pilot board *Le Géographe* until the ship was already at anchor just inside the Heads, again a typical occurrence. Flinders was also misrepresenting the situation. There were only about seventy officers and crew on board *Le Géographe*. By saying 'out of one hundred and seventy', Flinders was including in his statistic the crew of *Le Naturaliste*, who were currently fit and well and sailing for France.

news. He learnt that not only was *Le Naturaliste* not wrecked, but it had located the missing dinghy with Boullanger the hydrographer and the rest of the men alive and well.* In spite of his terrible health, Baudin's spirits began to lift. On Governor King's invitation, Baudin sent twenty-two of his sickest men to hospital.∞

The news of the impending peace made it doubly easy for King to assist the men of *Le Géographe*, honouring and exceeding his obligations as stated in Baudin's passport from the Admiralty. Baudin was thankful for King's reception: 'After having traversed the sea in different directions for nine months ... The succours which were lavishly bestowed, the affectionate and obliging cares of governor King ... I cannot pass in silence an act of humanity to which our situation gave rise.'

Baudin asked King whether they might be allowed to set up camp on shore. Baudin already had a

---

* Baudin learnt how Boullanger and the other men who had disappeared in the dinghy two and a half months before had been pushed by contrary winds and currents, slowly watching *Le Géographe* disappear from view. During the night Boullanger and his companions had sheltered behind a small island and the next day had been fortunate enough to sight a ship, which turned out to be the English brig *Harrington*. They managed to signal the ship and were rescued. While searching for *Le Géographe*, *Le Naturaliste* had come across the *Harrington* and the missing men transferred across. As Baudin had predicted at the time, the missing men had drifted north while *Le Géographe* wasted precious time searching the waters thirty miles to the south. Hamelin continued to search for Baudin and when he failed to locate him, had charted 'French Island' and other parts of Westernport Bay before running for Port Jackson.

∞ All survived but two – and these men died from dysentery, not scurvy.

site in mind: 'The place where Mr Flinders is located appears to be the most convenient, provided you see no objection.' King agreed and French tents soon joined the English tents on Bennelong Point (today the site of the Sydney Opera House). Although the colony was itself short of food, with recent floods on the Hawkesbury having destroyed the wheat harvest, King sent the Frenchmen ample fresh produce. Indeed, he asked his own colonists to reduce their ration by half in order to support the men with whom Britain had so recently been at war.

Flinders testified to the especially kind treatment received by the French: 'The distress of the French navigators had indeed been great; but every means were used by the governor … to make them forget both their sufferings and the war which existed between two nations.' In some ways, Flinders felt that the Frenchmen were catered for more favourably than his own expedition: 'The necessity of augmenting the number of cattle in the country had prevented the governor from allowing us any fresh meat; but some oxen belonging to government were killed for the distressed strangers.'

As soon as Baudin was well enough, Flinders paid him a visit: 'There was a friendly communication between us and I made it my business to shew the commandant that attention that was due to his employment and to his superior rank.' Flinders informed Baudin that he had given Hamelin his message, but that Hamelin had chosen to sail off anyway.

Then, not long after, *Le Naturaliste* reappeared off the Heads. Baudin welcomed Hamelin back warmly. Hamelin admitted that he had intended to return to France, but had encountered contrary winds on the southern coast of Van Diemen's Land. As Milius reported scornfully: '[He] had been forced to return to Port Jackson, to take on more food, not having enough board to continue the voyage! Mr Baudin was not annoyed at this reverse, and the reunion was happy for all of us.' Happy simply to be reunited, Baudin, it seemed, was more than willing to forgive and forget.

Since Flinders had arrived, his crew, with the help of several specialists sent by Governor King, had once again been busily repairing the increasingly leaky *Investigator*. As the Frenchmen recovered their health, one by one, they began to repair their own ships. Ronsard, the chief engineer, informed Baudin that *Le Géographe* needed to be careened in order to replace the copper lining the hull. *Le Naturaliste*, which would soon transport back the natural history collection gathered thus far, was so overrun by rats that the entire ship needed to be emptied out and fumigated and in the process at least 2,000 rats escaped or were killed.

Living so close to one another, on Bastille Day, 1802, Flinders invited Baudin and his officers to celebrate the French holiday in the English camp – the Peace of Amiens having finally been officially confirmed. Flinders watched the Frenchmen approach: 'Captains Baudin & Hamelin, with Monsieur Péron and some other French officers … were received under a salute of eleven guns. The intelligence of peace, which had just been received, contributed to enliven the party.' Flinders soon produced one of his charts which indicated the great bay that the Frenchman had missed: 'I showed to captain Baudin one of my charts of the south coast, containing the part first explored by him, and distinctly marked as his discovery. He made no objection to the justice of the limits therein pointed out; but found his portion to be smaller than he had supposed, not having before been aware of the extent of the discoveries previously made.'

Flinders was again keen to distinguish Baudin's discoveries from his own. He was also keen to see Baudin's charts and when Baudin did not reciprocate, Flinders was clearly disappointed: 'After examining the chart, he said, apparently as a reason for not producing any of his own, that his charts were not constructed on board the ship; but that he transmitted to Paris all his bearings and observations ... and from them the charts were to be made at a future time. This mode appeared to me extraordinary, and not to be worthy of imitation.'

Flinders received greater satisfaction from Lieutenant Henri Freycinet: 'Mons. Freycinet made use of the following odd expression, addressing himself to me in the house of governor King ... "Captain, if we had not been kept so long picking up shells and catching butterflies at Van Dieman's Land, you would not have discovered the South Coast before us!"' This remark was more like the kind of response Flinders had hoped for – a Frenchman conceding that he had beaten them in charting a great deal of the southern coast. Unlike the more temperamental Henri Freycinet, however, Baudin refused to reveal whatever disappointments he may or may not have felt.*

Henri Freycinet had an interesting time in Port Jackson. He challenged a British officer to a duel. It was not only Flinders who thought the Frenchmen were being given preferential treatment. After King had permitted Baudin to purchase 800 gallons of brandy previously denied the officers of the New South Wales Corps, Captain Kemp of the Corps accused Henri Freycinet of on-selling the brandy for profit on shore. Freycinet challenged Kemp to a duel, but the matter was eventually resolved non-violently with a begrudging apology from Kemp.

As Baudin and King compared notes on the headaches of having to deal with insubordination – King having to contend with the criminal antics of the Corps and Baudin with plenty of his own stories – the two men discovered they had much in common. They were of a similar age and King, who spoke fluent French, was sympathetic to most things French. Baudin moved into a house in town, not far from King's residence, and the two men began meeting on an almost daily basis. However, Baudin did not establish the same rapport with Flinders. The young English commander appeared very competitive, was overtly ambitious and a little too full of himself. For Baudin, he was not unlike many of his own haughty young officers.

Camped just a few tent flaps away from one

---

* Alas, few insights exist of Baudin's feelings while in Port Jackson as he ceased writing in his *Journal de Mer* while he stopped there.

another, the rivalries between the French and English camps were never far away. When Péron learnt that a few of the French sailors had given some shells collected in Van Diemen's Land to the British, he berated the men: 'It should be considered a crime to hand over the fruit of one's research to foreigners, in particular to the enemies of one's nation.' But Péron had no qualms about being the beneficiary of such a crime. On learning of the noble aspirations of the *Société des Observateurs de l'Homme*, Flinders' old friend, George Bass, happily donated a significant collection of Pacific Islander artefacts he had collected, for the benefit of the *Société*.

Péron had been entrusted with packing the expedition's natural history specimens collected thus far in preparation for *Le Naturaliste* transporting them back to France. After adding the 200 birds and 68 quadrupeds caught in Port Jackson, the collection was truly stunning, as Péron proudly described: 'We arranged in the most methodical manner 40,000 creatures of all sorts and descriptions ... 33 large packing cases were filled ... When only partially displayed in the house I occupied [it] excited the admiration of all the learned Englishmen of the colony, particularly the celebrated naturalist Colonel Paterson.' The French scientists continued their work with gusto. They surpassed in just a few months the energy and findings the British had made in the whole twelve years since the colony had been founded.

The lack of support for British science was demonstrated in the difficulties experienced by Robert

Brown, the naturalist on board the *Investigator*. Brown tried to remain optimistic, but he was deeply concerned for the welfare of his collection of over 750 specimens taken from the south coast, of which he estimated the number of new species to be about 300. He was bitterly disappointed that of the seventy live plants collected *en route*, only ten had survived. He even had difficulty in securing something as basic as boxes in which to store his samples. Having watched his specimens being consumed by mice on board the *Investigator*, in Port Jackson Brown was determined to have proper crates made. Indeed, Joseph Banks had promised him as much. But Brown found his commander unenthusiastic, not to say completely uninterested, in his work, as he later wrote to a friend: 'Whatever instructions Capt'n Flinders may have received concerning natural history, I think myself warranted, from my past experience, in assuring you that at no period of the voyage would he have been regulated … by my opinion.'

It was clear that Flinders was focused on charting, lending weight to the suspicion that his 'scientific' mission was little more than a cover for the Admiralty's far greater interest in colonisation. Day and night Flinders slaved away at his maps. He was very conscious of the need for urgency in completing and despatching his charts of the southern coast back to England.

The whaler *Speedy* was shortly departing for England. Flinders rushed to meet the deadline, but he missed it and the *Speedy* departed without any of his charts on board at all. Flinders sent a letter to Joseph Banks, apologising and assuring his patron that he had performed splendidly thus far in the race against the French:

> ... having met with the French national ship
> *Le Géographe* upon the coast of New Holland ...
> We were fortunate enough to save the
> principal and most interesting part of that coast
> from being first examined by foreigners,
> notwithstanding our long delays in England.

Flinders claimed that although sailing against the wind, he had still managed to chart not only the greater part of the southern coast, but the more valuable part as well:

> I am happy Sir Joseph in announcing to you ...
> that before we met the French national ship
> *Le Géographe*, the most interesting part of the
> south coast of New Holland had undergone
> the examination of the *Investigator* ... As was
> the case with Admiral D'Entrecasteaux, we
> were much opposed in our progress by easterly
> winds, from the time of passing his dangerous
> archipelago to past the situation of meeting
> *Le Géographe* ... These foul winds and our
> detention in England favoured Mons. Baudin, or
> no part of the south coast would have been left
> for him to discover ...

Flinders passed on all the intelligence he had gleaned of French progress thus far:

As far as I have been able to learn, the operations of the French have been confined to …
Van Diemens Land and to the west side of New
Holland … Mons. Baudin denied having visited
any of the more northern parts of New Holland.

Flinders then assured Banks that the faith he had
placed in him was well founded:

When the charts arrive, you will better judge,
Sir Joseph, how far the task has been well
performed … At these charts I am now
labouring assiduously in order to get copies
transmitted to the admiralty.

The problem was, Banks and the Admiralty
wanted the charts now. Missing his deadline with the
Speedy infuriated his superiors.

When the Admiralty learned that he had neglected to despatch his charts promptly, Banks had to
scramble to placate the First Lord of the Admiralty
from finding someone to replace Flinders. Sir Joseph
informed Flinders in a letter:

'Your charts and journals which I do not doubt
you have despatched home, have not yet been
received, this is a great misfortune to you, & a
great inconvenience to Public service … if I
had possessed only a few sketches of yours to
illustrate the statements I have been making in
your favour I should have been able to make a

much firmer and more lasting impression of the services you have done, than has been the case.'

Flinders' already diminished standing back in England would not be enhanced by his flagrant disregard of his sailing orders. Some in the Admiralty even began to deride the young commander as indolent and idle. It is unclear why Flinders did not place greater emphasis on despatching his all-important charts quickly. Perhaps in a desire to impress Banks and the Admiralty, Flinders had wanted to complete all of the charts, rather than just concentrating on the important ones of the south-east, in particular Port Phillip Bay. But in not sending any charts by the *Speedy*, Flinders left himself little chance of impressing anybody.

Flinders exacerbated his problems by another odd decision. On learning that the *Investigator* would soon be ready to sail, he prepared to depart Port Jackson to race north. Flinders knew that such a move was also contrary to his instructions: 'My instructions directed me to return ... to the South Coast, as the first step after refitting the ship at Port Jackson, but His Excellency was of opinion, as well as myself, that it would be unsafe to do this in the middle of the winter season; and that to remain six months in port waiting for the fine weather would be a sad waste of time ... it was decided to proceed to the northward.'

More likely Flinders had convinced Governor King rather than the other way around. Flinders' haste to head north may also have had something to do with what Captain Baudin had told him of his plans: 'I understood that [Baudin] meant to return to the South Coast, and after completing its examination, to proceed northward, and enter the Gulph with the north-west monsoon.'

Did Baudin perhaps 'help' Flinders make his decision by telling him where the French mission was ultimately heading? If so, the ploy worked. The Gulf of Carpentaria was a low priority in the sailing orders of both men, but Flinders was now determined to beat Baudin there – to the detriment of his other priorities, in particular the north-west coasts.

Meanwhile, Baudin had ordered the charting of the whole of Port Jackson. He soon had maps of the port far superior to anything the British themselves possessed. Many of the Frenchmen remained busy making a reconnaissance of the British settlement. Péron and Freycinet simply schemed its destruction. The pair threw themselves into the role of spies enthusiastically, gathering knowledge of the colony's defences and encouraging Lesueur to make detailed topographical sketches of its approaches – the kind of map that would be useful for planning a military invasion from land and sea.

Baudin's personal interest in Port Jackson was the indigenous people, the *Eora*. He noticed that the *Eora* had made far greater progress in the language of the English than vice versa. Baudin attended an *Eora* funeral and several corroborees where he encouraged his men to write down the musical notes to three chants. The Frenchmen's fascination with the *Eora* even extended to them sketching the local people having sexual intercourse. The French found some of the positions novel, as the bashful hydrographer Boullanger observed: 'The public roadway … scorning all modesty, serves for them as the nuptial bed, without dreaming to be surprised nor disturbed in their frolics.'

In July, the French watched their English neighbours packing up their camp. Flinders was ready to race north. The recaulking of the *Investigator* was complete and he had found crewmen to replace those lost at Cape Catastrophe. He welcomed a new Master, John Aken, as well as nine convicts and two *Eora* men. Whilst Flinders did not have the same scientific interest in indigenous people as Baudin, he had self-interest: 'I had before experienced much advantage from the presence of a native of Port Jackson, in bringing about a friendly intercourse with the inhabitants of other parts of the coast … Bongaree, the worthy and brave fellow who had sailed with me in the *Norfolk*, now volunteered again; the other was Nanbaree, a good-natured lad.'

As they were shown their quarters, Bongaree and Nanbaree came to experience at first hand life on the *Investigator*. Again, as departure from a European settlement neared, night after night below deck disappeared in a fog of sex, drunkenness and song. The stay at Port Jackson had allowed many of the men who had previously sailed with Flinders on the *Reliance* to rekindle old flames amongst the convict women. Having driven his crew hard repairing the ship during their three-month stay, Flinders let his crew bring their women on board and turned a blind eye to the debauchery below deck as couples tried desperately to squeeze every last embrace from their relationships before the men headed back out into the unknown. Some of the men were resentful of the short stay and their captain's zeal. The celebrations became so wild that Flinders was forced to have five of the men flogged for outrageous drunkenness and talk of mutiny.

Listening to the wild orgies, Flinders missed his wife. He had still not heard from her. Then, just before departure, the *Coromandel* arrived in port, bringing with it two letters. Flinders was elated to hold the precious correspondence in his hands. But on reading Ann's letters, he was thrown back into turmoil, shocked by the tortured words of his abandoned wife. He learned how Ann had become gravely ill after his departure. Constant weeping had inflamed one of her eyes to the point where the surgeon had almost been compelled to remove it. Three months had elapsed before Ann could even write her first letter to Flinders and a further three months went by before she could send it. He now read that first letter, together with another she wrote subsequently. The letters have not survived but they must have disturbed Flinders deeply, reminding him of the guilt he bore. He wrote back immediately:

> My dearest love ... oh my love, my love, how much do I sympathise in thy sufferings, that I could but transport myself to thee ...

In the letters Ann may have accused Flinders of abandoning her, betraying her, pursuing his ambition at the cost of his love for her. Flinders tried desperately to justify himself:

> My dearest Friend, though adducest me leaving thee to follow the call of my profession, as a poor proof of my affection for thee. Dost thou know, my beloved, that we could have barely existed in England? ... It was only upon the certainty of obtaining an employment, the produce of which would be adequate to thy support as well as my own, that I dared to follow the wishes of my heart and press thee to be mine ... look my dear Ann to the happy side. See me engaged, successfully thus far, in the cause of science and followed by the good wishes and approbation of the world ... hastening to thy love as the best reward for all my toils.

Flinders' words may have been cold comfort to Ann, the reward so distant; having to watch her friends having children; forced to survive on a meagre allowance; a married woman, stuck with her parents; a single woman – alone and lonely.

In Flinders' reply, written the day before he departed Port Jackson, he asked her to write to his father to keep him informed of progress. He was still too proud to do it himself following the feud over his hasty marriage.

On July 22, 1802 Péron watched the English pull up anchor: 'The intrepid captain Flinders, after effecting a junction with his companionship, the *Lady Nelson*, was getting ready to continue his grand voyage round New Holland.' Baudin watched his rival depart, his own ships still needing several more weeks of repairs. For Baudin there was no need to hurry, and he waited patiently for winter to pass in the south. Only Flinders was rushing.

Chapter 21

[IN THE SHADOW OF
CAPTAIN COOK]

L ike Baudin, Flinders now had two ships. He
watched the *Lady Nelson* struggling to keep up.
Young Lieutenant Murray commanded his consort vessel – the same Murray who had 'beaten'
Flinders by a mere ten weeks in discovering Port
Phillip Bay. Flinders knew he had no time to waste. If
his ships took too long to reach the north, he would
hit the Monsoon. That could be catastrophic. Regardless of the extensive repairs in Port Jackson, to his
horror the *Investigator* was still leaking. Flinders did

not need water attacking him from below, as well as above.

Heading up the east coast, he was now following in the footsteps of his great hero Captain James Cook. Flinders took great pleasure in seeing the same sights 'the greatest navigator of all time' had seen thirty-two years before. He stopped at Fraser Island: 'What is remarkable, on comparing my observations with those of Captain Cook, it appeared that little or no change had taken place in variation, during thirty-two years.' He discovered Port Curtis, to his great delight: 'This part of the East Coast had been passed in the night by captain Cook … [it had] escaped his notice, and the discovery of the port fell to our lot.'

At the prospect of improving upon the charts of his hero, Flinders could not help himself and started exploring another bay a little farther north. He became convinced that there was another great discovery to be made here that Cook had missed: 'My object in stopping at this bay was to explore two openings marked in it by captain Cook, which it was possible might be the entrances of rivers leading into the interior.'

Flinders scoured the mangroves. The going proved much tougher than expected: 'It would perhaps have been easier to climb up the trees, and scramble from one to another upon the vines, than to have penetrated through the intricate net work in the darkness underneath.' As darkness fell, Flinders spent the night in the mangroves: 'The swarms of musketoes and sand flies made sleeping impossible to all except

one of the boat's crew, who was so enviably constituted, that these insects either did not attack him, or
could not penetrate his skin.' Flinders found himself
under siege from another quarter as well. 'Some Indians had assembled … taking the advantage of a hillock,
[they] began to throw stones … nor would they
desist until two or three muskets were fired over their
head.'

Two other men became lost and had a far more
friendly encounter with the local *Darumbal* people, as
Flinders later learned: 'About twenty-five Indians …
surrounded and took them to a fire place. A couple
of ducks were broiled; and after the wanderers had
satisfied their hunger, and undergone a personal
examination, they were conducted back to the ship in
safety.'

Though he could sense it was near, Flinders
simply could not find the river. He knew it was
there, but he could not afford to spend any further
time looking. He called off the search and pressed on.*

Ego had cost Flinders almost two weeks in an
extremely tight schedule. Just as he had done on leaving King George Sound after first reaching New
Holland, Flinders was delaying his progress by charting
areas that had already been charted, at least nominally,
if not to Flinders' perfect standards. The east coast
barely figured in Flinders' instructions from the Admiralty at all. In his sailing orders, charting this coast was

---

* Through the misfortune of scaling 'West-arm Hill' rather than
'Broad Hill' only a mile to the north – Flinders missed one of the
continent's great waterways, the Fitzroy River.

the absolute lowest in order of priority.*

Continuing to chart and hug the coast north-wards, Flinders' progress was slow. He blamed the *Lady Nelson* for some of the delays. For the second time the *Lady Nelson* snapped off one of her movable keels and became stuck on a sandbar. For once Flinders was thankful of the huge tides they were encountering: 'At eleven, the flood came in, six or 8 inches perpendicu-lar, with a roaring noise … and presently set the brig afloat.' He had never seen tidal flows quite like these: 'I ordered particular attention to be paid to the tides during the night … the difference was no less than thirty-two feet!'

Indeed, Flinders had now entered a world ruled by tides, the Capricorn Channel. He continued to hug the coast, searching for something in particular. 'After passing Cape Capricorn, my first object on landing was to examine the refuse thrown up by the sea.' Flinders scoured the beach rubbish and found all manner of detritus: 'Coral … skeletons of fish and sea snakes, the fruit of the pandanus … cocoa-nut shells … but there were no marks of shipwreck.' Specifically, Flinders was searching for a French shipwreck: 'The French naviga-tor, La Pérouse, whose unfortunate situation, if in existence, was always present to my mind … the hope of restoring La Pérouse or any of his companions to

---

* From Cook's charting, the Admiralty and the British East India Co. already had a fairly good idea of what the east coast presented. They were far more interested in learning more about the north-west and western coasts, as a possible site for establishing a trading station, and of course to forestall the French. For Flinders' Sailing Orders – see Flinders' *A Voyage to Terra Australis*, Vol. 1, 1814, p. 9–10.

their country … could not, after so many years, be rationally entertained, yet to gain some certain knowledge of their fate would do away the pain of suspense.'

While searching for the wreck of La Pérouse, by hugging the coast so far north, Flinders had in fact set his own ships on a perfect course for shipwreck. Flinders soon found himself squeezed. To the west was the mainland, and to the east a vast reef. Flinders bravely pressed on, 'to ascertain their termination to the north-westward …' The problem was, there seemed to be no termination – the reef stretched on and on, day after day. 'By this time I was weary of them, not only from the danger to which the vessels were thereby exposed, but from fear of the contrary monsoon setting in upon the North Coast.'

Flinders could not afford any further delays and began sailing extremely close to the jagged edge of coral, searching for a way through. It was a very risky manoeuvre: 'We came to, in 35 fathoms … being surrounded by reefs, except to the westward from whence we had come … I therefore determined to remain at the present anchorage till low water, when the reefs would be dry, and the channels between them, if any such there were, would be visible.'

As the tide rushed out, Flinders decided to take a close look at his great adversary: 'In the afternoon, I went upon the reef with a party of the gentlemen; and the water being very clear round the edges, a new creation, as it was to us, but imitative of the old, was there presented to our view … mushrooms, stags horns, cabbage leaves, and a variety of other forms, glowing under water with vivid tints of every shade betwixt green, purple, brown, and white; equalling in beauty and excelling in grandeur the most favourite parterre of the curious florist … but whilst contemplating the richness of the scene, we could not long forget with what destruction it was pregnant.' As the tide flooded back in, Flinders continued on, bestowing an appropriate name on this massive living thing preventing him from reaching the safety of the open sea: The Great Barrier Reef.

On October 11, still hemmed in, Flinders lost his patience. Although the gap in the reef was narrow, Flinders instructed the *Lady Nelson* to attempt to pass through, the *Investigator* following behind. The two ships tried to sail against the tide rushing in. It was a disaster: 'We had scarcely entered … when Mr. Murray made the signal for danger … The *Lady Nelson* was carried rapidly to the southwest … We rode a great strain on the stream cable, and the ship taking a sudden sheer, it parted at the clinch and we lost the anchor.'

The tide and the current took command of Flinders' ships: 'The tide was, indeed, running past the brig at a fearful rate, and I feared it would pass over her bows; for she lay in one of the narrow streams which came gushing through the small openings in the outer reef …' Calamity was only avoided with the flood tide subsiding. Flinders realised he had made a mistake: 'My anxious desire to get out to sea and reach the North Coast before the unfavourable monsoon should set in, had led me to persevere amongst these intricate passages beyond what prudence could approve … I therefore formed the determination … to avoid all narrow channels, and run along, within side the larger reefs, until a good and safe opening should present itself.'

Flinders gambled that he would eventually find a gap through the reef further to the north. With every wasted day increasing the danger of running into the dreaded Monsoon to the north, Flinders decided to act. The loss of the last of her anchors presented Flinders with the perfect excuse: 'The *Lady Nelson* … not only caused us delay, but ran great risk of being lost … and in want of anchors and cables which could not be spared without endangering our own safety, she was become, and would be more so every day, a burthen rather than an assistant to me.'

Flinders had wanted to send the second ship back to Port Jackson for a while now. One of the *Eora* men asked to go back as well: 'Nanbarre … having expressed a wish to go back to Port Jackson, was sent to the *Lady Nelson* in the morning … At nine o'clock we got underway, and showed our colours to bid farewell … The brig was not out of sight when more reefs were discovered.'

The *Investigator* forged on alone. After two full weeks of following the inside of the reef northwards, Flinders finally saw what he hoped was another way through. 'And although caution inclined to steering back towards the land, this prospect of an outlet determined me to proceed … We were successful … we had at length gained the open sea.'

Flinders knew all too well how lucky he had been

to escape this enormous hazard. He named the last stretch he had just navigated The Labyrinth. His advice to those who might follow after him: 'If he do not feel his nerves strong enough to thread the needle … I would strongly recommend him not to approach this part of New South Wales …'

Flinders remained worried. He had survived The Reef, but the effort had cost him more precious time. The delays favoured his next adversary, The Monsoon.

Chapter 22

[FRIENDS AND LOVERS]

After five months in Port Jackson, Baudin was ready to leave. He had enjoyed his stay immensely. He had recovered his health, as had his men. *Le Géographe* and *Le Naturaliste* were now shipshape and ready to again take on the unknown. Governor King had even allowed him to buy a new little ship, the *Casuarina*, to replace *Le Naturaliste* which would soon be taking the scientific specimens so far collected back to France. The 30-ton *Casuarina* had been an absolute bargain – Governor King had parted with it for £50 and 150 gallons of rum.

Baudin had grown to like King a lot, and was sad to farewell this new friend. In stark contrast to the reception he had received at Île-de-France, Governor King had gone out of his way to help him. Baudin left a letter for the English Governor to pass on to the French Governor of Île-de-France. In the letter he described the hospitable treatment he had received, urging that the favour be returned should Flinders or any other British navigator need to stop there. Baudin then wrote King an affectionate farewell:

> It will … be a satisfaction to me to correspond with you from whatever country events may bring me to. It is, as you know, the only means which men who love and esteem one another can make use of, and it will be the one we shall reciprocally avail ourselves of, if, on your part, I have been able by my conduct to inspire you with the feelings which yours has inspired with me.

After the loss of Riedlé and Maugé, the new friendship had been very welcome, not to mention a relief from his still-troublesome relationship with his own countrymen. Baudin was not keen to lose King's company. All he had to look forward to for the next many months was the taciturn company of his officers and scientists.

And of course, the convict girl.

In the ship's log, Baudin described seventeen-year-old Mary Beckwith's arrival on board: 'At about

11 at night an English girl named Mary Bickaith appeared on board in men's clothing. I had known her during my stay at Port Jackson, and she had more than once asked me to obtain Governor King's permission for her to return to England ... he told me that if she wanted to leave, no inquiry would be made about her.' By that act alone, King had proved the depth of the two men's camaraderie. By turning a blind eye to one of his convicts leaving the colony, King breached his own regulations.

In his log, Baudin remained coy as to his reasons for smuggling the lass on board: 'I have embarked her to set her down somewhere in the Moluccas. Her youth will soon be noticed there and will find her some happy fate.' His men, however, were in no doubt as to the real purpose of the girl's presence in the captain's cabin, as Freycinet observed: 'The Citizen Commandant embarks a prostitute for his personal service.'

With Mary stashed safely below, on November 17, 1802, Baudin led his three ships out of Port Jackson to resume the exploration of the south coast. One officer was left behind. Baudin approved a request from Pierre Milius to quit the expedition at Port Jackson. Milius had had a nervous breakdown. His involvement in two small boat mishaps, one of which resulted in the disappearance of Vasse, had taken their toll. His nerves were shot.

Governor King promised to ensure that Milius was cared for and waved goodbye to his French guests. King too was sad to see Baudin go and had written the

French captain a warm farewell: 'I feel myself much gratified in your promise of corresponding with me. A debt this contracted I shall most religiously and with greatest pleasure discharge.'

No sooner had Baudin sailed through The Heads, however, when intelligence was delivered to Governor King that sent a shiver up his spine. According to the intelligence, his dear *friend* Baudin was not heading south to chart, but to colonise. King was stunned: 'A few hours after the French ships were out of sight I was informed that some French officers during their stay here had informed L't Col. Paterson and others that it was the intention of the French to make a settlement in … Le Canal d'Entrecasteaux.'

Captain Kemp of the Rum Corps added his voice, claiming to have overheard two young officers discussing an imminent French settlement to the south. Captain Kemp was the same officer who had been involved in the threatened duel following the sale of brandy. King was then presented with maps of the potential French settlement in Storm Bay, in Terre de van Diemen.

King was stunned and upset. He was suddenly suspicious that Baudin's amiability and supposed scientific passions were little more than a cover for French colonial designs on Nouvelle Hollande: 'I am inclined to think from his geographical pursuits that collecting alone is not the principal object of his mission, as it has very forcibly struck me that they have an intention of looking for a place proper to make a similar establishment to this.'

King was not only hurt, but worried. Flinders' discovery of Bass Strait, rather than consolidating English claims to Van Diemen's Land, had thrown them into uncertainty, and it would seem, jeopardy. The island's confirmed isolation from the mainland, coupled with the extent of d'Entrecasteaux's and Baudin's detailed surveys, gave the French a very strong claim to Terre de van Diemen. King had to do something. He sent for Lieutenant Robbins and ordered that the colonial schooner, the *Cumberland*, be readied to sail south, immediately.

Baudin was blissfully unaware of what had just transpired on his departure from Port Jackson and helped Mary Beckwith make herself at home in his cabin. Baudin was informed that his concubine was not the only British subject to have joined the mission. In all, nine convicts had stowed away on the ships. Baudin knew that his friend Governor King would be very disappointed to learn of their disappearance: 'Upon being questioned as to their motive in hiding aboard, they said it was to receive their liberty. I told them that they would be deposited on King Island.'

Baudin reached King Island on December 7, 1802. True to his word, he delivered the stowaways to a motley crew of eleven sealers already working the island. All of them except for Mary, that is.

Baudin sent a boat to circumnavigate King Island while his scientists continued their studies on shore. The scientists captured pelicans and from the sealers purchased some emus as well as a very tame male kangaroo and three wombats. In delivering the purchase,

195

the sealers took the opportunity to smuggle three of the convicts back on board *Le Géographe*.

It did not take long before the scientists were again annoying Baudin: 'The large dinghy set off, carrying the scientists, their knowledge and their baggage, for these gentlemen never move without pomp and magnificence. The cooks with their utensils, the pots and pans and the saucepans cluttered up the boat so much that not every one could fit in … they all returned at about nine o'clock, except for Mr Péron, who seeing nothing but molluscs at every step, had amused himself by missing the first boat.'

Baudin went on board *Le Naturaliste* to check up on the priceless cargo one last time: 'Since the *Naturaliste* was to leave on the morrow, I went aboard her … to examine the condition of the plants. We found them all healthy and the live quadrupeds and birds likewise.'

Baudin was extremely proud of the remarkable collection now stowed in the hold of *Le Naturaliste* – in total over 100,000 natural history specimens, including more than twenty living creatures; dingoes, wombats, black swans, cassowaries and four emus.

Captain Hamelin planned to sail immediately and Baudin bid him a fond farewell; the two men had become better acquainted at Port Jackson: 'On the imminent departure of Captain Hamelin and the *Naturaliste* we wished each other a safe journey and good health … I was truly fond of Captain Hamelin for his personal qualities, and when one has shared the same dangers for two years it was natural to feel as I did at his departure.' The feeling was mutual, as Hamelin recorded: 'Commandant Baudin gave us another and final proof of the generosity and kind-heartedness that characterises him, by sending a pig, two sheep and some chickens for the invalid Depuch.'

Hamelin saluted Baudin farewell as his commander climbed back down into his waiting boat. Hamelin watched Baudin row away into the darkness and then turned his attention back to what could only be described as his personal Noah's Ark. Soon after, Hamelin was surprised by a strange vessel approaching and docking beside the *Naturaliste*. In English, the strangers requested to board. The ship was called the *Cumberland* and was commanded by a young Lieutenant Robbins.

Hamelin listened carefully as Robbins explained that he just happened to be passing on his way to Terre de van Diemen. Hamelin was stunned, writing in his journal: 'There remains no doubt that the English are about to take from us the D'Entrecasteaux channel where it would however, interest the French Republic very much to have a settlement, as I shall try to prove in a report I shall send to the Minister of Marine.'*

Across the water, a few hundred yards away, Baudin also noticed the new arrival. An hour later, he watched the *Naturaliste* embark on its long voyage back

---

* It may be that this was exactly what Governor King had in mind when he so hurriedly dispatched the *Cumberland*. King knew that Hamelin was soon returning to France. King may have wanted Hamelin to report to Napoléon that the British had already begun settling Van Diemen's Land. With the two nations no longer at war, it would thus have required an act of aggression from the French to counter the British claim to Van Diemen's Land.

to France: 'This moment of separation was extremely painful for me and I felt a pang.' The newcomer approached his own ship the following morning. Robbins again introduced himself as Governor King's envoy and Baudin invited the young lieutenant to lunch. Robbins repeated what he had told Hamelin and handed Baudin a letter from Governor King. Baudin read the letter. Baudin stared at his young English visitors: 'Since I am reserving the right to reply in very few words to Governor King on this subject, I was very uncommunicative with these gentlemen.'

As word spread on board *Le Géographe* of the nature of Robbins' visit, several of Baudin's officers became very upset, one noting with rage that: 'We are forestalled everywhere! Discoveries and settlements! The English have done the southwest coast before us, will do the Gulf, and will establish themselves with impunity in the places we have discovered. Yet the *Investigator* left Europe a long time after us.' Ronsard, the chief engineer, was equally affronted: 'I hope that the French Government … will form a settlement in D'Entrecasteaux Channel, if only to avoid abandoning these vast regions to our arrogant rivals.'

It seems only Baudin saw Robbins for what he really was – a bluff. As Baudin read the letter delivered from Governor King again, his *dear friend* Governor King – Baudin realised it was not a very convincing bluff at that. King's letter read as follows:

To the Commander of the Expedition …
You will no doubt be surprised to see a ship so

close on your heels. You are acquainted with my intention to establish a settlement in the South; however it has been hastened by information communicated to me immediately after your departure. This information is to the effect that the French wish to set up an establishment in Storm Bay Passage or in the area known as Frederick Henry Bay. It is also said that these are your orders from the French Republic ...

I deem it my duty to declare to you ... that you cannot occupy any part of them without breaking the friendly relations which have been so recently established between the two nations ... HMS *Cumberland* has received orders not to leave you until the officer in command of her is convinced that your proceedings are wholly unconnected with any attempt at invasion of the British territory in these parts.

Baudin was curious as to what had prompted his friend to take this aggressive action. He read the date on King's letter and realised the Governor had dispatched Robbins at almost the same moment that they had bid one another such a warm farewell. He did not know that it was primarily Péron's boasting, that they were themselves sailing south to form a settlement, that had sent King into swift reaction. As Ronsard later learned, François Péron had made his ludicrous boast directly to one of the senior English officers, Colonel Paterson, that, 'We had the plan to make a settlement in the D'Entrecasteaux Channel.'

The next day the Frenchmen watched Robbins take possession of King Island, as Baudin wryly observed: 'I was some what amazed to see an English flag absolutely where our tents were set up. I thought at first, from the way in which it was hanging, that it had been put up to dry; but upon noticing a soldier in red uniform with a bayonet in his hand, I sought information as to what it could be. Our scientists then told me that roughly an hour earlier, Mr Robbins who had come ashore to dine with them, had placed it there in a way which I could see it. They did not know what it meant, unless to inform us that the island belonged to him.' Robbins even had to borrow the gunpowder from the French in order for his British marines to fire a salute while the flag was raised.

Baudin knew that it was all a show, that the main game lay to the south, as he wrote in his journal: 'The English claim on Van Diemen's Land was emphatically stated in the instructions of the schooner's Captain, but it rests merely on Governor Phillip's proclamation, the limits of which are recorded in what we know, from its beginnings of the present settlement. Therefore it seems to me to be no doubt that Governor King was afraid from whatever he had been told, that I was going to put someone on that land so as to occupy it first and that was his sole reason for dispatching a ship to observe us.'

Having mulled over the situation for a couple of days, Baudin decided to write Governor King two letters. The first letter was an official one, Frenchman to Englishman:

Sir,

The arrival of the *Cumberland* would have surprised me by reason of the contents of the letter you did me the honour of writing me, if Mr. Robbins, who commanded her, had not by his conduct made evident the real reason for dispatching him so hurriedly; but perhaps he has come too late, for several days before he hoisted his flag over our tents we had left in prominent parts of the island (which I still name after you) proofs of the period at which we visited it. The story you have heard, and of which I suspect Mr Kemp ... to be the author, is without foundation ...

Baudin went on to point out how unconvincing Robbins was in pretending to be off to found a colony, since he had obviously left in too much of a hurry to pick up the most basic of supplies:

I gave Mr Robbins, without regard to his having placed his flag over our tents, everything which he requested from me in the shape of gunpowder, sails, thread, needles, lead and sounding line, old ropes, &c. Our forge worked two days for him.

Baudin finished the letter and sealed it. Baudin then took a fresh piece of paper and wrote a second letter to King. This letter was for King's eyes only, friend to friend. As the quill scraped its way across the

parchment, black on white, Baudin wrote himself a **place** in history:

> I now write to you as, Mr King, my friend, for whom I shall always have a particular regard. It is on this ground alone I shall enter into details with you and tell you frankly my way of thinking … nothing in this letter will relate to the policy of the Governments and still less to your erroneous pretensions about Van Diemen's Land …
>
> To my way of thinking, I have never been able to conceive that there was justice or even fairness on the part of Europeans in seizing, in the name of their governments, a land seen for the first time, when it is inhabited by men who have not always deserved the title of savages or cannibals … From this it appears to me that it would be infinitely more glorious for your nation, as for mine, to mould for society the inhabitants of its own country over whom it has rights, rather than wishing to occupy itself with the improvement of those who are very far removed from it by beginning with seizing the soil which belongs to them and which saw their birth. These remarks are no doubt impolitic, but at least they are reasonable from the facts … not only have you to reproach yourselves with an injustice in having seized their land, but also in having transported on to a soil where the crimes and diseases of Europeans were unknown …

The issue Baudin raised was truly revolutionary. Not only does he raise the radical concept that indigenous people have land rights, but he commits these thoughts to paper. With this letter, Baudin proved his worth both as a man ahead of his time as well as his worth as a true friend. By committing these thoughts to paper, he questions not only England's right to claim the land of indigenous people, but France's right too. He thus risked undermining a large part of the justification for his own mission – and by committing it to paper, in a document sent to King – gave his friend ammunition, should King choose to use it, to undermine Baudin's credibility and legitimacy in this developing game of colonial upmanship.

As was his want, Baudin finished the letter with a friendly quip:

> ... I expect to receive one of your letters at the Isle of France, and trust afterwards we may meet in London or Paris ... the *Naturaliste* left to order the dinner for which you will have to pay.*

---

* What King thought of Baudin's letter is uncertain – apparently it had little effect on his plans. On Robbins' return, King immediately began to mobilise a proper expeditionary force to found a British settlement adjacent to the D'Entrecasteaux Channel, in Storm Bay, writing to the Admiralty that: 'My reasons for making this settlement are the necessity there appears of preventing the French gaining a foothold on the east side of these islands' (Walker, p. 22).

Chapter 23

[MONSOON]

F ar to the north, now deep in the monsoon
season, the leaky *Investigator* was finally disintegrating. As was Flinders himself. He tried to
share his incoherent thoughts with his wife, so far
away:

> ... for Mrs Flinders ...
> ... the poor ship is worn out, she is decayed, and
> rotten both in skin and bone ... Mankind being
> subject to change and I being one of them may
> indeed be suspected ... my mind retraces with

delight, our joys, our conversation, our looks, our everything of love. The loves, and alas! the fall of our first parents, told with such majesty by him whose eyes lacked all of what he threw with hand so masterly this great subject, dark before and intricate then with delight I last perused ... Eve in innocence, shewed me the excellence of my beloved wife; and think not Ann, my dearest, but that in innocence we yet remain ... Eve fallen, portrayed to me the consequences of the lapse from love and faith: – then bitter remorse, dissimulation, accusation and reproach, and final separation, – dreadful, dreadful consequence of womans fall from innocence and truth ...
There's misery in this picture, and not truth; I'll therefore quit it ...

In the eight months since leaving Port Jackson Flinders had charted in remarkable detail huge parts of the east coast as well as the immense Gulf of Carpentaria. The delays experienced heading up the east coast, however, meant that he now found himself in the predicament he had most dreaded. Here he was in a leaky boat literally rotting away in the dank, humid conditions, the Monsoon thundering above. Flinders was frustrated: 'Report after report was brought to me of rotten places found in different parts of the ship – in the planks, bends, timbers, tree-nails.'

He asked his carpenters to predict how much longer the ship might last. The news was not encouraging. The carpenters' report read:

... in a strong gale, with much sea running, the
ship would hardly escape foundering; so that
we think she is totally unfit to encounter much
bad weather ... under any unfavourable
circumstances, she would immediately go to
pieces ...

In the Arafura Sea, at this time of year, the *Investigator* was more than likely to encounter not one, but many tropical storms. Flinders was mortified: 'I cannot express the surprise and sorrow which this statement gave me ... with the blessing of GOD, nothing of importance should have been left for future discoverers, upon any part of these extensive coasts ...'

Flinders pressed on. 'Six months' the carpenters had said the ship might last. He estimated it would take three months to reach Port Jackson, sailing anti-clockwise around the continent, since it was now impossible to sail back through Torres Strait against the prevailing easterlies. If it took three months to sail back, that still left three months to keep charting. He might still reach the north-west coasts – the second priority as stipulated in his sailing orders. He was not ready to give up yet, convinced that the discovery of great new bays, islands, rivers lay just around the next corner, cape, inlet. So he pressed on.

Overall, Flinders was not unhappy with his work in the Gulf thus far, although: 'The increasing shallowness of the water made me apprehend that the Gulph would be found to terminate nearly as represented in the old charts, and disappointed the hopes found of a strait or passage leading out at some other part of Terra Australis.'

He made several trips ashore and saw some potential for settlement, although it was obvious that the land was already inhabited. Flinders found the people of the Gulf generally elusive: 'They always avoided us, and sometimes disappeared in a manner which seemed extraordinary.' Near Groote Island, Flinders walked past skeletons standing upright in the hollows of trees. 'The skulls and bones being smeared or painted, partly red and partly white … made a very strange appearance.'

On Chasm Island Flinders ventured deep into a series of caves where: 'Upon the walls … I found rude drawings … porpoises, turtle, kangaroos, and a human hand.' Soon after, he learnt that his men had shot and killed a man in a canoe. One of his own men died from sunstroke.

The next morning, they found the *Warnindil-yakwa* man that had been shot lying dead on a beach: 'The corpse was found lying at the water's edge, not lengthwise, as a body washed up, but with the head on shore and the feet touching the surf. The arms were crossed under the head, with the face downward, in the posture of a man who was just able to crawl out of the water and die.'

Flinders realised that the man had not died instantly in the water as the marines had told him, but had struggled to the beach where in the lapping waves life had drained from his body. The English expedition then treated the *Warnindilyakwa* man as just another specimen. 'A boat was sent … for the dead body, the painter being desirous of it to make a drawing, and the naturalist and surgeon for anatomical purposes …' The man was dissected on board the *Investigator* and his head preserved in a jar. The marine who had died from sunstroke was given a proper burial and the *Warnindilyakwa* island was named after him.

Not long after, an axe was stolen. The following day, some young Aboriginal men approached Flinders' camp. 'Two of them advanced, bringing some small fruits … on being invited to eat fish, they sat down and were immediately seized.' Flinders kept the younger of the two hostage until the axe was returned: 'In the evening I landed at the tents; and taking the native, a youth of fourteen named Woga, into the boat, rowed to the place most frequented by the Indians.' Enlisting the help of Bongaree, the *Eora* man who had joined the expedition at Port Jackson, Flinders tried to negotiate the return of the axe: 'Two came forward, bringing a young girl in their arms; and by expressive signs they offered her to Bongaree, in order to entice him on shore … [but] finding no axe likely to be brought, Woga was carried on board the ship, through a great deal of crying, intreating, threatening, and struggling … next morning, I took our prisoner to the tents … He struggled much, calling upon Bongaree to assist him; but after a while, became quiet, and I left him bound to a tree … He begged hard to be released, promising, with tears in his eyes, to bring back the axe.'

After two days, Flinders finally let the boy go: 'I determined to release the poor prisoner though the axe should not be restored.' Flinders' reasoning was interesting, revealing an inner turmoil: 'His detention ... might be an injury to those who should come after us, especially to captain Baudin, whom we daily expected to meet, according to what he had said at Port Jackson.'

A few days later, Flinders wrote Baudin a letter. He encountered a strange fleet he initially mistook for a buccaneers' lair: 'I set them down for piratical Ladrones who secreted themselves here from pursuit.' The vessels were in fact Malay *praus* fishing for *bêche-de-mer* which they sold to the Chinese as an aphrodisiac. Flinders met the Malay chief: 'A short, elderly man, named Pobassoo.' Flinders asked his Malay cook to act as interpreter while he grilled the old man with questions: 'According to Pobassoo ... sixty prows belonging to the Rajah of Boni, and carrying one thousand men, had left Macassar with the north-west monsoon.' Flinders asked the old man whether he had encountered any other European ships recently. Pobassoo shook his head. 'He had never seen any ship here before.' Flinders tried to describe to Pobassoo just how far the land extended to the south and told him that the British had established an outpost on the east coast many thousands of leagues away. The old man was surprised: 'They had no knowledge of any European settlement in this country; and on learning the name Port Jackson, the son of Pobassoo made a memorandum of it.' Flinders then wrote a letter and handed it to Pobassoo. 'A note to captain Baudin, whom it seemed probable he might encounter in the Gulph.'

Flinders pressed on. The bow of the *Investigator* continued to cut its way through the ocean and rain. Rounding Cape Arnhem, Flinders again noticed some prospect for settlement: 'If the East India Company have had any intention of making a settlement on New Holland, the good harbours in Cape Arnhem, the wild nutmegs, and perhaps the trepang which seems to bring the Malays a good many thousand dollars annually from the Chinese, might be additional incitements.' As one lightning storm after another tore across the sky, dumping torrent after torrent, the mood on board the *Investigator* deteriorated. Twenty-two men showed the early signs of scurvy. The sounds emanating from below deck were most worrying, not merely the cries of sick men but the groans of a dying ship. Flinders' men began to fear that their commander would continue regardless of the crew's wellbeing. Surgeon Bell became their spokesman, imploring Flinders to sail for Timor, for the sake of the sick:

> the ships company have been exposed to almost incessant fatigue in an oppressively hot climate … a body, though in health, may at the same time be losing strength; and consequently be likely to fall under any violent and long-continued exertions. If you should dread such an event, it would be well, if possible, to provide against it by refreshing the ship's company.

Flinders surveyed their predicament: 'We had continued the survey of the coast for more than one-half of the six months which the master and carpenter had judged the ship might run without much risk ... the remainder of the time being not much more than necessary for us to reach Port Jackson.'

Finally, Flinders relented: 'In addition to the rottenness of the ship, the state of my own health and that of the ship's company were urgent to terminate the examination here.' He realised that he would not be able to chart the north-west coast – in fact, he would be lucky to reach Port Jackson. But Flinders was more worried about the job left undone: 'It may well be said, that to leave such a coast as this without exploring it ... shews but very little of that genuine spirit of discovery which contemns all danger.'

Deep down, Flinders felt he had failed. He was devastated, damning himself as a man who: 'Must never boast of a single spark of that ethereal fire with which the souls of Columbus and of Cook were wont to burn! – I am not indeed such a Quixote in discovery as this, although since I was able to read Robinson Crusoe, it has been my constant pursuit.'

Chapter 24

[T U B E R C U L O S I S]

Baudin continued to battle constant delays and insubordination, especially on the part of Lieutenant Freycinet. 'This officer (who is insubordinate on principle) has not been able to carry out a single task nor even obey my orders to him! ... there is a strong possibility that I shall take his command from him.' Baudin had entrusted command of his new vessel the *Casuarina* to Freycinet, and was perplexed why he kept lagging behind, or got lost. When the expedition stopped to chart Kangaroo Island, Baudin sent Freycinet on an excursion to complete the charting of the gulfs to the north, with express orders to be back in twenty days.

Baudin then took the opportunity to build himself a new longboat. He was almost crushed as a tree was felled but brushed the mishap aside and took the first turn at sawing the timber into planks. He was the only officer, besides Ronsard, to do so. 'The other officers were careful not to show up … work, they say, is for the populace; a naval officer should know only how to guide a ship and rest when his watch is finished.'

Baudin's expedition completed the charting of Kangaroo Island. He noted that: 'If the English have the advantage over us in having reached it a few days earlier, we also have the advantage over them of having circumnavigated it and determined its geographical position in a way that leaves nothing to be desired for the safety of navigation.' As a result, Baudin claimed naming rights for the island, calling it Île Borda.* The arrival of Robbins at King Island had brought the French-English rivalry back to the fore.

The abundant wildlife on Kangaroo Island also allowed Baudin to fulfil that particular request from Napoléon's wife, as stipulated in his sailing orders:

> … a special collection for Mme Bonaparte, wife of the First Consul … You will make up this collection of living animals of all kinds, insects and especially of birds with beautiful plumage. As regards animals, I don't need to tell you how

---

* Another name in deference to the glory of Science – Charles de Borda was a famous French mathematician.

to choose between those intended for the menageries and those for a collection of pure pleasure.

For 'pure pleasure', it was hard to go past the kangaroos, so Baudin sent his convict stowaways on a nocturnal mission. The next morning he was delighted by their success. 'With the help of the dogs, the hunters caught twelve giant kangaroos of various sizes. Seven of them were taken alive and were put in pens aboard the ship to be kept. Amongst these ones are three females which have offspring and may prosper.'

The hold of *Le Géographe* was fast filling with an amazing collection of live creatures to rival even that already sent back on *Le Naturaliste*. Baudin became personally involved in helping to keep them alive. He liked the animals, even loved them. It was the humans he could not abide.

On January 31, he scanned the horizon for *Le Casuarina*. Freycinet had not reappeared. Baudin decided he would sail the following day, with or without Louis Freycinet. 'The 20 days allowed as the maximum period for the *Casuarina* were up. Nevertheless, I spent this day still at anchor in hope of seeing her return but the twenty-four hours were lost in vain.' The next morning, with still no sign of *Le Casuarina*, Baudin was true to his word. 'The crew were given breakfast, after which having hoisted our topsails, we weighed anchor and proceeded on our way, leaving the *Casuarina* to her good fortune, as she had chosen to leave us to ours.'

Just as *Le Géographe* set off, *Le Casuarina* was finally spotted in the distance. Baudin slowed his speed to allow the smaller ship to catch up. To his surprise Louis Freycinet sped away in the opposite direction. 'She continued running East, and so rapidly that by half past three she was out of sight. It is undoubtedly difficult to explain this manoeuvre on the part of Citizen Freycinet and he will surely tell us about it at our first meeting.'*

Baudin eventually turned back to search for *Le Casuarina* and over the coming days ordered his crew to climb hills to keep lookout. He lit bonfires. All with no success. Baudin pressed on towards the agreed rendezvous point in case of separation, King George Sound.

Le Géographe came more and more to resemble a floating zoo and botanical garden. Kangaroos, wallabies, parakeets and sulphur-crested cockatoos filled cage after cage. While journeying towards King George Sound, the health of the kangaroos began to suffer. Baudin ordered one of the scientists and another man to vacate their cabin to get the animals out of the sea spray. A few days later, to Baudin's relief, the kangaroos seemed to be recovering: 'During the morning I sent

---

* Louis Freycinet later presented a very different version of events, claiming to have seen the *Géographe* steering west at full speed. He would allege that he was unable to keep up and lost sight of Baudin's ship. But the ship's log confirms that the *Géographe* shortened sail to allow the *Casuarina* to catch up. Ronsard's private journal entry also supports this (Horner, p. 281). Freycinet appears to have lied. Péron's account supported his friend Freycinet's version, accusing Baudin of deliberately deserting the smaller vessel.

the little boat ashore to obtain grass for our kangaroos, which are all in very good condition, with a healthy appetite; but what was brought back did not suit them at all and none of them would touch it. As they are beginning to get used to maize, I am hoping that I shall soon be able to feed them entirely on that.'

The two men who had been evicted from their cabin were less happy and let Baudin know all about it. Baudin's fondness for the animals grew, at the expense of his fellow humans. Animals were grateful for small kindnesses and you knew where you stood with them. The same could not be said for people. That included Mary, the convict girl.

Young Mary had initially told Baudin that she had chosen to go to Port Jackson rather than be sent to a convent. This was not strictly true. At the age of fourteen, she had been convicted, with her mother, of stealing forty-six yards of calico prints worth £5. The storekeeper claimed he saw Mary hide the vast quantity of material under her dress. The storekeeper's testimony seemed ludicrous and may have stemmed from pretty Mary rejecting his advances. Either way, on June 11, 1800, the same day that Baudin was commissioned to lead his grand mission of discovery, Mary had faced her committal hearing. Unable to afford a defence counsellor, she had been convicted on the storekeeper's testimony and sentenced to death. Her sentence had then been commuted to transportation.

Whilst Baudin now intended to free her at the Spice Islands, Mary showed no gratitude for his actions. As the artist Lesueur described in his journal:

'Our commandant … had, as was known, secretly embarked a young woman at Port Jackson; it was also known the sort of girl she was. During the voyage she had affairs with several members of the crew, and she also caused the commandant's health to worsen again.'*

Baudin had hoped that Mary's presence on board would combat his loneliness and alienation from his men, but he was deeply mistaken. As Mary jumped from one bed to the next, her promiscuity further undermined the young officers' respect for their commander. Baudin's health deteriorated. Sailing west beneath the impressive cliffs of the Nullarbor Plain, Baudin was soon spitting blood. At some point, perhaps in Timor, he had contracted tuberculosis.

Three weeks after their separation near Île Borda, Baudin was finally reunited with *Le Casuarina* in King George Sound. Baudin boarded the smaller vessel to find it in complete disarray. He discovered that Freycinet's charting in the last few weeks had been rudimentary. Indeed Louis Freycinet was lucky to have made it at all. His supply of water had been almost completely exhausted while he sailed below the impenetrable cliffs of the Nullarbor Plain. The men of *Le Casuarina* had only survived due to the unusually favourable easterly winds pushing them westwards

---

* Indeed, Mary may not have confined herself to the crewmen. It seems strange that, but for Freycinet's one comment, neither he nor Péron refer to the girl or criticise Baudin for having brought her on board. Perhaps Mary had affairs with them as well. As author Anthony Brown suggests, there must have been an unsettling effect with 'a young and allegedly promiscuous woman in the midst of scores of presumably lusty French sailors' (Brown 1998a, p. 28).

quickly, covering 1,000 miles in less than two weeks. Baudin demanded to know Freycinet's reasons for the separation. Freycinet was evasive, suggesting it was not his fault. Baudin was flabbergasted: 'On this visit he received a scolding that I hope he will not forget, as much for the good of the Service as for himself.'

Freycinet's good friend Péron was also continuing to annoy Baudin: 'The gardener had collected more than 150 different species of plant during his stay shore and had sixty-eight pots of growing ones. This was work and not wit. I trust that Citizen Péron … will have composed sixty pages of writing which, for a different reason, will be all wit and no work.'

Leaving King George Sound, Baudin sent Louis Freycinet his sailing orders, with an unusual instruction for when they reached the north-west coast. 'From then on,' read the order, 'it rests with you alone whether to accompany me or not … you will have to be personally answerable to the authorities in France for the expenses incurred in the equipping of your ship since they will have grown burdensome for the government and pointless for the expedition.'

Almost as soon as the two ships departed King George Sound, Louis Freycinet ignored Baudin's orders to stay close to the coast. Again the *Casuarina* became separated from *Le Géographe*. On March 11, Baudin rounded Cape Leeuwin and approached the 'Bay of the Clumsy', twenty-two months after Timothée Vasse had disappeared there.

Baudin was reunited with *Le Casuarina* at Rottnest Island. Continuing on, Baudin tried to sail very slowly in order for *Le Casuarina* to keep up. The slow speed led to a severe roll resulting in the death of yet another kangaroo and an emu. Baudin's antipathy towards Freycinet grew, as it did towards Péron, whose ability to get himself lost while on shore persisted: 'Citizen Péron, the most thoughtless and most wanting in foresight of everyone aboard … who, until now, has caused us nothing but trouble and anxiety when he has been ashore with no-one to watch over and guide him … This is the third escapade of this nature that our learned naturalist has been on, but it will also be the last.'

For Péron, the irritation was mutual: 'Wretched man! In order to save his life in Timor, I had shared with his doctor the small supply of excellent quinine that I was saving for myself.' But quinine would not help Baudin now. The ache in his chest became worse: 'Until now I had paid little attention to the pains and discomfort that I was feeling, but on this day I was so weary that, scarcely able to stand I was obliged to resort to medicine.'

Baudin's ships rounded the north-west cape. It was now eight months since their departure from Port Jackson. In the Timor Sea, Baudin again crossed the path of Flinders, but this time they did not meet.

Chapter 25

[THE LONGEST VOYAGE]

Flinders stopped in Timor and received a more gracious welcome than the last British visitors who had been there. They did not become a Malay dinner. One afternoon, Flinders visited the grave of Baudin's gardener, Riedlé: 'Captain Baudin had lost twelve men from dysentery during his stay at Coepang, and I found a monument which he had erected to his principal gardener; but it was even then beginning to decay.' Flinders then loaded his ship with the contaminated water that caused so many of Baudin's men to die.

On April 8, 1803, a year after the two expeditions had met at Encounter Bay, the rotting *Investigator* weighed anchor and headed back into the rain. By now, Flinders had well and truly conceded that the deplorable state of his ship made the charting of the north-west coast impossible. He pressed on, hoping simply that his ship could survive long enough to reach Port Jackson. As he sailed, he watched his men, one by one, die.

The boatswain was the first to go: 'Mr Charles Douglas breathed his last ... I affixed his name to the two lumps of land, which seemed to offer themselves as a monument to his memory.' While burying the boatswain, the quartermaster died: 'William Hillier, one of my best men, also died of dysentery.' A week later, it was the sergeant: 'James Greenhalgh, sergeant of marines, died of the dysentery; a man whom I sincerely regretted.'

Just like Baudin's men, the Englishmen died in agony. Flinders named islands and other landmarks after the dead men. So far he had been fortunate with the wind, blowing consistently from the south which meant that the starboard side of the bow, the most rotten, was kept above the waterline.

Disappointed at the way this rotten ship had thwarted his mission, he considered conducting a little charting on the run as he passed back via Kangaroo Island. Surgeon Bell was stunned that Flinders would risk any delay in getting his sick men to hospital and wrote to his commander of his disgust. Flinders was taken aback by the surgeon's criticism. He replied:

The first part of your letter, appearing to be intended to raise yourself a character for humanity, by casting a malignant stigma upon mine it becomes necessary for me to know the causes which induced you to make use of the following sentence ... 'the sickly state of the ships company has not, nor appears likely to influence your speed', an explanation of these is what I am now expecting from you.

Surgeon Bell explained that he did not intend to question his commander's humanity, simply to point out the precarious health of his men, and the dangerous consequences of delaying their progress. Flinders wrote back again, like a dog with a bone:

Did you or did you not intend, by your first letter of yesterday, to reproach me with inattention to the state of the sick? ... I can forgive errors of the head, but those of the heart not so easily ... by interfering with the duty of a commander you get by much out of your depth.

The next day, the surgeon received another letter:

Amongst the errors that you have committed in your first letter of the 27th ... is the general one which you have committed in judging at all of what are or are not the motives by which my conduct is influenced ... Sir, I think you err in saying you have found me to be 'intent upon delaying our arrival at Port Jackson'; – you are also wrong in asserting that what you have already said regarding the sickly state of the ships company <u>has</u> not 'influenced my speed', as well as in saying that it does not 'appear likely' to do it … you have committed an error in judging how far the state of the sick ought to influence me … before you pronounce what 'ought to induce me to make all possible speed to port' … Your duty must necessarily coincide with humanity towards the ships company in all cases, whereas that of a Commander may be either diametrically opposite to humanity.

It was not enough. The following day Surgeon Bell received yet another:

I must demand answers to the following questions. Have you found that I am 'intent upon delaying our arrival at Port Jackson'? Have you found 'that what you have already said regarding the whole sickly state of the ships company has not' influenced my speed? Have you found that what you have already said 'is not likely' to influence my speed? Do you pretend to know what 'ought to induce', or 'it is fit' should induce, or 'it is necessary' should induce me to make all possible speed to port? Be advised, Sir … I have too much employment to have time for continuing a correspondence with a person who says he 'is convinced of the falsity' of a circumstance.

The surgeon's letter, however, must have weighed on Flinders' conscience, as he wrote in his journal: 'I wished to have completed the examination of Kangaroo Island ... but the sickly state of my people from dysentery and fever ... did not admit of doing any thing to cause delay in our arrival at Port Jackson ... when I contemplated eighteen of my men below, several of whom were stretched in their hammocks almost without hope, and reflected that the lives of the rest depended upon our speedy arrival in port, every other consideration vanished.'

Actually, Flinders had lost so many men and so many others were incapable of working, that he could barely sail the drowning *Investigator*.

Chapter 26

[SICK TO DEATH]

Off the north-west coast of Nouvelle Hollande, near Cassini Island in the Bonaparte Archipelago, Baudin encountered part of the same fleet of Malay *praus* that Flinders had met. He rowed in amongst the two dozen vessels and was received warmly by the Malays, but he was not given the letter Flinders had left with the old man Pobassoo.

Only four weeks after Flinders was there, Baudin reached Timor. Baudin learned that although his rival had charted the Gulf of Carpentaria, the condition of the *Investigator* made it highly unlikely that Flinders would have been able to do any further charting, including that of the north-west coasts. This pleased Baudin.

Baudin tried to rid himself of Mary in Kupang. He had grown weary of her antics, exacerbating his problems with his men. Lesueur described Mary's reaction to Baudin's plan: 'In no way would she agree to this, but rushed off headlong like a fury; she ran toward the bridge crossing the little river in Koepang, and threatened to throw herself from it. Reassured by two blacks sent after her by the Commandant, she allowed herself to be brought back to him, and it was agreed between them that she could continue … The same evening she was embarked, but meanwhile she had drowned her sorrows in drink, and had to be carried to the boat. She was in a truly horrible state; distraught, her hair dishevelled, her clothing in disorder, out of her mind … she was carried to the Commandant's cabin in front of all the crew.'

Baudin was humiliated. He decided it was about time he appointed a second-in-command, someone he could be confident would complete the mission, should he not be able to do so. Remarkably, Baudin had deferred the appointment since getting rid of Le Bas when he was last in Timor eighteen months before.

The continuing tension between François Ronsard and Henri Freycinet made the decision unavoidable. Ronsard had remained loyal to Baudin and would have been a sensible choice. Promoting Ronsard, however, would cause further friction with Freycinet, who strictly speaking was the next most senior officer and thought the appointment belonged to him. Indeed, he had already been acting as if he was the second-in-command for a while, much to Ronsard's irritation. With his health worsening, Baudin knew he could not defer the decision any longer. Baudin also thought he had come up with a solution to avoid a scene from Freycinet. He wrote to both men:

> I shall assemble the crew, in order that they
> should tell me which of the two of you
> they prefer to have as leader, and their choice
> will be irrevocable.

Freycinet and Ronsard were both stunned. Baudin's idea was again revolutionary – a vote by the seamen to choose their officer. The two men had never heard of such a thing, it was 'monstrous', but they nevertheless submitted to the vote.

The ballot was held and Ronsard lost – 12 to 60.

Baudin was shocked, as he had been confident that Ronsard would win. The vote had again backfired. Perhaps Ronsard had lost his popularity by recently being responsible for keeping order and awarding punishments. Whatever the reason, Ronsard was so appalled at the prospect of now being answerable to Henri Freycinet, ten years his junior, that he requested to be relieved of his duties in order to leave the mission. Baudin would not allow it. On June 3, 1803, the *Géographe* and *Casuarina* left Timor.

On June 10, 1803 Flinders could finally see the Heads of Port Jackson. It took another day to negotiate the entrance. During the slow manoeuvres Flinders watched another man die, one of the convict men who on landing would have received his pardon.

Flinders had just completed the first close circumnavigation of the continent. The feat would earn him immortality while it had cost the lives of eleven of his men. He immediately delivered the sickest of them to hospital. 'Four were too much exhausted, and died in a few days.'

In all, nineteen of Flinders' men had now died – one-quarter of his company. He himself was lame and hobbled off the *Investigator*: 'I left the ship at noon … and waited upon his excellency Governor King.' The sight that greeted King was appalling. Flinders' face was disfigured by scurvy, so that the young commander was barely recognisable. When King saw the state of the *Investigator*, he was doubly shocked. All the inhabitants of Port Jackson marvelled at the ghost-like appearance of the rotten ship and its ravaged crew.

For Flinders, there was worse to come. He picked up his mail. He learnt that his father, to whom he had not spoken since he had voiced his reservations regarding his marriage, was dead. Flinders broke down, torn by remorse, knowing that the moment of reconciliation had passed forever.

Flinders wrote of his pain in a letter to his old friend George Bass: 'My poor father has paid the last debt to nature … at a time when to my regret, our good understanding was not complete.' Flinders later learned that dear George had himself disappeared in the Pacific, presumed drowned.

Flinders felt surrounded by death. He wrote to Ann of his grief, his remorse:

> My dearest love ... how shall I express the anguish of my heart at the dreadful havlock that death is making all round ... my eyes can scarcely be turned when some victim does not die ... Thou has shewn me how very ill I have requited thy tender love in several cases. I cannot excuse myself now, but plead for respite until my return when in thy dear arms I will beg for pardon ... thou wilt see whether love or ambition has the greatest power over me ... believe me, oh truly believe me that I pursue discovery only to be able to avoid the future necessity of parting from thee.

Ann was lucky not to have been parted prematurely from her husband. A report on the condition of the *Investigator* declared the vessel dead on arrival:

> On the larbord side ... out of ninety-eight timbers we find eleven to be sound ... On the starbord side forward we have minutely examined eighty-nine timbers, out of which we find only five sound ... The above being the state of the *Investigator* thus far, we ... [are] unanimously of opinion that she is not worth repairing in any country, and that it is impossible

in this country to put her in a state fit for going to sea …

Governor King inspected the vessel personally and was in total agreement: 'The state of the *Investigator* is the worst I have ever witnessed … That she would have survived a Gale without dropping asunder is very doubtful to me as well as everyone who sees her.'

With the *Investigator* condemned as unseaworthy, Flinders found passage on another ship to rush his findings and charts back to England. 'Notwithstanding the reluctance I felt at returning to England without having accomplished the objects for which the *Investigator* was fitted out … I made to embark as a passenger in the *Porpoise*; in order to lay my charts and journals before the Lords Commissioners of the Admiralty, and obtain, if such should be their pleasure, another ship to complete the examination of Terra Australis.'

Several of Flinders' men, including Brown the naturalist and Bauer the artist, declined to sail on with Flinders, opting to remain in Port Jackson. By now wild tales of the *Investigator*'s harrowing trip had done the rounds of the rum houses of Sydney. Nor had the gipsy's prophecy been forgotten, namely that the expedition would eventually be shipwrecked in a different ship from the one in which they had originally embarked.

Samuel Flinders decided to stick by his brother's side. The two had drifted apart during the voyage, but in the last few days had been brought closer back together, as Flinders noted in his letter to Ann: 'My brother … is more friendly and affectionate with me since his knowledge of our mutual loss.'

With the prospect of soon being reunited with his dear wife, Flinders' spirits began to lift. Nor was the race yet over. Having learnt that Baudin was delayed in leaving Port Jackson, Flinders believed he must have given up his plans to chart the north coast.

Chapter 27

[AGAINST THE WIND]

Flinders was wrong. Baudin had not given up. He was indeed beating his way against the Monsoon.

Having learned in Timor that the condition of the *Investigator* made it unlikely that Flinders could do any further charting, Baudin discovered a new determination to complete his own task: 'I decided to continue with the work on the north coast of New Holland … although several sailors whom I had consulted were convinced that it would be impossible to make easting with the South-East monsoon.'

After the month spent in Kupang to 'recuperate', dysentery and malaria were again rife. Four days after leaving Timor, Pierre-François Bernier, the astronomer, became ill: 'During the afternoon the doctor came and warned me that Citizen Bernier had just manifested the most alarming symptoms, showing that the end was near.' Bernier, twenty-three years old, died the following day. Baudin mourned the loss of life: 'This death which can almost regard as a sudden one, made such an impression upon me that it would be difficult to express all that I suffered.'

Leschenault, the botanist, had been too ill to go on and had been left in Timor. Baudin wished he had been able to leave Mary behind too. After the episode on the bridge, Baudin felt like a laughing-stock, more than ever. He pressed on. He also changed his mind about letting Louis Freycinet and the *Casuarina* abandon the survey. 'I foresaw that I would have great need of her, if, later on, I managed to reach the Gulf of Carpentaria.'

Freycinet reacted by sailing the vessel more slowly than ever. Baudin suspected that he was deliberately delaying their progress: 'The *Casuarina*, which I have never been able to get to make good headway, no matter what means I have tried … is the sole reason for my not having reached the Gulf a long time ago.' Baudin was well aware Freycinet wanted to sail for Île-de-France. Baudin hated him. He hated Péron. He thought he hated them all, but realised their foolishness came from their youth: 'It is better to trust to experience rather than to the unimportant and thoughtless talk of young people, who see things only superficially or according to their slight amount of judgement.'

Baudin was not well. The tuberculosis was getting worse: 'During the night I was taken with a fit of spitting blood, similar to those I had already had on two different occasions, and the sputum that I brought up was so thick, that one would have said that it was pieces of lung coming away from my body.'

He forged on, trying to complete his mission, trying to reach the Gulf of Carpentaria. He slowed his speed for the sake of the *Casuarina*, causing the *Géographe* to again roll uncomfortably. Again it was the animals that suffered most. On that fateful morning of July 7, Baudin woke to some upsetting news: 'I was told that several of our quadrupeds and emus were very sick. We could only attribute this to the violent and incessant movement … which left them not a moment's peace. This news was particularly unpleasant, as I saw myself on the brink of losing them after giving them such attention as should have secured them a happier fate.'

Baudin was fond of his creatures of Nouvelle Hollande and, having kept them alive this long, he was not going to let them die now. Using supplies from his own private store he forced wine sweetened with sugar down the throats of the sick kangaroos: 'Although I was very short of these same things myself, I shall be very happy to have gone without them for their sake if they can help in restoring them to health.'

Baudin was willing the animals to survive, as he was himself: 'On this day I had a worse bout of spitting blood than I had had before … this spitting of blood was accompanied by such a weakness in all limbs, that I was compelled to go to bed.'

Baudin's orders had ambitiously predicted that his expedition would be back in France by March, 1803. It was now June, 1803 and he was still a long way from home. He made a note for the Minister of Marine: 'A proper exploration of this coast would take ten years, and even then I could not be sure it would be properly done in this time.' He was now sailing against the wind itself. He had pushed his health as well as that of his live animals and men, beyond all reasonable limits. The hold was so full of specimens that there was only room for enough water to last ninety days. Baudin knew he had to allow at least forty-five days to reach Île-de-France. And the animals were sick. These animals that he had himself cared for, like they were his own children. These animals destined for Joséphine Bonaparte's adoring looks and sweet caresses.

On July 7, 1803, he made his decision to return to France and announced it to his men. The reaction was instantaneous: 'The crew asleep below sprang up in a transport of joy, congratulating and hugging each other.' Péron described the sense of relief: 'This decision, for which we had all yearned for a long time and to which we had all looked forward as the sign of our deliverance, brought us a joy as lively as it was natural.' Celebrations continued into the night. Amidst the euphoria, only Baudin remained solemn: 'It was not without regret that I decided upon this step … Throughout the whole voyage no one has ever known where I was going or what I wanted to do …'

Baudin turned for home. In the hold of his ship was one of the most remarkable scientific collections ever assembled. In his cabin were unique charts of the western and north-western coasts, far more detailed than anything the British possessed.

Chapter 28

[R O B I N S O N   C R U S O E]

Flinders should have known the warning signs: 'If an unusual number of boobies and gannets be seen in the evening, there is strong suspicion of a bank and reef being near.' Only the day before, he had seen a lonely sandbank, practically in the middle of the ocean. Flinders had been nonplussed: 'Some apprehensions were excited … by meeting with this bank; but as it was more than two degrees to the eastward of the great Barrier Reefs … it did not therefore seem necessary to lose a good night's run by heaving to.'

The sound was truly terrible, a sort of moaning, wrenching howl. The sound of a ship dying, coral tearing huge holes in her underbelly. Flinders could hardly believe what he was seeing: 'The ship was carried amongst the breakers; and striking upon a coral reef, took a fearful heel over on her larbord beam ... a gun was attempted to be fired, to warn the other vessels of the danger.' It was too late. Minutes later, the other two ships in the convoy, the *Bridgewater* and the *Cato*, narrowly avoided colliding with one another, but not the reef: 'The *Cato* struck upon the reef about two cables length from the *Porpoise* ... [I] saw her fall over on her broad side, and the masts almost instantly disappeared ... the poor *Cato*, we could neither see nor hear any thing ...'

In the darkness, in the same waters where Flinders had searched for the wreck of La Pérouse, he met his worst nightmare. He and his companions clung to the decks of the *Porpoise* as they watched the carcass of the *Cato* being consumed by the waves: 'In a short time the decks and holds were torn up, and everything washed away; and the sole place left, where the unfortunate people could hope to avoid the fury of the sea ... they all crowded together ... some lashing themselves to the timber heads, others clinging to the chain plates and dead eyes, and to each other.'

Flinders scanned the darkness for signs of the *Bridgewater*, praying that she had escaped. There was hope. 'A light was perceived at her mast head, by which we knew she had cleared the reef ...' Flinders tried to reach the surviving ship, in desperation:

'I jumped over-board and swam.'

Others had managed to launch the cutter and as it passed, Flinders scrambled in. He ordered that the chest containing his precious charts be retrieved from his cabin and passed down into the boat. He and the other men then began to row towards the *Bridgewater*. But it was too far and the ship soon disappeared into the darkness. Flinders ordered the men to row back towards the *Porpoise*. One of the seaman described the general sense of terror:'There was no other appearance but of Death, there being such heavy seas ... In this mizarable situation we spent the night, every breast filld with horror, continual seas dashing over us with great violence, at length day light arriv'd.'

Remarkably, by morning, only three men had disappeared, though the death of one was especially heart-rending. In the words of Flinders: 'One of these poor boys, who, in the three or four voyages he had made to sea, had been each time shipwrecked, had bewailed himself through the night as the persecuted Jonas who carried misfortune wherever he went. He launched himself upon a broken spar with his captain; but ... was not seen afterwards.'

Flinders scanned the horizon for signs of the *Bridgewater*. Instead he saw a tiny fragment of land: 'A dry sand bank, not more than half a mile distant ... and the satisfaction arising from this discovery was increased by the *Bridgewater* being perceived under sail, and though distant ... she was standing towards the reef.' Flinders employed the cutter to ferry men and provisions that could be salvaged onto the sandbank:

'Before dark, five half hogsheads of water, some flour, salt, meat, rice and spirits were landed.' Flinders carried his own chest containing the papers so dear to him: 'The charts, with my log and bearing books and astronomical observations were all saved, though some of them in a wet and shattered state.' This chest contained Flinders' most treasured belongings, perhaps even a copy of his favourite book, *Robinson Crusoe*. The words that had bewitched him as a boy came back to haunt him:

> I poor miserable Robinson Crusoe, being shipwrecked … came on shore on this dismal unfortunate island, which I called the island of despair … having been excessively fatigued, I fell asleep, and slept as comfortably as, I believe, few could have done in my condition.

In his own book, Flinders' entry was like an echo: 'We laid down to sleep on the sand in tolerable tranquillity, being much oppressed with fatigue.' It seemed the future had been foretold. The gipsy's prophecy had come to pass.

With sand on his cheek and the sun in his eyes, a few hours later, Flinders woke to his nightmare. Passages from Defoe's book drifted like flotsam as Flinders now found himself living the life of Robinson Crusoe:

> … it was just punishment for my sin; my rebellious behaviour against my father … the general course of my wicked life … it spoke

to me like a voice; 'WRETCH!' dost thou ask
what thou hast done! Look back upon a
dreadful misspent life, and ask thy self what
thou hast not done?

Flinders stared at the mess of timber and rigging
that had been a ship. His hopes were now pinned
entirely on the return of the *Bridgewater*. 'A top-sail
yard was set up and secured as a flag staff on the highest part of the bank, and a large blue ensign hoisted …
as a signal to the *Bridgewater*. We expected … that she
would come to relieve us from our critical situation so
soon as the wind should be perfectly moderate.'

But the *Bridgewater* did not come. As the hours
stretched into days, Flinders began to face the awful
fact that Captain Palmer: 'Neither attempted to work
up in the smooth water, nor sent any of his boats to see
whether some unfortunate individuals were not clinging to the wrecks, whom he might snatch from the
sharks or save from a more lingering death …' Palmer
had abandoned them, giving them all up for dead and
sailing on towards Batavia.

As awareness of this abandonment spread, Flinders
watched many of his ninety-three companions become
listless, succumbing to despair. Here they were on a
sandbar barely above the high-water mark, 150 miles
from an unknown coast, 740 nautical miles from Port
Jackson. Flinders knew he had to do something, had
to take control. He realised that the greatest danger
was not starvation or drowning, but despondency and
disintegration.

With the consent of the other two captains, Flinders officially assumed command. 'I called a council of all the officers ... captain Palmer's want of energy and humanity had left us exposed; and it was finally determined, that an officer and crew in the largest of the two six-oared cutters, should endeavour to get to Port Jackson.' Most of those present were well aware of Flinders' earlier exploits with Bass in the tiny *Tom Thumb*, so: 'It seemed to be the general wish, that I should undertake the execution of the task; and ... the hope of being instrumental to the general safety induced me readily to comply.' A few provisions and a compass were loaded into the cutter, followed by Flinders and thirteen other men. He stared back at the lonely group of eighty men on the sandbar, surrounded by the vast blue. They were distant now, but Flinders could still see them waving. He had sworn to return.

The first day was rough but the wind favourable. The second day Flinders could see the mainland coast. He did not land. He knew it was safer not to and continued south. The winds were a godsend to begin with, blowing fairly consistently from the north. After a few days, though, they turned southerly and the men manned the oars, heaving against the wind. Flinders' burden weighed heavily: '[You have] perhaps never gone 250 leagues at sea in an open boat, or along a strange coast inhabited by savages; but if you recollect the eighty officers and men upon Wreck-Reef Bank, and how important was our arrival to their safety ... you may have some idea of the pleasure we felt, but particularly myself, at entering our destined port.'

In an extraordinary show of seamanship, achieved in a mere twelve days, Flinders sailed the cutter 734 nautical miles and entered Port Jackson Heads on September 8, 1802. Flinders steered straight to the wharf nearest Government House and led his dishevelled group through the streets. The stunned Sydneysiders watched them pass. He interrupted a shocked Governor King at dinner.

King immediately did everything in his power to help Flinders organise the rescue of the remaining survivors. Flinders planned to rescue the men on Wreck Reef and then sail on to England. In his urgency to be off, he accepted a rather inferior vessel, the tiny *Cumberland*, the same schooner that Lieutenant Robbins had used to pursue Baudin to King Island. Flinders had heard of the vessel: 'This schooner was something less than a Gravesend passage boat, being only of twenty-nine tons burthen … [but] joined to some ambition of being the first to undertake so long a voyage in such a small vessel, and a desire to put an early stop to the account which captain Palmer would probably give of our total loss, they proved sufficient inducements to accept the governor's offer.' For the love of his wife, he wanted to contradict Captain Palmer's inevitable report of his shipwreck reaching England as soon as possible. For the sake of his career, of course, he would not mind setting another world sailing record. It seems ambition as well as love still had a firm hold on Flinders.

On September 21, 1803, in the company of two other ships, the *Rolla* and the schooner *Francis*, Flinders headed back out of Port Jackson to rescue his men. Almost immediately, he realised that the schooner was worse than he had thought. 'The *Cumberland* is exceedingly crank … in one hour-and-half's cessation from pumping, the water washes on the cabin floor … I am now sitting on the lee locker, with my knees up to my chin for a table to write on, and in momentary expectation of the sea coming down the companion.' If anything, the vessel was leakier than the *Investigator*. It also made him itch: 'Of all the filthy little things I saw, this schooner, for bugs, lice, fleas, weavels, mosquitos, cockroaches large and small, and mice, rises superior to them all … I have at least a hundred lumps upon my body and arms; and before this bug-like smell will leave me, must, I believe, as well as my clothes, undergo a good boiling in the large kettle.' It was not an auspicious beginning to the final leg of the race and hardly 'lead me to think favourably of the vessel, in which I had undertaken a voyage half round the globe'.

Two and a half weeks after sailing out of Port Jackson, Flinders approached Wreck Reef, this time in daylight, and this time very carefully. As Flinders stepped back onto the sandbar, he was hailed as a hero: 'On landing, I was greeted with three hearty cheers, and the utmost joy by my officers and people; and the pleasure of rejoining my companions … made this one of the happiest moments of my life.'

Flinders wasted no time, he asked all the men to gather round and filled them in on their options: 'The people were assembled on the bank, and informed that such as chose to be discharged from the service might return to Port Jackson in the *Francis* schooner; and that the rest would be taken on board the *Rolla* and carried to China, with the exception of ten officers and men whom I named, to go to England with me in the *Cumberland*, if they would risk themselves in so small a vessel.'

One of the ten men named did object. The clerk Mr Olive did not like the look of the *Cumberland* at all. The other nine, however, were honoured to be able to serve Captain Flinders, hero and great navigator. Flinders was not offended by Olive's reluctance to join him, indeed even the great navigator had grave doubts about the seaworthiness of the *Cumberland*. But Flinders was feeling good and ready to take the gamble. 'Notwithstanding what had been discovered of the bad qualities of the schooner, I determined to proceed, at least so far as to reach some port where a passage might be procured in a better vessel without losing time.'

It was a brave decision. He still had two oceans to cross, not to mention the treacherous waters of Torres Strait, the Arafura Sea and the Timor Sea. No sooner had Flinders left the others when he sailed into yet another maze of reefs. He avoided further disasters, but realised he was surrounded by coral: 'This space might be very appropriately called the Corallian Sea.' Flinders pioneered the 'outer route' through the Coral Sea and the route he sailed through the Torres Strait is still known as 'Cumberland Passage'. Amazingly, the charts Flinders drew of the 'Eastern Fields' of Torres Strait were to remain in use until 1969. Flinders was keen to do some charting here on his second pass. It had been one of the priorities of his sailing orders and he had neglected it the first time he passed through when racing the Monsoon.

Two weeks later, Flinders navigated a new route through Torres Strait. Having been here before, he was very wary of the fierce Murray Islanders and rushed on: 'I steered WNW to avoid going near Murray's Islands, lest the small size of the *Cumberland* should tempt the Indians to make an attack … many were standing on the shore with their canoes seemingly in readiness.'

Sailing through the Wessel Islands, the same place where he had abandoned his earlier survey, Flinders spotted the wreckage of another boat washed up on the beach. He landed to investigate. 'And whilst the boat's crew was busied in cutting the wreck for fuel, the Indians approached gradually, and a friendly inter-course took place … they were presented with our axes after the work was done, and we got under way soon after ten o'clock.' These were the last 'Australians' Flinders would ever meet. Flinders left the coast of New Holland and headed for Timor. He was desperate to repair his constantly failing pumps, his only defence against the sea which threatened to consume his leaky tub.

Flinders replenished supplies in Kupang, but the lonely trading post simply did not have the tools to repair the ailing pumps. He decided to chance it and sail on, spurred by an interesting piece of news learned in the town: '[The Governor] informed me that captain Baudin had arrived at Coepang near a month after I had left it in the *Investigator* ...' More importantly, Baudin had then passed Timor again: 'They struggled against the trades near two months ... seeing it was impossible that he could get into the gulph ... and being moreover extremely ill, Mr. Baudin bore up for the Isle of France.'

The race was not over yet: 'My anxious desire to reach England ... induced me to leave ... It was my intention on quitting Timor, if the leaky condition of the schooner and the north-west monsoon did not oppose it, to pass ... direct for the Cape of Good Hope.'

Flinders left Timor behind. Ahead lay 5,800 miles of ocean. Below were 4,700 fathoms of water, and two faulty pumps.

Chapter 29

[FROM HERE
TO ETERNITY]

On the far side of the Indian Ocean, Baudin
lay in his bed. He had indeed been very ill
when they reached Île-de-France, but he was
feeling better now. He had been pleased to learn that
the *Naturaliste* had passed safely through Port Louis and
was probably already back in France: 'Le *Naturaliste*
took forty-one days to go from King Island to Île de
France … Her collection of living animals and plants
were in excellent condition.'

After his initial disappointment at having to give

up his survey of Nouvelle Hollande, on reflection, Baudin could be extremely proud of what he had achieved. He had also had the presence of mind to secure all charts and journals for the Minister of Marine before they reached the island. As was the standard practice of a mission sponsored by the government, all private journals had to be surrendered. As Baudin notified his gentlemen by letter:

> Citizens,
> In accordance with the strict orders of the government, you are informed that you must assemble all the journals, memoirs and notes that each one of you must privately have kept from the beginning of the expedition until now. These works being the government's property I am expressly ordered to claim them.
> In your presence, they will be placed in a box that will be sealed and addressed to the Minister of Marine. In response to this letter each one of you will have to declare on his word of honour that he has retained no journal or writing relative to the expedition.
>
> Greetings, N.B.

Baudin wrote another letter to the Minister of Marine, Forfait, expressing general satisfaction with his mission's achievements. He knew that his superior charts of the west and north-west coasts as well as his detailed charts of Terre de van Diemen could only assist any claim by Napoléon to these parts of Nouvelle

Hollande, should the First Consul chose to make such a claim. But Baudin was most proud of his mission's scientific findings. Whether or not science had been his government's prime objective, it had certainly become his. Baudin knew that his mission could only bring honour to France, as well as himself – as the Minister's sailing orders had promised: 'It is you, above all to whom it is reserved to reap most of the glory in this expedition, since your name will be attached, so to speak, to everything done in the course of your navigation.' In his letter to the Minister, Baudin promised that his mission would depart Île-de-France as soon as the weather was better – in order not to risk the health of his precious live animals.

One afternoon, Baudin received a surprise visitor. Pierre Milius stared at Baudin. He hardly recognised the gaunt person propped up by pillows. Baudin stared back. After recovering from his nervous breakdown, Milius had made his own way to Île-de-France, via Macao. He asked Baudin if he could rejoin the mission. Baudin told him that he had enough officers.

Milius noted the strange jar standing beside Baudin's bed. The jar contained an awful red mess. Baudin noticed Milius staring at what were fragments of his own lungs, coughed up in horrific pain, and scoffed: 'Are the lungs essential to life? You see I no longer have any. Yet I still exist!'

Baudin decided to write another letter, to his English friend, Governor King, to let him know how he was getting on:

Sir,

… Since I had the honour of seeing you I spent nine months in exploring the coasts of New Holland, which work is at last completed …

I was twice taken ill, and so badly too that the doctors often predicted that my career was at an end; but they made a mistake.

But the doctors had not made a mistake. For once, Péron's account was more accurate: 'Since our arrival in the colony his condition had become much worse; for a long time all hope of a cure had been lost.' Baudin spent his last agonising days at the home of Madame Alexandrine Kerivel, an old friend and some-time lover.

Of course he knew he was dying. He recalled the last three years. He recalled the last forty-nine. He recalled the little boy who had gone to sea, the young man who had wanted to make a name for himself. A man who had made a name for himself. Baudin knew that this last chapter of his life was safely recorded in his *Journal de Mer*. This book, safely secured with all the other journals from the voyage, would be his legacy. Like his other missions, this one too was, in the end, a success, even if it had cost him his life. He had learned a lot, about the world, about himself. He had seen amazing things. The cost of that experience was no more, and no less, than what Maugé and Riedlé had paid. It was the going rate. He was paying the same price as Dufresne, St Allouarn, La Pérouse and D'Entrecasteaux. The curse on French commanders, it seemed, was intact. If you stepped onto the soil of Nouvelle Hollande, you paid the ferryman. Perhaps the sixth in line would be luckier, whoever that might be. Baudin had done enough. He would not personally deliver his findings to Napoléon, but that did not diminish their value.

In his journal, Péron finally referred to his commander by name, the one and only time: 'At last the moment arrived, and on 16 September, 1803, around noon, Mr Baudin ceased to exist.'

Chapter 30

[LIFE AFTER DEATH]

Louis Freycinet was equally brief in describing his commander's death: 'Mr Baudin, commandant of our expedition, died as a result of a long and cruel illness. He was buried the following day with all the honours due to his rank in the navy.'

All the men that Baudin had come to despise attended his funeral. Nicolas-Tomas Baudin, *officier bleu*, man of humble birth, received a State Funeral. The new Governor of Île-de-France, General Charles Decaen, was there to pay his respects, as was the chief of all French naval forces in the Indian Ocean, Rear

Admiral Charles Linois. Pierre Milius was there, sad to farewell his laconic commander: 'He had to give up fighting any more against so many obstacles at once ... overwhelmed with fatigue and devoured by care ... death came to end all his pains.'

As had occurred on Baudin's first stop in Port Louis, Île-de-France then threatened to dismantle Baudin's mission. News that the Peace of Amiens had been broken reached the island. France was back at war with Britain and Admiral Linois had need of every ship he could muster. The *Géographe* was, after all, a corvette. Decaen ordered that it be placed on a war footing and that its natural history cargo be unloaded. Fortunately, he then changed his mind and allowed the *Géographe* to continue its voyage back to France.

Pierre Milius was appointed to captain the *Géographe* on the last leg of its voyage. Henri Freycinet was outraged, feeling that the job should have passed to him. Thirty-one-year-old Milius was the logical choice for command. Besides having far more experience than 25-year-old Freycinet, the older man had the essential ingredient to be a commander: 'Milius commanded a respect mixed with fear; he was, besides, a great seaman.' He was also determined not to suffer another breakdown and perhaps in an attempt to forestall criticisms from another quarter, Milius made a tactical appointment in nominating the person to be in charge of the scientific collection: 'All natural history objects gathered and cared for by M. Baudin, both for the collection of Mme. Bonaparte and for the Museum, were placed by my orders in the care of

M. Péron.' Péron accepted the responsibility willingly. He had done very well out of the voyage. He had joined the mission as a lowly assistant-zoologist; he would now return to France as *the* senior naturalist. Freycinet was relieved of his command of *Le Casuarina*, the ship paid off, and he was ordered to rejoin *Le Géographe*.

On December 16, 1803 the *Géographe* was finally ready to sail. Milius ordered the lines be cast off and sailed out of Port Louis to complete Baudin's mission.

On the very same day that the *Géographe* departed the north coast of Île-de-France, a small English schooner, the *Cumberland*, rounded the south.

§ § §

The situation on board the *Cumberland* had been unbearable for weeks. The port pump had been the first to go. Flinders and his ten companions had then listened to the laboured heartbeat of the last pump. 'The starbord pump, which was alone effective, was obliged to be worked almost continually, day and night.' The schooner was lucky to stay afloat: 'Had the wind been on the starbord side, it is doubtful whether the schooner could have been kept above water … This state of things made it necessary to take into serious consideration the propriety of attempting the passage round the Cape.'

Flinders realised that he was endangering not only his own life and that of his crew, but also his precious charts. He was not well, and '… affected with a bilious remitting fever ... Having no medical man on board, our getting to a port receives an additional object to hasten it ... Besides these, there are several subordinate reasons ... Learning some further intelligence of the *Géographe* and *Naturaliste*.'

Flinders consulted his chart of the Indian Ocean. There was only one other place in this part of the world where he might find relief, as well as intelligence concerning his rival's ships. On December 6, 1803, he made a decision to steer for the small French island to the north-west: 'Necessity, and not inclination, obliged me to put into the Isle of France.' Having been so long at sea, Flinders did not know that the truce had been broken, that France and England were once again at war.

Chapter 31

[THE TIDES OF WAR]

s Flinders approached Île-de-France, he tried
to follow a smaller vessel in order to safely navigate the many reefs surrounding the island.
The only map Flinders had was the crude sketch in his
Encyclopaedia Britannica, his farewell gift from Sir Joseph
Banks. In light of his recent experiences, it seemed
wiser to rely on local knowledge. The vessel Flinders
was following, however, did not sail on to port but
instead made a panicked dash for the nearest bay. Not
a good sign. The next occurrence only increased his
anxiety. 'Presently we saw several men with muskets on

the top of the hill ... [this] caused me to apprehend that England and France were either at war or very near it.'

Flinders' worst fears were confirmed on sending Aken, his Master, ashore with the passport. A French corvette soon arrived to escort the *Cumberland* to the main port. During the journey, Flinders examined his passport closely, having not done so previously: 'My passport was in French ... and my knowledge of its contents was very imperfect ... I set myself to consider it attentively; and so far as I could make out, it seemed to be solely for the *Investigator* ... it appeared that if the governor of Mauritius should adhere to the letter of the passport and disregard the intention, he might seize the *Cumberland* as a prize; and the idea of being detained even a week more than necessary was intolerable.'

He tried to remain optimistic: 'During this passage to Port Louis, my mind was occupied in turning over all the circumstances of my situation ... The breaking out of the war ... the conduct of a governor appointed by the first consul Bonaparte, who was a professed patron of science ... the testimony which the commanders of the *Géographe* and *Naturaliste* had doubtless given of their treatment at Port Jackson.' The last would surely be his saviour. If he received just half of the kind treatment Baudin had received in Port Jackson, if that generosity was reciprocated, he would be fine: 'I went into the boat in my frock uniform, and was conducted to the government house.'

At 6.00 pm Flinders was escorted to meet the

Governor, General Decaen. He was asked to wait: 'The captain-general was at dinner and I was kept waiting until eight o'clock.' Feeling edgy and feverish, Flinders was not impressed: 'They took me to a shady place which seemed to be the common lounge for the officers … they asked if I had really come from Botany Bay in that little vessel … Others asked questions of monsieur Baudin's conduct at Port Jackson … and also concerning the voyage of monsieur Flinedare, of which, to their surprise, I knew nothing, but afterwards found it to be my own name which they so pronounced.'

Not recognising the pronunciation of his own name was a great mistake. The seemingly innocuous conversation with the French officers in the shady lounge was actually the first part of his interrogation. Next, he was ushered in to meet the Governor: 'At length the interpreter desired me to follow him, and I was shown into a room.'

Flinders came face to face with a man thirty-four years old, five years older than himself. The two men stared at one another. Flinders noted the rosy glow to Charles Decaen's cheeks, presumably from the wine he had consumed during the dinner that had kept him waiting: 'The captain-general De Caen, fixed his eyes sternly upon me, and without salutation or preface demanded my passport.'

Flinders was offended. Such a greeting was certainly nothing like the hospitable reception Baudin had received from Governor King at Port Jackson. In response, Flinders did not remove his hat. Decaen duly noted the discourtesy, as did his *aide-de-camp*. They asked him to remove it. The meeting did not get off to a good start.

Flinders struggled to contain his own outrage: 'Consider all the circumstances of my situation: my voyage, shipwreck … Let him suppose himself to have executed so much of the same task, escaped the same dangers … to be arrested … and this is done by the representative of a government which … owed him a return for the kind treatment recently experienced by Frenchmen in the port from whence he came.'

The main problem was, Flinders did not realise what one of those Frenchmen had said to Decaen. Péron had told Decaen that Flinders was actually a spy.

When Decaen had quizzed Péron on the French expedition's stay at Port Jackson, Péron had cooperated enthusiastically, with a 28-page report, '*Coup d'oeil rapide sur l'éstablissement des Anglais de la Nouvelle Hollande*.' The report encouraged Decaen to launch a pre-emptive attack on the British colony: 'Port Jackson should be destroyed as soon as possible. Today we could do so easily; we shall not be able to do so in twenty-five years' time!'

Péron, the 'Observer of Man', had broadened his expertise to include the strategies of war. He had outlined all the intelligence he had gathered concerning the state of the colony, including the military-styled topographical maps he had encouraged Lesueur to sketch. His report stated: 'Once the English Colony is conquered it can easily be defended by our troops against any attack with great force, and since the colony has enough subsistence it won't starve of hunger because of enemy warships.'

Interestingly, Péron had hinted to Decaen that Baudin's mission had indeed been pursuing 'secret instructions' all along, issued directly by Bonaparte: 'To conceal it from the governments of Europe, and especially from the Cabinet of St James ... It was necessary that ... all our natural history researches, extolled with so much ostentation by the Government, were merely a pretext for its enterprise ... Our expedition ... was one of those brilliant and important conceptions which ought to make our present government forever illustrious.'

Péron had then gone on to accuse Flinders of being a spy, suggesting that the English navigator's rival mission was actually one of traversing the Pacific looking for strategic points from which the British could launch an attack on Spanish America, France's ally. Finally, Péron had told Decaen all about the episode at King Island. He had described in detail how an arrogant young British officer called Robbins sailing in the *Cumberland* had arrived to spy on them and forestall the French mission from making a claim on Terre de van Diemen.

In front of Decaen now stood an arrogant young Englishmen who had arrived in the *Cumberland*. Flinders soon felt the full force of Decaen's ire: 'He expressed himself unsatisfied with my answers ... saying that I was imposing upon him, for it was not probable that I should be here in so small a vessel.'

For Decaen, busily preparing his colony for war

with the British, the very timing of the *Cumberland*'s arrival seemed suspicious, as Flinders noted: 'He asked in an impetuous manner why I came here in a <u>small</u> <u>schooner</u> with a passport for the *Investigator*, and after many other questions put with much acumen … why I appeared … without my officers & scientific gentlemen … why I shewed the colours that I did – why I chased a vessel in sight of the island.'

Although ignorant of what Péron had informed Decaen, Flinders slowly began to appreciate the acute nature of his predicament: 'I found myself considered in the light of a spy …' Found guilty, spies were of course shot.

As was his want, Flinders did not skirt the perilous waters in which he now found himself, rather he ventured deeper. Deliberately, inexplicably, he steered straight towards the reefs. Ordered back to collect his journals and charts as evidence, Flinders told his French escorts in no uncertain terms what he thought of their Governor: 'I expressed to them my sentiments of general De Caen's manner … and added, that the captain-general's conduct must alter very much before I should pay him a second visit.' The polite French officers no doubt reported the comments back to Decaen. That night, at 1.00 am, the French officers returned and escorted Flinders and Aken, his second-in-command, off the ship: 'We were taken to some place which we expected was to be a tavern, but it had a most prison-like appearance and a soldier was placed over our chamber.' The two men were confined to a room in the Café Marengo. Flinders continued to stew.

'The injustice, the haughtiness, and the Bastille-like mystery with which I am treated. I am kept from my voyage of discovery, from my country, from my family ... This is indeed some return for the hospitality and assistance which the French ships *Géographe* and *Naturaliste* but now received at Port Jackson.' Flinders finally realised that there was nothing to do but try to rest: 'I stripped and got into bed; but between the mosquitoes above and bugs below, and the novelty of our situation, it was near daybreak before either of us dropped asleep.'

The following morning, the interrogation continued. 'A gentleman who spoke some English put various questions to me from a paper and wrote down my answers ... My answers to all these being taken down, and, together with my letter from governor King relating to the *Cumberland* shewn to the general, I found that they began to be more satisfied concerning me.'

After five hours of interrogation, Decaen did begin to believe that Flinders was who he claimed to be – that he was not Robbins, nor a spy. Decaen had realised that some of Péron's accusations had to be taken with a good dose of salt. And it was dinner time.

At 5.00 pm, Flinders was just about to be escorted back to the Café Marengo when Decaen's *aide-de-camp*, Monistrol, came back into the room. Monistrol's message caught Flinders unprepared. 'To my surprise, an invitation was brought me to go to the general's table, his dinner being then served up.' A gap had opened in the treacherous reefs surrounding Flinders.

An invitation to dinner indicated Decaen was prepared to treat him as an officer. But for the haughty Flinders it was too late. He had a fever. He was not thinking straight. His frustration had transformed into a white-hot anger; anger at having stopped here; anger at having embarked in the atrocious *Cumberland*; anger at being interrogated; anger at being treated like a spy; anger at being delayed in getting back to see Ann; anger that he was treated so differently to Baudin; anger that his fate now rested solely in the hands of a Frenchman.

Monistrol stared at the Englishman. He could not understand the hesitation. The gap loomed in the reefs, but Flinders ignored it and veered straight towards the terrible coral: 'This invitation was so contrary to all that had hitherto passed … that I at first thought it could not be serious … my reply was, that under my present situation and treatment it was impossible … when I should be set at liberty, if His Excellency thought proper to invite me, I should be flattered by it, and accept his invitation with pleasure.'

Monistrol was stunned. He tried to change Flinders' mind. To no avail. Monistrol delivered Flinders' rejection of the dinner invitation to Decaen. The Governor promptly sent Monistrol back with a cryptic response to Flinders: 'When the aïde-de-camp returned … he said that the general would invite me when set at liberty.' There would be no more invitations.

It had come to this. The same doggedness that had allowed him to circumnavigate a continent and survive shipwreck had brought his race undone. Flinders knew it, as he later confided in a letter to Ann:

> You know, my dearest, that I always dreaded the effect that the possession of great authority would have upon my temper and disposition … between men dependent and men in power, any man who has any share of impartiality must fear for himself. My brother will tell you that I am proud, unindulgent, and hasty to take offence … there is more truth in the charge than I wish there were … In this island, those malignant qualities are ostentatiously displayed and I am made to feel their sting most poignantly.

Now, as the days turned into weeks, Decaen kept Flinders locked up on the legitimate grounds that Flinders had breached his passport. Flinders recorded that: 'The captain-general being convinced … that I had absolutely changed the nature of the mission for which the First Consul had granted a passport … he ordered colonel Monistrol to go on board the *Cumberland* … to collect … all other papers which might add to the proofs already acquired … even to letters received from my family and friends during several years, were all taken away, locked up in a trunk, and sealed.'

Decaen wanted Flinders to justify a particular passage in his journal, in obvious contravention of his passport. Flinders pleaded his defence:

Sir … I find, that the plea for detaining me is …
that I have violated the neutrality therein
required, by having given in my journal as an
additional reason for putting into this port, that
'it would enable me to acquire a knowledge of
the periodical winds and of the present state
of the French colony' … upon this incorrect and
worst supposition I have, I think an example of a
similar conduct in your own nation, unless you
can assure me that the captains Baudin and
Hamelin made no such remarks upon Port
Jackson …

The main problem with the letter was the way he
finished it:

Now, Sir, I would beg to ask you whether it
becomes the French nation, even independent of
all passport, to stop the progress of such a voyage
of which the whole maritime world are to
receive the benefit? How contrary is this with
her conduct some years since towards Captain
Cook. I sought protection and assistance in your
port, and I have found a prison. Judge for me as
a man, Sir – Judge for me as a British officer
employed in a neutral occupation, Judge for me
as a zealous philanthropist, what I must feel at
being thus treated.

Not a courteous letter. Decaen did not respond,
so on Christmas Day, Flinders sent another:

SIR ... it appears that Your Excellency had
formed a determination to stop the *Cumberland*,
previously even to seeing me ... a mean action,
and altogether unworthy of you or your nation
... you told me impetuously that I was imposing
upon you ... that an officer of your rank and
judgement could act either so ungentlemanlike,
or so unguardedly ... unless his reason had been
blinded by passion.

This time, Flinders did receive a response from
Governor Decaen. 'In the evening, a letter was brought
me ... from general De Caen, and the haste with
which it had been sent inspired favourable hopes ...'
The hopes were soon dashed as Flinders read Decaen's
response:

Your undertaking as extraordinary as it was
inconsiderate, to depart from Port Jackson in the
Cumberland ... more for the private interests of
Great Britain than for what had induced the
French Government to give you a passport ...
had already given me an idea of your character;
but this letter overstepping all the bounds of
civility, obliges me to tell you until the general
opinion judges of your future or mine, to cease
all correspondence tending to demonstrate the
justice of your cause; since you know so little
how to preserve the rules of decorum.

Decaen was insulted. He was also correct in some of his observations. The *Cumberland* had arrived without a single scientist on board. Flinders thereby hardly constituted a scientific mission, as stipulated by his passport. Furthermore, Flinders had indeed rushed off in the *Cumberland*, pursuing his personal desire to rush his charts back to England as soon as possible to counteract Baudin. Decaen had also discovered that Flinders had, in complete contravention of his passport, been carrying secret dispatches from Governor King to the Admiralty. In the dispatches King requested more troops in order to, amongst other purposes, defend Port Jackson if attacked by Decaen.

In fact, if Flinders had had more time to make his usually detailed observations of a coast new to him, describing Île-de-France's ports and approaches in his normally meticulous detail, Decaen might have had to try him as a spy, and executed him. Decaen felt little pity for one arrogant young Englishman, when thousands of upstanding young Frenchmen were dying on the battlefields of Europe.

Flinders could not admit defeat, or even an error of judgement. He was, again, like a dog with a bone. Contrary to Decaen's orders he wrote back to him, requesting he be given his private books, letters and charts, especially those of the Gulf of Carpentaria. He wanted to rework the charts while he could still remember the lost details, the originals having been destroyed in the wreck of the *Porpoise*. 'A compliance with the above requests will not only furnish me with a better amusement in my solitude, than writing letters to Your Excellency, but will be attended with advantages in which the French nation may sometime share.'

Surprisingly, Decaen granted the request. All the documents that Flinders asked for were delivered, except for the third volume of his journal.* Amongst the documents was also his Naval Signals book which Flinders destroyed the minute he was alone. With at least most of his papers returned, he was a little more content, as he wrote to his brother: 'Their rage is disarmed of its sting, for they cannot make me very unhappy whilst I have useful employment. To external appearance they are doing me the greatest imaginable injury, but I will so contrive it, that it shall prove to have been of the greatest advantage to me in the end ... Although I use the expressions they and them, there is but one man here who I believe is my enemy. The governor both hates and fears me.' Flinders raced on. He knew that the contest was still far from over. There had been the race to discover, now there was the race to publish. By now, he had his own suspicions as to the real reason for his incarceration: 'Some odd opinions were started relative to the real cause of my confinement ... in matters of discovery, I should think that he kept me here to give time for captain Baudin's voyage to be published before mine, and as no probable reason has yet been given for my detainer it may possibly be so.'

---

* Flinders would never see this book again; it was not relocated until the 1900s when 'discovered' in the British National Maritime Museum.

Chapter 32

[HOME AT LAST]

On March 23, 1804, the *Géographe* was almost home. Not a moment too soon. Pierre Milius watched the coast of dear France drawing nearer. The trip from Île-de-France to here had been horrendous, as Milius noted: 'The hardships and pains of all kinds that I endured on this voyage led to the complete breakdown of my health. It is pointless to name here those responsible for all my ills.' Prime amongst the troublemakers had been both Freycinet brothers, whose insubordination had led Milius to relieve them of all duties. Milius had received a great insight into the sort of headaches Baudin had experienced for three years. The conflicts on board had taken their toll on his nerves. He had a fever and as they approached the end of their saga, he once again tottered on the edge of a breakdown.

He was equally nervous of being intercepted by the Channel Fleet enforcing the British blockade of French ports. He decided not to try to reach Le Havre, but instead docked at Lorient. Baudin's mission was home. As he had promised, Milius had delivered Baudin's precious charts, journals and natural history specimens back to France. Finally he could surrender to his shattered mental state. For the second time, Milius broke down.

News of the *Géographe*'s return spread quickly and a crowd gathered to watch as crate after crate was unloaded. The live creatures were the most dazzling. Out of the hold of the *Géographe* emerged seventy-two living animals. Amongst them, two of Baudin's beloved kangaroos had survived, as had emus, parrots, a cassowary, tortoises and various other types of birds. Sadly, the two wombats had died.

The live creatures were followed by almost 300 living plants that had also endured the ravages of life at sea. After them came the preserved zoological specimens, over 2,500 of which would be claimed as completely new to Science. When the total cargo from the *Géographe* was tallied and added to the specimens already brought back on the *Naturaliste*, Baudin's expedition had brought back over 200,000 specimens. The collection would double the total holdings of the

Muséum. Members of *Le Institut* and the men from the *Muséum* marvelled at the quality and sheer quantity of riches brought back, proclaiming it as 'the greatest collection ever to be brought into France'. The man now responsible for that collection, François Péron, was pleased to receive the compliments and when Joséphine Bonaparte inquired whether she could sequester the live animals for her 'collection of pure pleasure', Péron happily obliged.

Joséphine Bonaparte was well known as a passionate collector of exotic plants and animals and it was not unusual for her to become involved in the affairs of State if she required something for her collection. There was already a standing order that any exotic seeds found on board captured English ships should be dispatched directly to her. She had already requisitioned a large part of the collection brought back on the *Naturaliste* and she now did the same with the riches unloaded from the *Géographe*.

With Péron's willing support, the kangaroos, emus and other creatures of Nouvelle Hollande were introduced to their new home, the royal residence *Château de la Malmaison*. Joséphine already possessed one of the most beautiful and impressive menageries of exotic flora and fauna in Europe. The black swans, kangaroos and emus would become its shining centrepiece. Joséphine also secured seeds and seedlings of eucalyptus trees, banksias, bottlebrush, kangaroo paws and melaleucas which she planted in the gardens of the *Château*. On the outskirts of Paris, a small part of Nouvelle Hollande had invaded France. No doubt

Joséphine had little idea how many men had died in order for these few live creatures to reach her garden, where they soon ranged freely, rubbing shoulders with llamas, a zebra, a gnu and an orangoutan.

Napoléon had been away conquering the Egyptians when Joséphine wrote to him that she had bought the country estate on the banks of the Seine, even though they had agreed it was too expensive. He had been livid. He was happy now that he was the leader of France, and rich. It had not taken long for the estate to cast its spell over him too. The *Château* proved a convenient sanctuary from his hectic career of running one country and waging war on many others. Joséphine did a beautiful job of the gardens and Napoléon enjoyed the quaint emus and kangaroos reclining in the shade. The black swans were remarkable, a true inversion of the natural order courtesy of the far side of the world.

However, in the first half of 1804, Napoléon did not have a great deal of time to spare to ponder the achievements of Baudin's expedition. He had far bigger fish to fry. Planning his invasion of England consumed him day and night.

Péron was one of the first to note the changed atmosphere in Paris. The capital now seemed focused far less on science and much more on war. Péron was disappointed. The return of their expedition received little fanfare from Napoléon. Péron understood that perhaps the emperor was disappointed that yet another French mission to Nouvelle Hollande had cost the life of the commander. Péron argued that the life of that commander was not worth much anyway. Nor was he the first to express such sentiments.

Having returned to France before Baudin's ships, many of the deserters who left the mission on the voyage out had been keen to have themselves exonerated of any wrongdoing. Hence, many of them had already painted an extremely unflattering picture of their deceased commander. One of them, Bory de Saint-Vincent, an aristocrat with powerful and influential family connections, had just published a book in which, to defend himself, he claimed to have foreseen the expedition's inevitable disintegration due to the obvious shortcomings of its leader. Another of the deserters, Gicquel, had already advised the ministry that: 'M. Baudin has no qualities, either moral or social. He is neither naturalist nor mariner. His hair stands on end in the least squall.'

Péron soon added his voice to these, agreeing that Baudin had been a useless commander, and if the mission had fallen short of any of its objectives, the reason had been due solely the failings of their stubborn, authoritarian, conveniently deceased captain.

Sadly, there were few to contradict the stories. Maugé, Riedlé and Levillain were dead. Milius was confined to hospital. Once he had recovered, his views were taken with a grain of salt. Although they had parted as warm friends at King Island, Captain Hamelin of the *Naturaliste* remained silent on the Baudin issue. He was, after all, a career man and did not want to be landed in the same boat with a dead, and if they said so, flawed commander. Hamelin did not denigrate his commander's reputation, but nor did he spring to his defence. After the last 'voting' episode in Timor, Ronsard too seemed content to hold his counsel on what he thought of Baudin as a leader.

France's leader, Napoléon, appreciated the distraction of kangaroos and black swans, but was not interested at that stage in weighing up the pros and cons of Baudin and his expedition. There was a whole world to conquer, with only the British Navy standing in the way. Once a few logistical issues had been sorted out, the great victory would be at hand. With Britain defeated, France would be the sole remaining global super-power and Napoléon would rule the world. British colonies and unknown lands would be his for the taking. France would simply inherit far-flung colonies as a matter of course: Gibraltar, Bombay, Malaya … Port Jackson.

Chapter 33

[THE HOME FRONT]

ews of Flinders' imprisonment reached England in mid-August, 1804. For Ann, it was the most joyous of news. She had thought Matthew was dead. As Flinders had feared, the news of his shipwreck had reached her first. Ann had been shattered. So the news of his imprisonment came as a happy surprise. Sir Joseph Banks was similarly surprised and wrote to inform Robert Brown, still in Port Jackson: 'Poor Flinders is a Prisoner & I fear not very well treated; he put, in the little *Cumberland*, into l'Ile de France for water and Provisions & some Repairs, wholly ignorant of the War, the Governor … accused him of being a Spy & maltreated him.'

Banks immediately did what he could to secure Flinders' release, contacting his colleagues at the *Institut National*. He had recently helped secure the release of the *Naturaliste* which had been stopped by the British Navy in the Channel. Banks's colleagues at the *Institut National* assured him that they would present Flinders' case to Napoléon's councillors, *Le Conseil d'Etat*. Banks was then informed that the *Conseil d'Etat* had recommended the release of Flinders, as an act of generosity, but that the decision, however, needed to be ratified by Napoléon who was currently away in Italy. Banks was asked to be patient, that the matter would be sorted out soon and the delay would last only a little longer.

On Île-de-France, Flinders remained under lock and key. The longer he was kept a prisoner, the more suspicious he became: '[An acquaintance] lately arrived from France, called to breakfast on his way to town. He gave me to understand that I should not be set at liberty until after the voyage of Baudin was published.'

One afternoon, eight months after he had arrived, Flinders received a surprising visitor: 'The brother of the French commodore Baudin called today upon me, and was exceedingly kind and civil in offers of service in every way, whether in accommodating me with money or in any other away.' Augustin Baudin, captain of a Danish vessel, had received a letter from his brother prior to his death which advised of Baudin's courteous treatment by the English at Port Jackson. Flinders was grateful that someone had noted the contrast: 'Augustin Baudin … testified the grateful sense his brother had always entertained of the generous reception and great assistance received from governor King at Port Jackson, and expressed his own regret at not being able to do any thing for my release.' Augustin visited Flinders again one week later, to ask the Englishman for advice on a delicate matter. 'Captain Baudin called upon me to take his leave, and to ask concerning the propriety of taking a young woman to India whom his brother had brought hither from Port Jackson.' The convict girl, Mary Beckwith, was still at Île-de-France. Flinders did not record what he counselled Augustin to do.

Flinders had been released from the Café Marengo and transferred to the *Maison Despaux* or 'Garden Prison' where all British prisoners of war were kept. Initially, there had been a lot of other British officers, but as prisoner-of-war exchanges were made, the number dwindled. Flinders had himself, successfully, helped his second-in-command, John Aken, petition for his release.

As Aken prepared to depart on an American ship, Flinders slipped his fellow officer sixteen of his precious charts, including the very first that depicted western New Holland and New South Wales as one discrete landmass.* Flinders enclosed a letter for Joseph

---

* Since Flinders had not mapped the north, north-west and west coasts, he relied on the earlier Dutch charts to fill in almost 3,000 miles of otherwise blank coastline. Of course Flinders did not, at this stage, have access to Baudin's charts which were at that time the most detailed and accurate charts depicting the west and north-western coasts.

Banks, including a suggestion as to how the confusion of names could be clarified:

> I send you, Sir Joseph, a copy of my general chart of New Holland which is lately finished … The propriety of the name Australia or Terra Australis, which I have applied to the whole body of what has generally been called New Holland must be submitted to the approbation of the Admiralty and the learned in geography. It seems to me an inconsistent thing that captain Cook's New South Wales should be absorbed in the New Holland of the Dutch …

To leave Banks in no doubt which name he preferred, Flinders wrote 'Australia' as the main title, with 'Terra Australis' a secondary one.

Flinders was delighted for Aken, but simultaneously the walls of despair began closing in. Flinders had protected his charts from the elements and even shipwreck and had looked forward to proudly laying them before the Lords of the Admiralty. Here he was, sending them away to an uncertain future, to face not only the perils of the sea, but the war raging upon it. Flinders had written another letter to Banks a month earlier. It was hard to believe that this was the same man who had braved every hazard, afraid of nothing and no one. This letter revealed a man feeble, wrecked, grasping desperately:

If I do not prove myself worthy of your patronage, Sir Joseph, let me be thrown out of the society of all good men. I have too much ambition to rest in the unnoticed middle order of mankind ... although I cannot rival the immortalized name of Cook, yet if persevering industry, joined to what ability I may possess, can accomplish it, then I will secure the second place ... if you, Sir Joseph, as my guardian genius will but conduct me to the place of probation. The hitherto obscure name of Flinders may thus become a light by which even the illustrious character of Sir Joseph may one day receive an additional ray of glory.

Later, Flinders heard a rumour that Sir Joseph was on his deathbed, so he fired off another letter:

I sometimes fear – and it is a sickening thought – that I may be kept here until my patron, my conductor on the road to fame, shall be no more. Where, Sir Joseph, shall I find another disinterested friend to humble exertion under whose auspices I might be able to proceed in the career which you have opened to me? No – it is not to be hoped. Without fortune, rank, or connexions, what can I hope for ... 'The world forgetting, by the world forgot ...'

On receiving this letter, Banks was perhaps less rather than more reassured about the faith he had placed in his protégé. Flinders finally received his first letter back from England, a return letter from Joseph Banks. The news was not encouraging:

> From the moment I heard of your detention,
> I have used every effort in my power towards
> affecting your release. As the enmity between
> the Governments of France and England is
> carried to such a height that no exchange has
> on any pretence been effected, they could do
> nothing for you ... Unfortunately, the Emperor
> of the French was in Italy, where he still remains
> when my letter arrived. I confess, however,
> I entertain sanguine hopes of a favourable answer
> when [Napoléon] shall return to Paris, from the
> marked and laudable attention His Imperial
> Majesty has always shown to scientific men.

Aken had been the last of Flinders' men to be released at General Decaen's discretion. Flinders however could not now be released at Decaen's whim, since he had himself insisted that his case be referred directly to France. Flinders soon realised that he had done himself few favours by this tactic: 'General Decaen ... remitted the judgement of my case to the French Government, and cannot permit me to depart, or even send me to France, until he shall receive orders.' Flinders had helped make himself an exception by his own actions. He was now at the mercy of Paris and the long delays in seaborne correspondence travelling between France and Île-de-France.

Chapter 34

$$\left[\begin{array}{c} \text{THE WORLD} \\ \text{FORGETTING} \end{array} \right]$$

Flinders' race had come to a standstill. The man who had once voyaged beyond the known world, now struggled to see past the back fence. He described a day in the life in his personal New World:

> August 18, 1805 … Rose at half past six. Slipped on my shoes and morning gown, and went down to walk in the garden. Met the sergeant and bid him bon-jour … Meditated during my

walk upon the extreme folly of general De Caen
keeping me prisoner here ... but this will
not bear to be dwelt upon, it leads almost to
madness ... Got up into the tall almond tree to
see if there was any ship off; none to see ...
General De Caen's conduct must have
originated in unjust suspicion, – been prosecuted
in revenge, his dignity being injured at my
refusing to dine with him, and continued from
obstinacy and pride ... stripped myself naked,
and washed from head to foot in the little
tub ... Took three pinches of snuff whilst I sat
thinking of my wife and friends in England.
Mem. Must not take so much snuff when I
return ... drank three glasses of Madeira ... Find
myself a little sleepy. Don't know whether to go
down and play a game of Billiards with the
old sergeant, to drive it off; or take a nap.
Determined on the latter and laid down my
bed ... Waked. Had a head–ach and looked very
pale. Went down to the gate and sat down in the
sentry box, looking at the people who passed
by ... The sentry talking with his comrade said
Bonaparte was only 38 years old when he made
himself Emperor ... Went to bed at half past
nine. Lay for some time considering for some
time upon the causes of the trade and the
westerly winds, especially upon the earth's
revolution round its axis ... must have some
kind of trap set for that rat, which comes
disturbing me every night ... Dropped asleep

soon after ten. Waked about one by the noise of the soldiers in the guard house, who are playing about and running after each other like children … Wish that loud-voiced fellow had taken a dose of opium. Fell asleep again … Dreamed that General De Caen was setting a lion upon me to devour me, and that he eat me up. Was surprised to find devouring so easy to be born …

Thomas Pitot, his new friend, was worried about the Englishman's state of mind. Pitot convinced Governor Decaen to allow him to move to a sugar plantation in the middle of the island. Flinders packed up his few personal belongings and moved inland, climbing higher towards the Wilhelm Plain.

Things began looking up, considerably. The sugar plantation was owned by a widow, Madam D'Arifat, also sympathetic to Flinders' plight. Madam D'Arifat had five children, including three lovely young daughters. The eldest was the particularly lovely Delphine, twenty years old.

Madam D'Arifat inquired as to Flinders' 'situation'. Flinders was elusive: 'Madame was a little inquisitive concerning my voyages, the causes of my imprisonment here, my shipwreck, and finally of my family in England … I added nothing more than answered the questions: I did not say, that amongst my other grievances I had a beloved wife in England who was expecting my return in sickness and in tears …'

Indeed, on October 22, 1805, Flinders received

his very first letters since being imprisoned, from his beloved, tearful wife. It would take Flinders a full month before he wrote back to her. The same day that he received Ann's letter, however, he wrote to Madame D'Arifat: 'She had before made me an offer to live with her without expense, which I declined; but I find the family so very agreeable and interesting, that I am become desirous of being as much with them as possible.'

Previously, Flinders had declined to live in the house, saying he preferred a bungalow out the back. The same day that he received Ann's letters, Flinders agreed to move inside the house, just down the corridor from Delphine's bedroom. His days spent with Delphine and her sisters were soon keeping him awake at night: 'After dinner … I join the ladies again, either in a walk, or in conversation before the house. After tea … we retire to the parlour for the evening … sometimes in singing and flute playing, or sometimes at cards. At nine we sup, and at ten retire to bed; where the agreeable employments of the day often occupy so much of my thoughts as to prevent me from sleeping.'

Flinders wholeheartedly approved of the young ladies' attire, the latest fashions from Revolutionary Paris: 'In the dress of the ladies I remarked nearly the same singularity as I have before noticed in the account of them at the comedy: Very delightful to behold …' His night at 'the comedy' had been a rare excursion while he had been at the 'Garden Prison'. Flinders had been permitted, in the company of some French officers, one night at the Opera, where it had not been so much the show, but the audience, that had enthralled him: 'The younger women were some of them very pretty, and there was one that might be very well called a beauty … The necks of almost all, and the shoulders, and bosoms, and nearly half the breasts were uncovered, as well as the arms nearly to the shoulders. They seemed to have good clear skins, and well turned necks and bosoms for the most part, and large eyes that were by no means destitute of power. An equal number of women, equally dressed, would I think raise an uproar in one of our English theatres.'

Flinders had grown to like French people. And he especially liked the D'Arifat family: 'This family, particularly Mademoiselle Delphine, become daily more interesting. She is indeed an extraordinary young lady, possessing a strength of mind, a resolution, and a degree of penetration which few men can boast of.' Some French customs baffled him, though. A few days later, after a dinner party, Flinders and another guest offered to walk Delphine and her sister home: 'Our principal purpose was to conduct home the two young ladies … but it appeared that they dare not trust themselves with us for half a league … Thus the same ladies who dance with naked bosoms before a whole society, feared to walk half a league in open daylight with two gentlemen of their acquaintance.'

Flinders finally sat down and wrote to Ann:

Thy dear letters of May 12. And June 14, 1805 I received, my best love … What a relief did these letters bring to me! Since Sept. 1802 I had

known nothing of thee or any one of my
relations; and my letters of that date had told
me of the death of my dear father and of the
miserable state of thy health. I knew not what to
fear … now I can dwell upon the domestic
scene my imagination continually raises with a
solid and heartfelt satisfaction. I know that I have
still a beloved wife whose ~~bosom~~ healthful frame
is agitated only by her sighs at my absence …
Receive my best beloved, my thanks for thy
communications, but especially for thy sweet
assurances of unaltered affection; and with them
receive my vows of ~~fidelity continued~~ constant
unabated love.

The words crossed-out are as they appear in
Flinders' *Private Letters* book, in which he wrote a draft
before penning the final pages he would send. At least
Ann did not see the last two words he had felt compelled to cross out, and did not need to agonise as to
the reason why. Flinders' letter continued:

… it is with the eldest son, of about 27 years,
and the eldest daughter of about 20 that I have
more particularly attached myself. Thou canst
not conceive how anxious they are to see and be
acquainted with thee, ~~to have thee amongst~~
~~them~~. Though unknown, I scarcely think thou
art less dear to Mademoiselle Delphine D'Arifat
than to many of thy relations: She talks of
making a voyage to England in the peace in

order to see more of our English manners and to make acquaintance with thee.

One can imagine how Ann felt on receiving this letter, learning that her husband was not only free on parole, but in the company of a charming, beautiful young woman, while in a frail and vulnerable state of mind. All the other threats her husband had faced suddenly paled into insignificance as this new threat appeared on the horizon. She had almost lost him to shipwreck and scurvy but he had survived; would she now lose him to another woman? The Unknown had suddenly found Ann, right in her living room, confronting her from the sheets she held in her trembling hands.

Ann sat down and wrote her husband another letter. In this one, she offered to sail out to Île-de-France, to be with him, that their prisons might converge and be the same.

That letter, however, like all correspondence from Europe, would take a long time to arrive. In the meantime, Flinders spent the evening dancing with Delphine and her sister: 'I adventured to waltze for the first time, with my two fair instructresses. The contra-danses and waltzes continued till midnight … what is more surprising Miss Delphine rose at six as usual and went out to bathe.'

Suddenly, on Boxing Day, 1805, Madame D'Arifat sent her eldest daughter away to visit her brother on the far side of the island. Flinders was upset and wrote Delphine a letter on New Year's Day. He enclosed a gift:

My dear Miss D'Arifat … do me the favour of accepting a little fan … the smallness of its price is by no means a measure of my regard, but will demonstrate the sense I entertain of your delicacy … for my own interest I wish you may have a little solitary time in which to remember the absent … there is a certain unfortunate Englishman at the Refuge scarcely less anxious of a place in your recollection … if you know my heart, you will remember, that in my evening walks, I am thinking with admiration and gratitude of those individuals in this island … who have received me into their bosom, and of which, my friend, you are so bright an ornament … Remember the expression <u>à jamais,</u> and if the word <u>doucement</u>! escapes your lips, remember the pain it once caused me. Your beauty – but this is the affair of your lover, and therefore no concern of mine … Adieu, my dear Miss D'Arifat.

Delphine eventually returned from exile, but her relationship with Flinders then disintegrated. Flinders was coy as to the reasons for the collapse: 'The conduct of one of my friends in this house has continued to give me much pain … keeping just within the rules of decency …' During Delphine's absence, Flinders may have had time to reflect on what he owed to the woman he had left behind in England, and how desperately he wanted to see her again after an absence of almost five years. Delphine had simply been a distraction: 'Delphine has not recovered from the state of sadness … I believe she sheds many tears in secret: she is changed considerably.'

The days dragged on, into weeks, months, years. Flinders received Ann's letter in which she offered to sail out to join him. He hesitated. He considered the idea: 'What a joyful event will this be for me! Nothing in the world could give me so much satisfaction. How swiftly shall I fly to thee, my best life! Oh how my heart pants for the moment!' He changed his mind: 'Of all things in the world, I most desire thy presence here, since I cannot come to thee; but of all things in the world I should most dread thy undertaking such a voyage … No my dearest, it cannot be. I ask thee not to undertake it.' He dared not risk her life on the treacherous seas – seas still gripped by war. His depression deepened, as he confided to his private journal:

> … there is a weight of sadness at the bottom of my heart, that presses down and enfeebles my mind … I am satisfied nowhere. When in company I wish the time came to break up, and when alone I am no more happy … I may truly say, that I have no pleasure in life … the energy of my mind is I fear lost for ever …

Chapter 35

[BAUDIN THE TERRIBLE]

I n August, 1806, Napoléon gave his royal decree for an official account of Baudin's voyage to be written. As early as June, 1804, Jussieu had urged the government to fund the publication of an account of Baudin's voyage: 'It will be glorious for France to forestall, by the publication of this voyage, a nation which despite its settlements and resources in this new region has published nothing that approaches the work of our naturalists.' Two years later, still nothing had happened.

Normally, the commander of an expedition writes the historical account of a voyage of discovery.

But Baudin was dead. In the absence of the commander, the task of writing could be handed to one of the next most senior officers. Both Hamelin and Milius, however, were busy prosecuting the war. Even after the disaster of Trafalgar, the French Navy still had to struggle on and desperately needed every experienced officer it could get. So Péron applied for the job.

Péron had worked tirelessly since his return to France, handing out parts of Baudin's magnificent natural history collection to anyone who might assist his cause. After he helped Joséphine secure most of the live animals, the *Société des Observateurs de l'Homme* was disbanded, so Péron then sent her a gift of another 206 items: 'A great quantity of weapons, implements and clothing of the savage people of Van Diemen's Land, Maria Island, New Holland and the many archipelagos of the South Seas.' The artefacts from the South Seas were those donated by George Bass.* Péron hoped that Joséphine's passion for exotica could win him a powerful patron, and perhaps even curry favour with her husband. Péron beseeched Joséphine to whisper in the ear of her 'glorious spouse' and to intercede on his behalf to secure funds to publish: 'More than ever you are indispensable to us … our work is suspended … we have obligations of honour to meet.' In France, with Napoléon the self-declared Emperor, the culture of self-promotion was on the rise, and Péron felt right at home. He even penned letters directly to Napoléon,

---

* The entire priceless collection was later lost forever when it was auctioned, together with Joséphine's furniture, after her death in 1814 (Horner p. 330).

reminding the Emperor of the eucalyptus seedlings that had been planted and how one day, 'seated in the shade of these gigantic trees, and meditating on the wonders of your reign, will not our nephews one day say: "And these forests also, are among the blessings of the great Napoléon!"'

Péron was not afraid of hyperbole. The moment the mission had returned, he had been quick to write a letter to the new Minister of Marine, Decrès, presenting himself as the person solely responsible for delivering back to France the magnificent natural history collection transported in the *Géographe*. In the letter he claimed to be the only surviving naturalist not to have died or left the mission. He implied that he alone had collected most of the animals and cared for them during the voyage.

After the desertions and deaths of so many of the other scientists on board the *Géographe*, he had worked hard during the voyage, taking on extra responsibilities and duties. He was partly responsible for the sheer size and quality of the natural history collection returned to France. But his letter to Decrès was an outright lie and had started him on his slippery slide away from the truth.

Péron's handling of the vast natural history collection entrusted into his care by Milius was lamentable. Many of the dried and preserved specimens were entrusted to Labillardière, the chief naturalist of the d'Entrecasteaux expedition. Labillardière only published a few of the findings of the expedition and Baudin's collection was ultimately mixed up with that of the d'Entrecasteaux expedition. Much of the collection remained disorganised and inaccessible to scientists for years. Labillardière eventually appears to have claimed the entire Australian collection as his private property which was then sold to private collectors along with the d'Entrecasteaux collection after Labillardière's death. Much of what Péron did not hand out to secure favours, he kept for himself. Later, Georges Cuvier would lament that the Baudin collection never realised its scientific potential: 'The Baudin expedition to New Holland, where Messrs Péron and Lesueur made immense collections ... did not give us, for science proper, fruits proportional to the rich materials it procured.' Cuvier had no hesitation in laying the blame at the feet of Péron: 'To assure for himself the sole glory for his discoveries ... he kept carefully to himself all the manuscripts, and even all the pictures accompanying them, though he could not claim they were his own work.'

Péron's tireless lobbying finally paid off. On August 4, 1806, Napoléon signed a decree commissioning an official account of Baudin's voyage and findings, to be written in three volumes by Péron. A task was even found for Louis Freycinet who would prepare the charts. Péron had written to the Freycinet brothers seeking their collaboration a few months earlier. So the story of Baudin's voyage would be written by his worst enemies. The chest containing Baudin's journal as well as all the other journals, charts and findings of the mission was entrusted to Péron and Freycinet.

Writing with Baudin's journal open beside him, Péron could address his commander's criticisms of him one by one, presenting his own, far more lively account of all the times he got himself lost. These episodes were now described as dangerous adventures where only the quick thinking, resourcefulness and sheer dogged determination of intrepid Péron saved the day. Sometimes, Péron even felt obliged to correct Baudin's writing. Where Baudin had written: 'Throughout the whole voyage no one has ever known where I was going or what I wanted to do …' Péron is suspected to be the person who scribbled '… nor what I was doing'. In Péron's book, remarkably, he refused to refer to Baudin by name, preferring instead to call him the commandant, often preceded by an adjective, such as 'incompetent' or 'wretched'. The only time Péron mentioned Baudin by name in his account of the expedition, was in describing Baudin's death. Nor was he prepared to give Baudin's name any recognition when he and Freycinet renamed the charts. They threw themselves at this task with gusto, naming hills and bays after one another. They were fair about it; Péron's name was honoured in ten different places on the French charts and Freycinet's name also appeared in ten places. Only one feature was named after their commandant, the 'Baudin Islet', a tiny speck of land within the massive 'Freycinet Estuary'. Of course, Péron and Freycinet did not forget to honour their patrons. Baudin's Golfe Misanthropie became Golfe Joséphine and Flinders' 'Spencer's Gulf' became Golfe Bonaparte. What Flinders had called 'Kangaroo Island' and Baudin had called Île Borda became Île Decrès.

Péron realised that his own professional reputation now hinged intimately on the perception of Baudin's expedition. In his book he adopted the strategy of blaming any of the mission's perceived shortcomings on the now deceased commander. Péron accused Baudin, now unable to defend himself, of having been the root of all problems, a man who had caused the deaths of his own best friends Maugé, Riedlé and Levillain, a man who had 'lost all rights to the confidence of the government, and of honourable men'.

In 1807, the ever-so-honourable Péron completed the first volume of his masterpiece *Voyage de Decouvertes aux Terres Australes*. He personally presented a copy to Napoléon who then, supposedly, made his famous observation: 'Baudin did well to die; on his return I would have had him hanged.'*

After all his hardships, including the ultimate sacrifice of his life, rather than securing the admiration of Napoléon and the scientific community, Baudin's reputation was mud.

---

* This damning of Baudin by Napoléon, no doubt gave Péron great satisfaction, assuming Bonaparte actually said it. The quote comes from Péron's biographer. The original source of the quote was presumably Péron's version of the meeting, and not Bonaparte's — and as can be seen by much of what Péron wrote, the veracity of the story must be open to question (Horner, p. 338).

Chapter 36

[GULF IN THE TRUTH]

In 1808, still imprisoned on his sugar plantation, Flinders read in an old Parisian newspaper that Péron had published a narrative of the French expedition. Flinders was desperate to know what was written in the book: 'The voyage of M. Baudin is in publication. I am curious to know how the work will speak of me and the treatment he received at Port Jackson. The contrast of his and my reception is so great that some management will be required not to expose French honour to too much criticism.'

The publication of the French book reminded

Flinders how long he had been delayed in completing his own mission. Frustratingly, little by little, further details of Péron's book began to reach Flinders. On January 7, 1809, Pitot brought him some fresh newspapers from France. The news was old in Paris, but completely new to Flinders and what he read made Flinders suspect that the French were still determined to win the race, by fair means or foul: 'In a *Moniteur* of July 1808, I read a letter of M. Henri Frécynet; by which it appears that that part of the South coast of Australia discovered by me, as well as that first seen by Lt. Grant and M. Baudin is to be called <u>Terre Napoléon</u>; that Kangaroo Island is to be called <u>Isle Decrès,</u> and my two gulphs are to be named <u>Golphe Bonaparte</u> and <u>Golphe Joséphine</u>.'

Incensed, Flinders wrote to Ann: 'Whilst general De Caen keeps me a prisoner here, they have taken possession in France of a considerable part of my discoveries. The before unknown part of the south coast of Australia was principally discovered by me; but at Paris they have given it the name of <u>Terre Napoléon</u>.'

Flinders felt that his suspicions regarding the reasons for his internment were practically confirmed. 'I know not whether to attribute these incroachments to the editors of the Voyage [Péron, Freycinet, Lesueur] or to the French government. If it arises from the latter, there is very probably some connexion between them and my long detention in this island.'

Furious and helpless he wrote to Banks: 'In my charts transmitted to the admiralty, the parts discovered by Mr. Grant, by Mr. Baudin, and by me, are distinctly and impartially marked; and what is more, I shewed these charts to Mr. Baudin at Port Jackson, and he raised no objection to the division.'

In March, 1809, Flinders was informed that he would soon receive a surprising visitor: 'Captain Hamelin ... desires to see me, but fears to displease the captain general in coming into the country for that purpose.' Hamelin, former commander of the *Naturaliste*, had been promoted dramatically during the war and now arrived to replace Admiral Linois, to take command of the French Fleet in the Indian Ocean. Hamelin did not wish to meet Flinders face to face, but Flinders managed to get a message to Hamelin inquiring whether he might have a copy of Péron's book: 'I suppose that he would have on board his ship the voyage of Captain Baudin, but he says not. The first volume only was published when he left France, in which honourable mention is made of me ... the parts of the south coast of Australia lately made known, are entitled <u>Discoveries of M.M. Flinders and Baudin</u>.'

This news eased Flinders' fears to a great degree. Pitot then brought Flinders further good news: apparently his old rivals were doing everything in their power to try to help him. 'He tells me also from captain Hamelin, that all the officers of the *Géographe* and *Naturaliste*, but particularly M.M. Hamelin and Péron, had made application with the marine minister for my liberation, and that the minister had several times answered, that an order had been sent out for that purpose.'

Indeed, Flinders' release had been ordered, by

Napoléon himself. Following the lobbying by Joseph Banks and Thomas Pitot, members of *Le Institut* had finally requested an audience with Emperor Bonaparte. Flinders' case was presented by the venerable, now 77 years old, Louis-Antoine de Bougainville, who had found the Emperor in a good mood. It had taken years for Flinders' case to reach Napoléon. It took a few minutes for Napoléon to make up his mind to release him. Three copies of the order were then immediately dispatched on three separate ships destined for Île-de-France.

The first ship had been captured by the British a few weeks later. Without reading any of the dispatches the English officers threw the order overboard. The second ship had been intercepted some months later, the dispatches suffering the same fate. The third ship sailed on.

Finally, the order for Flinders' release arrived. Though the order came from the Emporer himself, Decaen at first ignored it. Decaen now viewed Flinders as a hostage and only when the British invasion of Île-de-France looked imminent, did he finally release his prisoner.

On June 13, 1810, Flinders boarded the *Harriet* and sailed out of Port Napoléon: 'After a captivity of six years, five months and twenty-seven days, I at length had the inexpressible pleasure of being out of the reach of general De Caen.'

It appears that Decaen made a secret deal with his British adversary, Major-General Abercromby, to secure his own liberty in exchange for Flinders, should the island fall. And fall it did.

In the same month that Flinders finally departed Île-de-France, Napoléon dispatched reinforcements to the island. Interestingly, the reinforcements were not solely for the defence of the island, but also for another purpose as Napoléon outlined in a letter: 'It is proposed, on the arrival of these expeditions, to take the English colony of Port Jackson.'

The arrival of Napoléon's letter, however, was followed all too quickly by the British. The British invasion arrived on December 2, 1810. British Naval superiority delivered 10,000 troops to march on the island's capital. As Decaen had feared, he was heavily outnumbered with only 4,000 troops. There were 10,000 militia on the island, but as Decaen had also feared, these men were inadequately trained and too ready to desert. Soon after, he capitulated to Abercromby.

Flinders had been detained for six weeks at the Cape of Good Hope by Vice-Admiral Bertie, who was assisting with the plans to invade Île-de-France, and persuaded Flinders to draw a map of the island's defences. Flinders initially declined, reminding Bertie that such an act would be in breach of his parole. Bertie insisted and Flinders succumbed.

Chapter 37

On October 24, 1810, Flinders stepped back onto the wharf at Spithead. The next day, he came face to face with Ann Chappelle.

The couple were finally in the same part of the world, the same country. The same room. Alone together. In a hotel in London the couple found themselves in a new unknown. They had to navigate what was essentially a new relationship. Ann had been thirty-one when he left. She was now forty-one. There was pain and joy in the reunion. It was, for Flinders, an extremely private moment: 'I need not describe to you our meeting after near ten years absence …' Husband and wife, friends and lovers. They were briefly interrupted by one of Flinders' shipmates, who quickly made his excuses, as he later wrote to his commander: 'I felt so sensibly the affecting scene of your meeting Mrs Flinders that I could not have remained any longer in the room under any consideration.'

Ann took Flinders back to Lincolnshire, to show him off: 'I went with Mrs Flinders to visit her old friends … to all of whom she wished to show her lion.' Again and again, to an open-mouthed audience, Flinders told the tale of his adventures. At Ann's request he left out some of the details of his story; his incarceration, the invalidity of his passport and his attitude to Decaen.

Flinders then secured a copy of Péron's book. He sat down and began to read. When he had finished the book, he was in shock.

The audacity of the conspiracy amazed him: 'It was kept out of sight that I had ever been upon the coast; and in speaking of M. Péron's first volume the newspapers asserted, that no voyage ever made by the English nation could be compared with that of the *Géographe* and *Naturaliste*.' Péron had even asserted that the French had not missed Port Phillip Bay, but had actually seen it from the masthead of *Le Géographe*.

Flinders was tormented with questions. Who precisely was responsible for this, was it the French government, was it the author, or had Baudin himself misrepresented the facts as far back as Port Jackson?

Flinders struggled to determine exactly where to lay the blame. He suspected the author: 'Péron was present at Port Jackson, when I showed one of my charts of this coast to captain Baudin, and pointed out the limits of his discovery ... How then came M. Péron to advance what was so contrary to the truth? Was he a man destitute of all principle? ... The motive for this aggression I do not pretend to explain. It may ... be intended as the fore runner of a claim to the possession of the countries so said to have been first discovered by French navigators.'

The Royal British Navy had their own suspicions, as stated by an anonymous reviewer of Péron's book, believed to have been John Barrow, a member of the Admiralty:

> The perusal of M. Péron's book has convinced us that ... the passport was fraudulently obtained; that there never was any intention to send these vessels on a voyage of discovery ... but that the sole object of it was to ascertain ... what our colonists were doing, and what was left for the French to do ... a strong suspicion arises that the whole has the effect of a premeditated design to snatch the merit of the discovery from its rightful possessor, for the purpose of setting up a claim, at some future day, to this part of New Holland. The circumstances of Captain Flinders' unjust detention, as a prisoner, on the isle of France, was an admirable incident to favour this design.

For Flinders, regardless of who was to blame, the solution to this outrage was obvious. He intended to write his own book to set the record straight.

Soon after, Flinders visited Sir Joseph. By chance, Captain William Bligh was there. The three men examined the charts Flinders had sent back from Île-de-France several years before. Bligh complimented Flinders on the quality of his work. To Flinders' surprise, his old adversary 'said more in favour of my charts than I expected'. Only then did Sir Joseph look closely at the charts that Flinders had sent to him, only then did he seem to appreciate Flinders' considerable charting achievements. Flinders was bemused: 'He seemed scarcely aware before of the extent of my examinations.'

The two men then tackled the thorny issue of 'names' – in particular, the name Flinders had suggested to eliminate confusion regarding 'New South Wales' versus 'New Holland'. Flinders again advocated the name 'Australia'. Sir Joseph did not like it. The cartographer Aaron Arrowsmith was also present and agreed with Sir Joseph, preferring to maintain 'New Holland'. Flinders was frustrated: 'New Holland and New South Wales were known to form one land, there should be a general name applicable to the whole.'

As a compromise, Flinders suggested adopting a French idea: 'A neighbouring, and even rival nation ... speak of these countries under the general term of Terres Australes ... and having no reference to either of the two claiming nations, appears to be less objectionable than any other …'The two 'claiming nations' were of course France and England. Banks and Arrowsmith finally agreed on the compromise, though they insisted on latinising it to Terra Australis. Flinders still felt aggrieved: 'Had I permitted myself any innovation upon the original term, it would have been to convert it into AUSTRALIA.'

Flinders and Banks also discussed the idea of Flinders writing an account of his voyage. Flinders was then dismayed that although the Admiralty were interested in publishing his charts, they were not interested in funding him to write a book.

He had already met disappointment from the Admiralty in trying to secure back-pay for his promotion to post-captain, to include the time he had been locked up on Île-de-France. Flinders was hurt that certain members of the Admiralty seemed not only to underestimate what he had been through, but did not appreciate the enormity of the task they had originally set him: 'I beg leave to observe, that I was deputed to examine the coasts of a country, which, in a superficial extent, is little inferior to all the kingdoms of Europe; and this … was expected to be performed in about four years, including the passage out there and home of near six months each.'

Ann too was indignant. 'In addition to the misfortune of shipwreck – of being nine years cast off from society and the bosom of his family … he was by this last stroke made to feel that this, instead of obtaining for him any extraordinary reward for his services, had in reality deprived him of six years of that rank in the Navy to which he was so justly entitled.'*

Some in the Admiralty felt that Flinders got what he deserved. He had not dispatched his charts of the south coast back quickly from Port Jackson as ordered, he had not charted the west and north-west coasts of New Holland and instead he had wasted time charting areas not stipulated in his sailing orders. He had done a heroic job following shipwreck, but his attitude when meeting Decaen had been plainly foolish. Some members of the Admiralty even insinuated that Flinders had collaborated with his captors, or at any rate, was too friendly with them. Many felt that he should have 'considered it a naval officer's duty to attempt to escape, not to live comfortably on the enemy's charity on parole'.

Most importantly, following Trafalgar, the French were not a threat on the oceans. For the moment, the Admiralty did not need Flinders' story to counteract French claims to New Holland. If the French tried to make a colony on the west coast, the Royal Navy would just blast them out of the water.

The fact that the Admiralty would not help him

---

* Flinders pursued back-pay for his time in prison like a man on a mission. After receiving promotion to 'post-captain' as had been promised by the Earl St Vincent on his departure, Flinders continued to argue for his promotion to be backdated to 1803. This was the date he would have returned had he not become a prisoner-of-war on Île-de-France. But St Vincent's successor, Charles Yorke, was only willing to backdate the promotion until May 7, 1810, the time at which he himself became the new First Lord of the Admiralty. Yorke was also reluctant to set a precedent of awarding full pay to prisoners-of-war. Britain currently had thousands of them abroad (Ingleton, p. 400).

publish a book to counter Péron's claims was a bitter pill for Flinders to swallow: 'No means were spared by the French government to enhance the merit of their voyage ... but the *Investigator*'s voyage seemed to obtain as little public notice in England as in France ... It would ill become me to say that in one case there was an ostentatious munificence, or in the other, injustice and neglect ... the extreme difference made between the two voyages could not but add to the bitterness of my situation.'

Flinders was determined to set the record straight. He retired from the Navy on half-pay, determined to write his book, virtually at his own expense.

Chapter 38

[RACE TO THE FINISH]

Flinders began work on his *magnum opus*, *A Voyage to Terra Australis*. If he completed the book he would be paid by receiving a share of the profits. Flinders was optimistic: 'After my task is completed, if nothing better turns up, I intend to purchase a small house, with a garden, in the country; and there retire with my books to live upon my little income … I go no more to sea, unless it is upon discovery.' The young lieutenant who had thought that his voyage would be only the beginning of an illustrious career as a navigator and explorer, now realised he had made his last voyage. Flinders, once so young and ambitious and focused on what the future might hold, was now forced to dwell on the past. Ten years had been a lifetime.

Flinders reported on April 1, 1812: 'This afternoon Mrs Flinders was happily delivered of a daughter; to her great joy and to mine.' The little girl was christened 'Anne' in honour of her mother. Flinders described the new addition on the family scene in the same economical language he used to describe a new headland or bay: 'The child is a little black-eyed girl, without blemish, neither fat nor lean and has a decent enough appearance.' The baby girl was in good health. The same could not be said of her father. Ann was worried: 'To write an account of his voyage & discoveries ... this object after immense labours, by depriving himself of the necessary exercise conducive to health, curtailed his natural rest ...'

Flinders incorrectly assumed that he had a stone in the bladder. He was in a lot of pain, as he recorded in his journal: 'Continue to pass gravel, consisting of oblong small crystals, some bright, others discoloured with blood ... these crystals have always been more or less enveloped in mucus forming a pulpy mass ... the detached pieces feeling to be too large for the passage.'

The pain became worse and worse. In his journal Flinders recorded passing urine no less than fifty-two times in twenty-four hours. Soon, Ann hardly recognised her dashing young lieutenant: 'So dreadfully was he altered, he looked full 70 years of age, & was worn to a skeleton.'

Flinders raced on. He was pleased to learn that the publication of the next volumes concerning the French voyage had been delayed: 'Baudin's voyage is not yet finished. The funds destined for it have been diverted to other purposes. Péron's second volume is in slow progress … when they will be published seems quite uncertain … [my] publication is likely to take place in the spring of 1814; and I do not think that the French voyage of Baudin will be completed published before that time.'

Flinders then learned that Péron had died. Péron had known since arriving in France what he was suffering. He had seen the symptoms before. It began with tiny specks of blood on his handkerchief. It ended with Péron coughing up fragments of his own lungs, without which he died at the age of thirty-five. Louis Freycinet took over the preparation of the second and third volumes of the French publications. Indeed, in 1811 Freycinet published the second volume of *Voyage de Decouvertes aux Terres Australes* in which appeared the very first published chart to depict the whole continent of Terres Australes. In this the French did beat the English.

Flinders' finances continued to dwindle. The family moved from home to home in order to save money. The finishing line, however, was in sight.

On October 21, 1813, the printer delivered a copy of Flinders' 'Introduction' to his book. Flinders was working hard, but he was happy. During this new pursuit, Ann was travelling by his side, as was his daughter. Flinders watched his daughter grow: 'She now runs stoutly, and though able to say very few words makes herself understood.' The girl's mother was a little more effusive: 'She is, if you can credit the word of a Mother, very articulate, intelligent. She often reminds me of her dear father.'

Flinders raced on, finally racing death itself: 'Morning, noon and night I sit close at writing, and at my charts, and can hardly find time for anything else.' Flinders finished the book and sent it to the publisher.

The publishers set to work, rushing furiously. In the meantime, Flinders ordered a new copy of another book, his favourite, the one that helped to set him on the course of his life, *Robinson Crusoe*. As the last chapter read, 'I have given the first part of a life of fortune and adventure ... Beginning foolishly, but closing much more happily ... I could not keep the country out of my head, and had a great mind to be on the wing again.'

On July 10, Flinders began to take flight. He made his final entry in his private journal. It was a Sunday: 'Did not rise before two being I think, weaker than before.' The pain had become truly horrendous and Flinders began to drift in and out of consciousness. Ann watched her husband hopelessly. His doctor said he overheard Flinders murmuring; 'It grows late, boys, let us dismiss ...' His very last words before he lapsed into unconsciousness were, 'My papers!'

On July 18, 1814, the first printed copy of Flinders' book was rushed to his bedside. The following morning, Ann's sister, Isabella, described the scene:

I was awakened, by my Sister rising, she was going to the sick room – I begged her to let me go first – The sun shone brightly on me as I went down the stairs, – all seemed so still! … I went in … Dear Flinders! – I stood at the foot of the bed contemplating the scene for a few moments, then rushed up stairs to my Sister. She was in the room of death & pressed his cold lips to hers … it was a heartbreaking effort … Her dear babe … the poor child felt that something dreadful had happened, but did not know what, & putting her little fingers to wipe the tears from her mother's eyes, she said 'Don't cry Mamma.'

Chapter 39

[E N D   G A M E]

The year after Flinders' death, Napoléon was deposed. He was imprisoned on an isolated island, St Helena, where his only solace was the garden he built with his own hands, planting exotic plants, many of them the strange species of Terres Australes.* In the evenings, from his window at Longwood, Bonaparte watched the British convict ships stopping off on their way to Port Jackson.

Following the restoration of the monarchy, many

---

* One of them, the paper daisy, quickly spread across the whole of his prison 'Longwood' and today is across the entire island.

of the names Péron and Freycinet had imposed on Baudin's charts, especially names such as 'Terre Napoléon' and 'Golfe Bonaparte', were soon despised in France as much as in Britain.

Freycinet blamed the choice of names on the deceased Péron. In reward, Freycinet was eventually entrusted with his own mission that led him back to the west coast of Nouvelle Hollande in 1818. France had, by no means, lost interest in the unclaimed west coast. Freycinet was followed by Dumont d'Urville in 1826. The French continued to reconnoitre possible sites for a settlement, this time in King George Sound. The British had had enough. Two months after d'Urville's visit, marines were sent from Sydney to form a garrison at King George Sound. In 1826, the British extended their claim west from their original line of 130° longitude – claiming all of the continent that came to be known by the name Flinders had suggested – 'Australia'.

Flinders was fortunate. He had the chance to write and publish his own version of events. Baudin never had that chance. France's claim to Nouvelle Hollande, like Baudin's great achievements, was buried deep in the National Archives of France. Deep within this building, within the unread pages of Baudin's *Journal de Mer*, French claims were lost, as was Baudin the man.

Lost was his remarkable resilience and perseverance in securing unique charts of the western and north-western coasts of Australia, a coast today still peppered with hundreds of French names bestowed by his mission. Lost was Baudin's passion for zoology and botany, resulting in one of the greatest natural history collections the world has ever seen, crucial in laying the foundations of oceanography, ecology and anthropology. Lost were Baudin's enlightened observations on the land rights of indigenous people. Lost was the genuine 'Observer of Man' who remained true to the ideals of the *Société des Observateurs de l'Homme*, to observe without judgement. Lost was a man who struggled to prevail, fearless in the face of Death, succumbing with good humour.

[EPILOGUE]

Initially, the importance of Flinders' mission was also overlooked. *A Voyage to Terra Australis* did not sell as well as expected and Ann was eventually presented with a bill from the publishers to cover the shortfall in the costs of printing. Flinders did not acquire the financial security he hoped for his wife and baby daughter. Indeed he left his finances in a mess. Concerned that he might not be recognised for his great efforts, Flinders had asked that £100 from his estate be used to build a monument to commemorate himself. In his 'Last Will and Testament' Flinders was generous to all his relatives, to the point where his widow was constantly harassed by relatives seeking their inheritance. Flinders had overestimated what he would earn from the sale of his book and in honouring her husband's bequest Ann and her daughter's humble allotment of £1,200 soon vanished. Flinders left £500 to his brother. Ann forgave him: 'Had my dear Captain F_ seen his danger, he would never had left me in such a situation, with neither a bed nor a chair to call my own; his attention was particularly bent to concluding the voyage, without ever reverting to his own concerns, otherwise he would have provided for our comfort without leaving so much to others.'

In desperation, Ann wrote several times to the Admiralty seeking the same widow's pension that Captain Cook's wife had received. It took four years of persistence, but finally her case was settled. Her claim was rejected.

Learning of her plight, the governments of New South Wales and Victoria eventually granted Ann a pension of £100 per year. The first payment finally arrived in 1853, a year after she had died.

The memory of Flinders as a great navigator languished. In 1879, author John Shillinglaw planned to write a book telling the story of Flinders' life, proclaiming in a pamphlet to raise the funds: 'In the grand old Navy List of Britain, the names of James Cook and Matthew Flinders should ... stand side by side ... The Life and Voyages of Cook are to be found on every man's bookshelves ... No Life of Flinders has yet been published ...' The pamphlet failed to secure financial backing and Shillinglaw never wrote the book.

§ § §

It was only in the lead-up to Australia's Federation in 1901, exactly 100 years after Flinders had set off on his circumnavigation of the continent that he called 'Australia', that he began to receive his due recognition.* As a proud young country celebrated its birth, the searchers for national heroes dusted off the name 'Matthew Flinders' and began to polish it to a great sheen. In Australia, from 1901 onwards the name 'Flinders' embarked on its journey to becoming a household name. Today the name is honoured by a university, numerous towns, islands, national parks, schools, streets, a vast mountain range, and at least one pub. Modern-day hydrographers are in awe of his achievements. Some of the remarkable charts Flinders drew were still in use during World War II.

In contrast, in England, the country of his birth, Flinders still awaits such recognition. The situation has changed little from the day that his daughter Anne tried to find her father's gravestone. The search was futile, as Anne explained: 'The churchyard remodelled, and quantities of tombstones and graves with their contents had been carted away as rubbish, among them that of my unfortunate father, thus pursued by disaster after death, as in life.'

Today the site of Baudin's grave is also unknown.

---

* The name 'Australia' was officially adopted several years after Flinders' death. When copies of Flinders' book finally reached Port Jackson in April, 1817, the Governor Lachlan Macquarie liked the name 'Australia' as did the colonial-born inhabitants. The name quickly became the popular choice in NSW, and when Flinders' successor, Phillip Parker King, returned with his charts of exploration to London in 1823, they all bore the name 'Australia'. Finally the Hydrographic Office began to accept the name and published it for the first time officially in 1830.

For almost two centuries, so was any sense of Baudin's great achievements. But little by little, step by step, he has been discovered.

In 1878, Jules Verne published *Histoires des Grands Voyages et Grands Voyagers*. Verne's book seems to have been the first historical text to even include Baudin's expedition in telling the history of notable French explorations. Yet Verne did not read Baudin's own *Journal de Mer*, relying instead primarily on Péron's book. Verne's history did little to improve the perception of Baudin.

In 1910, in Australia, Ernest Scott published *Terre Napoléon*, in which the hitherto insignificant role of Baudin's expedition in the exploration of Australia was first questioned. English history until that point had been only too ready to minimise the importance of French explorations of the continent that the British had claimed exclusively. Scott questioned Péron's credentials and his version of events, but he did not have access to Baudin's personal *Journal de Mer*.

§ § §

In 1927, Arthur Jose, an Australian, discovered a copy of Baudin's *Journal de Mer* and began piecing together a very different version of events, concluding that 'altogether Baudin, to use a colloquialism, has not had a fair spin'. Alas, Jose died suddenly and the paper he had been preparing to deliver was instead delivered by the Australian naval historian Francis Bayldon. One author suggests that Bayldon then rewrote Jose's presentation to again denigrate Baudin as an incompetent and poor commander. Jose's defence of Baudin was eventually furthered in France by the research of Bouvier in the 1940s and Faivre in the 1950s. In the 1960s, John Dunmore lent his voice to the debate.

Events accelerated in 1963 when microfilm reels of Baudin's *Journal de Mer*, made by the National Archives of France, were brought to Australia through the initiative of Brian Baldwin from the State Library of South Australia. Author Christine Cornell then began work on translating the microfilm, which was published in 1974. Based on this translation, Baudin's reputation and character were rehabilitated by Frank Horner in his authoritative book *The French Reconnaissance*, published in 1987.

In the year 2000, author Anthony Brown was the first to highlight just how intimately Baudin's expedition was linked to Flinders.' The same year, having waited almost two centuries, through the initiative of Jacqueline Bonnemains, curator of the *Muséum d'Historie Naturelle* at Le Havre, Baudin's *Journal de Historique*, which focuses on the expedition's scientific findings until the first arrival in Timor, was published for the first time in October, 2000.

Baudin's *Journal de Mer*, however – Baudin's version of events as opposed to Péron's, the journal from which almost all Baudin's quotes in this book have been derived – has yet to be published in France.

In July, 2001, a historian objected to the erection of a statue honouring Baudin in Western Australia. The statue was to have been erected near Perth, part of the coast on which Baudin's expedition bestowed 240 French names still in use. The historian's objections have so far been successful and as this book goes to press, plans for the erection of the statue near Perth have been deferred indefinitely.

On a trip to France in September, 2001, I had trouble locating Baudin's original *Journal de Mer* while visiting the National Archives of France. When the staff finally found the precious four volumes containing Baudin's own version of the voyage, in his own handwriting, the volumes were literally in the basement, on the bottom shelf, hidden in shadow at the end of an aisle where the light-globe was on the blink. At last I saw the charts where Baudin's original names 'Ance des Regrets', 'Pointe de la Misère' and 'Golfe de la Misanthropie' had been crossed out in red ink and replaced by Péron and Freycinet's names.

Today, the name 'Flinders' is honoured in Australia in more than ninety places. The name 'Baudin' appears in only eight.

[ACKNOWLEDGMENTS]

This book could never have been written if not for the efforts of several other authors and historians. I am particularly indebted to Christine Cornell who completed the monumental task, in 1974, of translating Baudin's *Journal de Mer* from French into English. Tina kindly allowed me to quote extensively from her impressive translation thus enabling Baudin's own voice to feature prominently in this book. For similar reasons, I am equally indebted to Warwick Hirst from the Mitchell Library who provided me with transcriptions of Flinders' *Private Letters Books* and *Private Journal*. Warwick's work allowed me to read these documents with ease, as opposed to the painstaking task of trying to decipher Flinders' beautiful but practically illegible original writings. I am also grateful to the Libraries Board of South Australia which published a facsimile of Flinders' *Voyage to Terra Australis* in 1966, enabling me to read Flinders published book in the comfort of my home, rather than spending my whole life reading the two-hundred year old publication in libraries.

In terms of secondary sources about Baudin and Flinders, there are two 'Bibles' on which I have relied very heavily – Frank Horner's *The French Reconnaissance* and Geoffrey Ingleton's *Matthew Flinders:*

Navigator and Chartmaker. These two meticulously researched, authoritative texts provide the secondary foundation on which this book has been built. Horner and Ingleton are both responsible for definitive biographies of Baudin and Flinders, covering vast background material not included in the primary sources. I have quoted extensively from both these monumental works and I am most grateful to these two men.

I am also greatly indebted to the charming and generous Anthony Brown, author of *Ill-Starred Captains*. Though Anthony knew I intended to write a 'rival' book to his own, during the making of the documentary and writing of this book, he has constantly given liberally of his time and knowledge. Anthony was the first to publish a book that paralleled the Baudin and Flinders story in equal measure and during my research we had numerous enjoyable conversations and many of Anthony's skillfully researched 'Discoveries' are quoted in this book.

I am also grateful to the authors Catherine Retter and Shirley Sinclair. Catharine spent many hours in the Greenwich Maritime Museum sifting through Flinders' early correspondence while researching *Letters to Ann: The love story of Matthew Flinders and Ann Chappelle*, from which I have quoted several extracts. Thanks also to Paul Brunton from the Mitchell Library who shared with me many interesting details on Flinders' life based on his own extensive research and knowledge. Based in the Rare Books department at the State Library of Victoria, Des Cowley also gave generously of his time and expertise, as did Jacqueline

Bonnemains, author of several works regarding the achievements of Baudin's voyage and curator of the *Collection Lesueur* at the *Muséum d'Historie Naturelle*. Thank you Jacqueline for allowing me to film the magnificent Le Havre collection and to quote from your research.

For the research and ideas of so many authors that feature in this book – thank you John Dunmore, Arthur Jose, Alan Schom, Brian Baldwin, Ernest Scott, Miranda Hughes, Ann Moyal, Jill Duchess of Hamilton, Susan Hunt and Paul Carter, Sidney Baker, Edward Duyker, Carmelo Amalfi, Tim Flannery and the very charming sisters Madeleine Ly-Tio-Fane and Huguette Ly-Tio-Fane Pineo. Thanks also to the publishers of the *Encyclopaedia of Aboriginal Australia* and to Dr Philip Jones, anthropologist at the South Australian Museum.

It is fair to say that I would never have become aware of this story if I had not been approached to make a documentary about Matthew Flinders, hence I am also very grateful to the person who first initiated the idea of making the television program, Dione Gilmour, Executive Producer of the Natural History Unit at the Australian Broadcasting Corporation.

Many thanks to Ken Oldis and Catherine Hannebery who provided valuable preliminary research of the Baudin story for the documentary. Catherine's fine research skills and knowledge of French were a great help as was Ken 'Ned Kelly' Oldis' research and unique and passionate way of viewing the historical world and that of Revolutionary France in particular. Making the documentary has definitely helped shape the drama presented in this book, so thank you Michael Brindley for editing my early scripts for the documentary, which has similarly benefited this book. The same must also be said for the terrific efforts of Bruce Permezel, fellow TV producer and editor of the documentary – whose talent and endurance, not to mention good humour, has benefited both documentary and book.

Michael Duffy, your terrific and speedy editing skills were very much appreciated as was your support in recognising the potential of this book. Thanks to Ian Cruickshank, mariner and Flinders buff, who proof-read the manuscript and who first suggested the idea of giving the fabled strait a name, leading to this book referring to the mythical feature as 'Williamson's Strait'.

Last, but never least, I must thank my long-suffering family, not only for direct contributions to the book, but also for putting up with my long absences away filming as well as my absences research-ing and writing when I should have been home, sharing the load of looking after two wonderful, bois-terous daughters. To my amazing, darling wife Lee, who also holds down a job as a solicitor, I thank you tenderly for your incessant proofreading, clear-thinking, advice and love. Thank you to my cherished daughters, Madeleine and Natalie, for your love, for making me laugh and keeping me sane, almost.

[BIBLIOGRAPHY]

Primary Sources

Baudin, Nicolas (translated from the French by Christine Cornell): *The Journal of post Captain Nicolas Baudin, Commander-in-Chief of the corvettes Géographe and Naturaliste, assigned by order of the government to a voyage of discovery.* With a foreword by Jean-Paul Faivre. Adelaide: Libraries Board of South Australia, 1974.

Historical Records of New South Wales: *Letters from Commodore Baudin to Governor King.* Vol. 5, 1803–1805.

Historical Records of New South Wales: *Letters from Commodore Baudin to Governor King.* Vol. 4, 1800–1802.

Flinders, Matthew. *A Voyage to Terra Australis: undertaken for the purpose of completing the discovery of that vast country, and pros- ecuted in the years 1801, 1802, and 1803, in His Majesty's ship the Investigator* … London: G. and W. Nicol, 1814. (Republished by the Libraries Board of South Australia, Adelaide, 1966.)

Flinders, Matthew. '*Private Letters Books, 1801–1814, including letters from his wife Ann, 1814–1821.*' Vols. 1–3. (ML S1/55–57) Unpublished manuscripts transcribed by Warwick Hirst, held at Mitchell Library, Sydney.

Flinders, Matthew. '*Private Journal, 1803–1814.*' (ML S1/58) Unpublished manuscript transcribed by Warwick Hirst, held at Mitchell Library, Sydney.

Flinders, Matthew. *Extracts of letters etc. from the Admiralty and Colonial Officer recorder.* Transcribed by William Petrie. Latrobe Library Australian manuscripts collection, Melbourne.

Milius, Pierre Bernard. *Recit du voyage aux terres Australes par P.B. Milius Second sur le Naturaliste dans l'expedition Baudin (1800–1804).* Transcribed by Jacqueline Bonnemains &

P. Haughel; Muséum d'Histoire Naturelle Le Havre, 1987.
(Excerpts quoted from translations by Frank Horner, 1987
and Anthony Brown, 2000.)

Péron, François. *A Voyage of Discovery to the Southern
Hemisphere performed by Order of the Emperor Napoléon during
the years 1801, 1802, 1803 and 1804*. English translation by
R. Phillips. B. McMillan, London, 1809. (Republished by
Marsh Walsh Publishing, Melbourne, 1975.)

Secondary Sources

Baldwin, Brian S. *Flinders and the French*. In *Proceedings of the
Royal Geographical Society of Australasia*, SA Branch, Vol. 65,
1964.

Baldwin, Brian S. *French sources for South Australian history*. In
Proceedings of the Royal Geographical Society of Australasia, SA
Branch, Vol. 64, 1963.

Brosse, Jacques. *Great voyages of exploration: Circumnavigators and
Scientists, 1764–1843*. Translated by Stanley Hochman, preface by Fernand Braudel. Doubleday, Lane Cove, NSW, 1983.

Baker, Sidney J. *My Own Destroyer. A biography of Matthew
Flinders*. Currawong Publishing, Sydney, 1962.

Bonnemains, J., E. Forsyth & B. Smith. *Baudin in Australian
Waters: The artwork of the French voyage of discovery to the
Southern Lands 1800–1804*. Oxford University Press,
Melbourne, 1988.

Brown, Anthony J. *Ill-Starred Captains: Flinders & Baudin*.
Crawford House, South Australia, 2000.

Brown, Anthony J. *Friends of Humanity: The scientific Origins,
Objectives and Outcomes of the Voyages of Nicolas Baudin and
Matthew Flinders*. In *South Australian Geographical Journal*,
Vol. 98, 52–60, 1999.

Brown, Anthony J. *The Captain and the Convict Maid: A
Chapter in the Life of Nicolas Baudin*. In *South Australian
Geographical Journal*, Vol. 97, 20–32, 1998(a).

Brown, Anthony J. *Flinders, Baudin and the Unknown Coast*.
Paper presented at the *Encounter 2002 Public Forum*,
South Australia, 15 July, 1998(b).

Bruce, Evangeline. *'Napoléon and Joséphine. An Improbable Marriage'*. Phoenix Giant, London, 1996.

de Beer, Gavin. *The Sciences were never at War*. Nelson, London, 1960.

Defoe, Daniel. *Robinson Crusoe*. Penguin, 1965.

Dunmore, John. *French Explorers in the Pacific*, Vols. I&II. Oxford University Press, London, 1965.

Dunmore, John. *Pacific Explorer*. The Dunmore Press, New Zealand, 1985.

Dunmore, John. *Visions and Realities; France in the Pacific 1695–1995*. Heritage Press, New Zealand, 1997.

Duyker, Edward. *In search of Madame Kerivel and Baudin's last resting place:* National Library of Australia News (September, 1999), NLA, Canberra, 1999.

Encyclopaedia of Aboriginal Australia. Edited by David Horton. Aboriginal Studies Press. Canberra, 1994.

'Gazetteer of Australia, 2001'. By the Committee on Geographic Names in Australia. www.auslig.gov.au/mapping/names/natgaz.htm (24.1.2002).

Gurney, Alan. *Below the Convergence*. Pimlico, London, 1997.

Hamilton, Jill, Duchess of. *Napoléon, the Empress & the Artist*. Kangaroo Press, Sydney, 1999.

Horner, Frank B. *The French Reconnaissance: Baudin in Australia 1801–1803*. Melbourne University Press, Melbourne, 1987.

Hughes, Miranda J. *Philosophical Travellers at the Ends of the Earth*. In *Australian Science in the Making. Bicentennial Essays*. Cambridge University Press, Melbourne, 1988.

Hunt, Susan & Carter, Paul. *Terre Napoléon: Australia through French Eyes 1800–1804*. Historic Houses Trust of NSW & Hordern House, Sydney, 1999.

Ingleton, Geoffrey C. *Matthew Flinders: Navigator and Chartmaker*. Genesis, UK, 1986.

Jose, A.W. *Nicolas Baudin*. In *Journal & Proceedings*. Royal Australian Historical Society. Vol. 20, 1934.

Kelly, Michael. *François Péron's hatred of Nicolas Baudin*: address to W.A. Historical Society, August 27, 1965.

King, Jonathan. *The Passionate Circumnavigator*. Article in *The Australian*, Sept. 21, 2001.

Ly-Tio-Fane Pineo, Huguette. *In the Grips of the Eagle: Matthew Flinders at Ile de France, 1803–1810*. Moka, Mauritius, 1988.

Mack, James D. *Matthew Flinders 1774–1814*. Nelson, Melbourne, 1966.

Moyal, Ann. *A Bright & Savage Land. Scientists in Colonial Australia*. Collins, Sydney, 1986.

Owens, Susan. *Napoléon's Grand Passion*. Article in *The Australian Financial Review*, p. 11. July 7–8, 2001.

Plomley, N.J.B. *The Baudin Expedition and the Tasmanian Aborigines 1802*. Blubber Head Press, Hobart, 1983.

Retter, Catharine & Shirley Sinclair. *Letters to Ann: The love story of Matthew Flinders and Ann Chappelle*. Angus & Robertson, Sydney, 1999.

Rousseau, Jean Jacques. *The Social Contract – Discourses*. Aldine Press, London. 1961.

Schom, Alan. *Napoléon Bonaparte*, HarperCollins, New York, 1997.

Scott, Ernest. *The life of Captain Matthew Flinders, R.N.* Angus & Robertson, Sydney, 1914.

Scott, Ernest. *Terre Napoléon: A history of French Exploration and Projects in Australia*. Methuen London, 1910.

Shillinglaw, John J. [Prospectus] *Preparing for publication … Flinders the Navigator. A memoir from original sources*. 4 pages. Melbourne, 1879.

Verne, Jules. *Grands Voyages et Grand Voyagers*. Vol. 4, Paris, 1878.

Walker, James Blackhouse. *Early Tasmania: papers read before the Royal Society of Tasmania …* H.H. Pimblett, Government Printer, Hobart, 1950.

Williams, Glyndwr & Alan Frost (editors). *Terra Australis to Australia*. Oxford University Press in association with the Australian Academy of the Humanities, Melbourne, 1988.

Williams, Nadine. *Discovering Love*. Article in *The Adelaide Advertiser*, June 23, 2001.

[NOTES]

The chapters in this book rely heavily on the following sources, to whom I am most grateful. See bibliography for publication details.

Prologue
Frank Horner's *The French Reconnaissance*; Faivre in Cornell/Nicolas Baudin's *The Journal of post Captain Nicolas Baudin*.

Chapter 1
Frank Horner's *The French Reconnaissance*; Geoffrey Ingleton's *Matthew Flinders: Navigator and Chartmaker*; Anthony Brown's *Ill-Starred Captains*; Nicolas Baudin's *The Journal of Post Captain Nicolas Baudin*; François Péron's *A Voyage of Discovery to the Southern Hemisphere*; John Dunmore's *Pacific Explorer*.

Page 4
The greatest … to Europe From *Le Moniteur*, 27 July 1798, 9Th erm VI, quoted from Jose, p. 341.

Page 8
Some part … the experiment Walker, pp. 4–5.

Page 10
Napoléon and La Perouse expedition Dunmore (1985), p. 203 & Hamilton, p. 69.

Napoléon and platypus Hamilton, p. 9.

Page 11
Hoist the … colony Walker, p. 8.

The natural … Port Jackson Dunmore (1965), Vol. II, p. 11.

Page 15
It might appear … respective labours Flinders 'Private Letters Book', p. 53.

Chapter 2
Catharine Retter & Shirley Sinclair's *Letters to Ann*; Geoffrey Ingleton's *Matthew Flinders: Navigator and Chartmaker*; Matthew Flinders' *A Voyage to Terra Australis*; Anthony Brown's *Ill-Starred Captains: Flinders & Baudin*.

Chapter 3

Nicolas Baudin's *The Journal of Post Captain Nicolas Baudin*;
Frank Horner's *The French Reconnaissance.*

Page 33

Observations … anthropologists Rhys Jones, in Bonnemains *et al*, p. 38.
Just let me … can do Yves Laissus, in Bonnemains *et al*, p. 31.

Page 34

Irresponsible … hurt anyone Yves Laissus, in Bonnemains *et al*, p. 31.
The obstinacy – and irreparable Péron, p. 26 & p. 29.

Page 38

Sided with … officers Jose, p. 346.

Chapter 4

Matthew Flinders' *A Voyage to Terra Australis*; Geoffrey Ingleton's
Matthew Flinders: Navigator and Chartmaker.

Page 44

My father … me Defoe, pp. 1–2.
induced to go … Robinson Crusoe Brown, 2000, p. 38.

Page 47

Mr. Flinders … without my orders Retter & Sinclair, p. 139.
About 5 … know not Flinders 'Extracts of Letters …', p. 19.
My employments … mankind Flinders 'Private Journal 1803–1814',
      p. 82; Oct 13, 1805.
I trust that … to do it Retter & Sinclair, p. 34.

Chapter 5

Nicolas Baudin's *The Journal of Post Captain Nicolas Baudin*; Frank
Horner's *The French Reconnaissance: Baudin in Australia 1801–1803.*

Page 53

Secret instructions Dunmore, 1985, p. 190.

Page 54

Explore the … settlement Walker, p. 6.

Chapter 6

Matthew Flinders' *A Voyage to Terra Australis*, Vol. I; Geoffrey
Ingleton's *Matthew Flinders: Navigator and Chartmaker.*

Page 59

daily ration of grog allowed in 1801 Gurney, p. 49.

Page 60

Write to me … best love Retter & Sinclair, p. 37.

Chapter 7

Nicolas Baudin's *The Journal of Post Captain Nicolas Baudin*;
François Péron's *A Voyage of Discovery to the Southern Hemisphere*;
Frank Horner's *The French Reconnaissance*.

Page 73

Milius and death of Vasse Kelly, p. 4.

Page 74

One can readily ... state of depression Brown, 2000, p. 123.

Page 77

To visit ... equal size Dunmore (1985),Vol. II, p. 10 – translated from
   Péron's *Voyage* and his version of the expedition's sailing orders.

Chapter 8

Nicolas Baudin's *The Journal of Post Captain Nicolas Baudin*;
François Péron's *A Voyage of Discovery to the Southern Hemisphere*;
Frank Horner's *The French Reconnaissance*.

Page 83

The women are ... type of commerce Milius, pp. 26–27, quoted
   from Brown, 2000, p. 146.

Page 87

Incapacitated ... a duel Jose, p. 378.

Chapter 9

Matthew Flinders' *A Voyage to Terra Australis*,Vols. I & II.

Page 91

Flinders and the *Minang* people 'Encyclopaedia of Aboriginal
   Australia', p. 1011.

Chapter 10

Nicolas Baudin's *The Journal of Post Captain Nicolas Baudin*;
Frank Horner's *The French Reconnaissance*.

Page 94

This terrible ... dead bodies Péron, p. 136.

Page 97

The experience ... last two Horner, p. 36.

Chapter 11

Matthew Flinders' *A Voyage to Terra Australis*,Vol. I.

Page 101

From ... Baudin Flinders 'Private Letters Book',Vol. 1, p. 5.

Chapter 12
Nicolas Baudin's *The Journal of Post Captain Nicolas Baudin*; François Péron's *A Voyage of Discovery to the Southern Hemisphere.*
Page 106
The science ... existence Rhys Jones, in Bonnemains *et al*, p. 36.
The philosophical ... society Hughes, M., pp. 25–28.
Natural man Hughes, M., pp. 25–28.
Man is born ... they Rousseau, p. 3.
Page 114
There is no ... area Hughes, M., p. 36.
Page 115
They were treacherous ... of madness Brown, 2000, p. 214.

Chapter 13
Matthew Flinders' *A Voyage to Terra Australis.*

Chapter 14
Matthew Flinders' *A Voyage to Terra Australis*; Nicolas Baudin's *The Journal of Post Captain Nicolas Baudin.*
Page 122
In the shade ... me Plomley, pp. 57–58.
Several of them ... we did Plomley, p. 84.
Page 123
In vain ... evokes Plomley, p. 64.
Like most animals ... intermittent periods Horner, p. 205.
One of our ... founded Hughes, M., p. 37.

Chapter 15
Nicolas Baudin's *The Journal of Post Captain Nicolas Baudin.*
Page 133
Most of them ... swallows them up Brown, 2000, p. 79.

Chapter 16
Matthew Flinders' *A Voyage to Terra Australis*; Nicolas Baudin's *The Journal of Post Captain Nicolas Baudin*; Geoffrey Ingleton's *Matthew Flinders: Navigator and Chartmaker.*
Page 137
As the point ... courage Péron, p. 244.

Chapter 17
Matthew Flinders' *A Voyage to Terra Australis*; Nicolas Baudin's

The Journal of Post Captain Nicolas Baudin; Geoffrey Ingleton's
Matthew Flinders: Navigator and Chartmaker.
Page 143
Monsieur Baudin … tramp Baldwin, 1964, p. 54.
Page 144
There were figures … of the negroe Brown, 1998(b).

Chapter 18
Matthew Flinders' *A Voyage to Terra Australis*; Geoffrey Ingleton's
Matthew Flinders: Navigator and Chartmaker.
Page 151
I was … with you King, p. 16.
Page 153
It surprised … this Flinders 'Private Letters Book', Vol. 1, p. 4.

Chapter 19
Nicolas Baudin's *The Journal of Post Captain Nicolas Baudin.*
Page 157
Golfe de la Misanthropie Personal observation of Baudin's original
    charts held at the National Archives of France in Paris.
Page 159
Our commander … among us Péron, p. 257.
Page 160
More than … engulf us Jose, p. 383.
Page 161
Their faces … feeling Hamilton, p. 161.

Chapter 20
Matthew Flinders' *A Voyage to Terra Australis*; Matthew Flinders'
*Private Letters Books, 1801–1814, including letters from his wife Ann,
1814–1821*; Frank Horner's *The French Reconnaissance*;
Geoffrey Ingleton's *Matthew Flinders: Navigator and Chartmaker*;
Nicolas Baudin's *The Journal of Post Captain Nicolas Baudin*;
Catharine Retter & Shirley Sinclair's *Letters to Ann.*
Page 165
Captain Hamelin … but himself Brown, 2000, p. 239.
Page 167
The place … objection Historical Records of New South Wales,
    Vol. 4, p. 948.
Page 168
rations in colony Walker, p. 13.

Page 169

ship repairs Historical Records of New South Wales, Vol. 4,
  p. 953 & p. 955.

Page 177

Péron and Freycinet become spies Hunt *et al*, p. 23.

Eora music See Péron's *Atlas*, 1824 ed.

Page 178

The public … frolics Rhys Jones, in Bonnemains *et al*, p. 60.

Page 180

The intrepid … New Holland Péron, p. 276.

Chapter 21

Matthew Flinders' *A Voyage to Terra Australis*.

Chapter 22

Nicolas Baudin's *The Journal of Post Captain Nicolas Baudin*;
Anthony Brown's *The Captain and the Convict Maid*; Anthony
Brown's *Ill-Starred Captains*; Frank Horner's *The French
Reconnaissance*.

Page 192

It will … with me Historical Records of New South Wales,
  Vol. 4, p. 1006.

Page 194

map presentation to Kemp Walker, p. 16.

I am inclined … to this Hunt *et al*, p. 56.

Page 199

I deem … these parts Walker, p. 18–19.

Page 201

Sir … foundation Historical Records of New South Wales,
  Vol. 4, p. 1009.

I gave … him Historical Records of New South Wales, Vol. 5, p. 831.

Page 202

I now … unknown Historical Records of New South Wales,
  Vol. 5, pp. 830–831.

Page 203

I expect … pay Historical Records of New South Wales,
  Vol. 5, p. 831.

Chapter 23

Matthew Flinders' *A Voyage to Terra Australis*; Geoffrey Ingleton's
Matthew Flinders: Navigator and Chartmaker.

Page 205

For Mrs Flinders … it Flinders 'Private Letters Book', pp. 24–25.

Page 211

If the … incitements Flinders 'Private Letters Book', p. 21.

The ships … company Mack, p. 148.

Chapter 24

Nicolas Baudin's *The Journal of Post Captain Nicolas Baudin*; Frank Horner's *The French Reconnaissance*; Anthony Brown's *Ill-Starred Captains*.

Page 217

Mary's crimes Williams, p. 4.

Chapter 25

Matthew Flinders' *A Voyage to Terra Australis*, Matthew Flinders' *Private Letters Books, 1801–1814, including letters from his wife Ann, 1814–1821*.

Chapter 26

Matthew Flinders' *A Voyage to Terra Australis*; Frank Horner's *The French Reconnaissance*; Geoffrey Ingleton's *Matthew Flinders: Navigator and Chartmaker*.

Page 228

In no way … all the crew Brown 1998(a), p. 28.

Chapter 27

Nicolas Baudin's *The Journal of Post Captain Nicolas Baudin*; Frank Horner's *The French Reconnaissance*.

Page 238

poor health and lack of water Brosse, p. 105.

Chapter 28

Matthew Flinders' *A Voyage to Terra Australis*; Matthew Flinders' *Private Journal, 1803–1814*; Geoffrey Ingleton *Matthew Flinders: Navigator and Chartmaker*.

Page 243

There was no … light arriv'd Brown, 2000, pp. 481–2.

Page 244

I poor … condition Defoe, p. 67 & p. 45.

It was … not done Defoe, p. 85 & p. 89.

Chapter 29
Nicolas Baudin's *The Journal of Post Captain Nicolas Baudin*;
Frank Horner's *The French Reconnaissance*.
Page 255
Are the lungs ... exist Baldwin, 1963, p. 28.
Page 256
Sir ... a mistake Baldwin, 1964, p. 57.

Chapter 30
Frank Horner *The French Reconnaissance*; Matthew Flinders'
A Voyage to Terra Australis.
Page 262
Necessity ... Isle of France Flinders 'Private Journal 1803–1814', p. 10.

Chapter 31
Matthew Flinders' *A Voyage to Terra Australis*; Matthew Flinders'
Private Journal, 1803–1814; Matthew Flinders' *Private Letters Books*;
Frank Horner's *The French Reconnaissance*; Geoffrey Ingleton *Matthew
Flinders: Navigator and Chartmaker*.
Page 266
Coup d'oeil ... Nouvelle Holland Hunt *et al*, p. 22.
Port Jackson ... time Scott, 1914, p. 464.
Once the ... enemy warships Hunt *et al*, p. 54.
Page 271
You know ... most poignantly Retter & Sinclair, p. 51.

Chapter 32
Frank Horner *The French Reconnaissance*; Anthony Brown's *Ill-Starred
Captains*.
Page 279
The greatest ... France William & Frost, p. 228.
Joséphine's menagerie Bruce, pp. 393–4.
Joséphine's flora Owens, p. 11.

Chapter 33
Matthew Flinders' *A Voyage to Terra Australis*; Matthew Flinders'
Private Journal, 1803–1814; Geoffrey Ingleton's *Matthew Flinders:
Navigator and Chartmaker*.
Page 288
From the ... scientific men Baker, p. 88
General Decaen ... orders Scott, p. 348.

Chapter 34

Matthew Flinders' *Private Journal, 1803–1814*; Matthew Flinders' *Private Letters Book*; Geoffrey Ingleton's *Matthew Flinders: Navigator and Chartmaker*.

Chapter 35

Frank Horner's *The French Reconnaissance*.
Page 303
place names by Péron and Freycinet Kelly, p. 3.
the Baudin Islet Kelly, p. 3.

Chapter 36

Matthew Flinders' *Private Journal, 1803–1814*; Matthew Flinders' *Private Letters Book*; Huguette Ly-Tio-Fane Pineo's *In the grips of the eagle: Matthew Flinders at Ile de France, 1803–1810*.
Page 309
It is proposed … Port Jackson Horner, p. 344.

Chapter 37

Matthew Flinders' *A Voyage to Terra Australis*; Geoffrey Ingleton's *Matthew Flinders: Navigator and Chartmaker*.
Page 312
I need … absence Flinders 'Private Letters Book', Feb 2, 1811.
I went … line Flinders 'Private Journal 1803–1814', p. 252.
It was kept … Naturaliste Flinders, 1814, p. 470.
Péron's assertions Péron, p. 244.
Page 315
In addition to … so justly entitled Retter & Sinclair, p. 143.
Page 316
considered it … on parole Brown, 2000, p. 472.

Chapter 38

Matthew Flinders' *Private Letters Book*; Matthew Flinders' *Private Journal, 1803–1814*; Catharine Retter & Shirley Sinclair's *Letters to Ann*; Geoffrey Ingleton's *Matthew Flinders: Navigator and Chartmaker*.
Page 322
I have … wing again Defoe, p. 297.
It grows … my papers Scott, 1914, p. 396.

Chapter 39

Geoffrey Ingleton's *Matthew Flinders: Navigator and Chartmaker*; Jill

Duchess of Hamilton's *Napoléon, the Empress & the Artist*; Matthew
Flinders' *Private Letters Book*.
Page 327
Baudin's passion for zoology Amalfi, Carmelo. Article in *The West
    Australian*, June 2, 2001.

Epilogue
Page 330
In the grand … published Shillinglaw, p. 2.
Page 331
The churchyard … in life Scott, p. 397.
Page 332
All together Baudin … spin Jose, p. 338.
Bayldon's rewriting of Jose's presentation Kelly, p. 11.
Page 334
historian's objections Amalfi, Carmelo. Article in *The West Australian*,
    July 10, 2001.
'Flinders' vs 'Baudin' 'Gazetteer of Australia', 2001.